PRAISE FOR
BOTTOM SHELF

"Fred Minnick doesn't just know bourbon—he lives it. But this book ain't just about whiskey. It's about heart, healing, and finding meaning in the most unexpected places…like an old bottle of Old Crow. Fred's story is powerful, honest, and full of soul. I'm proud to call him a friend—and even prouder to recommend this book."

—Terry Bradshaw, Pro Football Hall of Fame quarterback

"An intoxicating mix of memoir and mystery, *Bottom Shelf* proves that the most powerful legacies are the ones we almost lose."

—Ian Somerhalder, actor and cofounder of Brother's Bond Bourbon

"While setting the record straight about a legendary whiskey brand and the Scotsman behind it, Minnick goes beyond bourbon to weave a true love story with his powerful and unforgettable journey after finding himself on the bottom shelf. It's a story of resiliency and the power of hope, fueled by focus and love. And like the finish of a vintage Old Crow, you'll remember this ride long after you turn the final page."

—Brian F. Haara, author of *Bourbon Justice: How Whiskey Law Shaped America*

"From the first page, this is an honest, fascinating, and moving discovery, not just of the great American spirit that is bourbon but of the great American spirit within Fred himself."

—Graham McTavish, actor and #1 *New York Times* bestselling coauthor of *Clanlands*

"This isn't just bourbon history—it's American history told with grit, passion, and a palate that refuses to forget. Fred Minnick gives Old Crow back its soul."

—Peggy Noe Stevens, master bourbon taster and founder of Bourbon Women

"In this moving and engaging blend of memoir and bourbon history, Minnick tells a fascinating tale of the power of spirits to shape both a vast industry and a single life. More than just finding solace at the bottom of his tasting glass, Minnick finds grounding, focus, and the importance of community and family for support and meaning. Fred Minnick's journey celebrates how great spirits bring people together and, even in our darkest moments, reminds us that we're never really alone."

—Martin Cate, owner of Smuggler's Cove and a James Beard Award winner

"*Bottom Shelf* opened my eyes to the world of bourbon. I found myself chasing new and interesting finds, savoring them, and wishing I had the palate and the storytelling chops of Fred Minnick. You will come out of this book wishing you could sit down and have a sip of bourbon with Fred. Of course, that's what this book is;

Bottom Shelf is the chance to sit down with one of the world's foremost experts, get inside his mind, and feel like you're right there with him, having a drink. In Fred's hands, the story of bourbon becomes smart, human, and fun. *Bottom Shelf* is part quest, part history, and part how-to book, and anyone who reads it will come out with one hell of a pleasant buzz."

—Daniel Barbarisi, author of *Chasing the Thrill* and *Dueling with Kings*

"Fred Minnick's masterpiece comes at the right time for the bourbon world. We need his personal, spiritual journey to remind us why we fell in love with bourbon in the first place."

—Chuck Cowdery, author of *Bourbon, Straight*

"A brutally honest, engaging, and fascinating account from our most foremost bourbon critic. I was hooked from page one and touched by this tale of heartbreak and ultimate triumph. This is a book about bourbon, but it is also a book about resilience and redemption and what drives a person to succeed."

—Edward Lee, chef and author of *Bourbon Land*

"Before I'd read a word of Fred Minnick's terrific new book, I thought, 'I hope this is a tale of hard-won redemption that follows a flawed man scraping rock bottom before finding love and understanding in the people he holds dear. I also hope it involves Old Crow.' I'm pleased to say I was rewarded on both counts. With wit and grace, Minnick offers a stirring reminder that we sometimes find courage in unlikely places and that by a strange twist of human emotion, our obsessions—even those widely dismissed as 'rotgut swill'—give us faith to carry on."

—John O'Connor, author of *The Secret History of Bigfoot*

"Fred Minnick has long been bourbon's most trusted voice. With *Bottom Shelf*, he shows us the man behind the palate, unearthing not just a forgotten whiskey but the truths that shaped him, and I'm proud to call him a friend."

—Dierks Bentley, country singer and songwriter

"*Bottom Shelf* is authentic and vulnerable. As someone who supports veterans, it makes me proud of my friend to be able to put his story out for people to read. Not all are willing to do so."

—Jared Allen, Pro Football Hall of Fame defensive end

ALSO BY FRED MINNICK

Camera Boy: An Army Journalist's War in Iraq

Whiskey Women: The Untold Story of How Women Saved Bourbon, Scotch, and Irish Whiskey

Bourbon Curious: A Simple Tasting Guide for the Savvy Drinker

Bourbon: The Rise, Fall, and Rebirth of an American Whiskey

Rum Curious: The Indispensable Tasting Guide to the World's Spirit

Mead: The Libations, Legends, and Lore of History's Oldest Drink

BOTTOM SHELF

How a Forgotten Brand of BOURBON Saved One Man's Life

FRED MINNICK

sourcebooks

Cover design by Faceout Studio, Spencer Fuller
Cover images © Paul Grossmann/Tetra Images/Getty Images, Vector pack/Shutterstock, LiliGraphie/Shutterstock, Vac1/Shutterstock
Internal design by Laura Boren/Sourcebooks

This book is a memoir. It reflects the author's present recollections of experiences over a period of time. Some names and characteristics have been changed, some events have been compressed, and some dialogue has been re-created.

Published by Sourcebooks
1935 Brookdale RD, Naperville, IL 60563-2773
(630) 961-3900
sourcebooks.com

Cataloging-in-Publication Data is on file with the Library of Congress.

Printed and bound in the United States of America.
MA 10 9 8 7 6 5 4 3 2

To Oscar and Julian,

I hope you find somebody who makes you

as happy as your mother makes me.

A Note from the Author

Portions of this text contain direct quotes from historical documents that are racially insensitive. Neither the publisher nor the author condone this language.

Note also that the author shares personal mental-health and self-harm stories.

Introduction

With seven American whiskeys before me and bourbon-filled oak barrels stacked all around, I felt a gentle breeze waft in from the open warehouse door. The wind carried rich caramel scents straight to my nose and sent a tingle down my spine.

I love that smell.

Caramel is bourbon's quintessential note, because this spirit must always be stored in new charred oak barrels. And much like wood does for barbecue, the burned oak imposes a plethora of wood sugar notes to the spirit aging in the barrel. This wood extraction gives bourbon all of its color and the majority of its flavors and aromas with caramel, and sometimes vanilla, being the most common.

I brought the bourbon to my nose. And there it was. Just as nature's breath promised me, caramel stood on shoulders above the other aromas of grain, maple, peanut butter, and cinnamon. I put it upon my lips, and there it was again. Can you say caramel bomb?

I closed my eyes, feeling the bourbon drop down my jawline and curling under my tongue. It tickled everywhere.

I smiled and looked around the room.

I was with my whiskey club—Club Marzipan—selecting a barrel of bourbon for the club. This caramel barrel would be available exclusively to them, my community, a representation of the great people who look to America's spirit as their hobby of choice. From the South and Midwest, Pacific Northwest, and the heart of New York City, they come from all walks of life and political affiliations. They don't care about your favorite sports team or who you voted for; all they want to do is sip a dram and talk bourbon.

When times were tough, this group saved my career, giving me an avenue to share my bourbon passions with strangers on zooms. There were few adventures I looked forward to more than sipping bourbon with these fine folks.

When I taste this barrel pick again, I'll close my eyes and remember this moment, surrounded by my Club Marzipan friends, and the love of my life—Jaclyn, who loves bourbon as much as me. I'll remember looking into her deep brown eyes and wondering if my boys are covered in ticks while playing in the creek looking for tadpoles and crawfish. Yeah, even when I travel for work, I try to bring my family, because they are my everything. And moments like this are sealed in a bottle to be relived again whenever I taste.

When people ask me "How are you?" I frequently reply "Living the dream."

Because it's true.

I have an amazing family and a career where I earn a living sipping bourbon. I've traveled the world and met so many cool people, educating them on how to taste bourbon like a pro. I even taught football icon Peyton Manning bourbon history and sipped the good stuff with Metallica backstage.

I've developed real friendships with people I've only previously seen on TV or the stage, such as *Vampire Diaries* star Ian Somerhalder and country star Dierks Bentley, both of whom are mega whiskey geeks.

My career is a story I never thought imaginable.

And it almost didn't happen.

PROLOGUE

ROCK BOTTOM

THE BELT WAS fastened around my neck, tied to a metal shower rod firmly bolted into the wall. I jumped off the edge of the porcelain tub. My feet dangled a mere inch from the ground.

This was it.

The leather cinched around my neck, folding my carotid artery, crushing my Adam's apple. I gasped for air. I once read that when people attempt suicide, they almost instantly regret it and try to save themselves. As I felt pressure in my eyes, like they were being sucked deeper into my skull, I knew I could stop it. If I wanted to live, all I had to do was plant my foot back on the edge of the tub. But I didn't.

I wanted to die.

I hated this world.

I hated the new me that had formed since I returned from Iraq. Once jovial and the life of a party, I no longer enjoyed my former hobbies. Music, sports, and get-togethers irritated me. The crowds and useless chatter drove me into corners, where I would focus on what plagued my mind: *Why had my friends died? Why had I lived? And why had we even been there in the first place?*

Every moment of every day, a darkness swelled deep inside me, pouring anger and hate into my soul. Intellectually, I knew I had signed up for the National Guard at age eighteen and that I swore an oath to protect and serve my country from enemies foreign and domestic, and that I had honorably served my country, to the point of making a true difference. But when I came home, I felt a mental and physiological change at every reminder of the war. And in 2005, I could not hide from anti-war signs, CNN debates, or random people sharing their unsolicited political beliefs with me.

When I could not hide, my darkness turned to rage. I once tried to fight a room full of college kids over their beliefs, nearly slammed a stapler into my boss's head for disagreeing with me, and stood outside a rich person's house screaming over protest yard signage that they had every right to display.

That's why this belt was around my neck. Every night, as soon as I closed my eyes, war haunted my dreams. Men in black robes tried to kill me. During the day, I cowered under rooftops in fear of snipers lurking overhead and shivered to flashbacks of helicopters blazing past, knowing a firefight would soon ensue.

Loud noises triggered the worst flashbacks. When a thunderous boom echoed directly behind me at the magazine office where I had recently taken a job as a food editor, my ears rang and my heart jumped out of my chest.

I thought:

What was the noise?

Iraq.

Am I back in Iraq?

I screamed and fell underneath my desk, shaking, grabbing my head, rocking back and forth, crying. My friends knelt to comfort me. "It's going to be okay," whispered Kevin Gibson, a coworker who'd become one of my best friends. I saw a couple of people snickering in the corner. Somebody always laughs when a veteran falls for cover.

When I ended myself, would they laugh then?

I put on a good front and hid my pain from most people. I fake-smiled and was great at my job, even uncovering a few scandals in the restaurant industry that made national news. I was the only restaurant reporter at the time to land exclusive interviews with Chipotle CEO Steve Ells and Panera Bread founder Ron Shaich. But despite what looked to be a healthy professional life, on the inside, I was dying.

The belt moved just above my Adam's apple, tighter. I was beginning to black out when I started thinking of my wife. It was all happening so fast that I had not even thought about her.

How sad is that?

I loved Jaclyn, but she would be better off without me. How often had she canceled plans because of my anxiety? Could she even count the number of times I had grown so irritable that I'd leave our apartment after an argument? Still, as my final breath drew near, I saw her in my mind, as if for the first time. In my final seconds of life, I wanted to remember my happiest moment since returning from Iraq, the moment I met Jaclyn.

—∞—

When Jaclyn and I first started talking on the phone, after matching on eHarmony, we shared our past relationship stories. It turned out she had dumped her past boyfriends. All of them. Since she broke so many hearts, I nicknamed her "Manbreaker."

I stood in the Milwaukee airport holding the sign "Manbreaker," wondering, *Is this too much? Will this be funny?*

People rushed by me with their suitcases, in a hurry to reach their planes, and I gripped the sign more tightly, trying to stay calm. In Iraq, large crowds were easy targets for car bombs. Three months after returning from the war, I avoided crowds. In fact, I avoided all things.

But today I was in the airport. For her. Waiting to see the most intriguing woman I had ever met. She looked beautiful in her pictures. Brown eyes. Black hair. I loved her nose. But looks had nothing to do with why I was falling for her; it was her voice on our phone calls that made me, well, *feel*. Since Iraq, I had felt a barrier around my feelings for loved ones. I became distant with my family and my old friends, and even stopped enjoying my passions, like sports. Except for her. Jaclyn pierced that barrier like a hot knife in butter.

And here I was holding this damn sign. What if she didn't like it?

I looked for funny things in the crowd to take my mind off my fears. I scanned until the perfect distraction appeared in all his shimmering permed-up glory—a perfect specimen of the patented Wisconsin man mullet. While this hairstyle eventually faded in most parts of the country, flannel shirt Wisconsinite males carried this 1980s hairdo through the tough times. They proudly walked into bars, lit a cigarette, and barked, "I'll have Miller," and then went on complaining about Brett Favre throwing interceptions. I imagined an entire room of mullet men arguing over the Green Bay Packers, and that soothed me.

Jaclyn appeared in a sea of passengers. Her hair was braided, she was smiling from ear to ear, and she walked confidently toward me. She's tiny, so her model-like strut doesn't draw the same attention as that of a six-foot model, but I was wowed with each step. In my head, I sang "here she comes" to the tune of the La's "There She Goes."

I stood close to a foot taller than Jaclyn, looking down at her, watching her shoulders sway. She touched the sign. "I love it," she said, tipping up on her toes and kissing me on the cheek.

She loved the sign! *Okay, I am good. I can retire from this dating game now and marry her.*

Now, that day seemed so long ago. My arms tingled as my blood circulation slowed. I saw Jaclyn at the altar of the church where we had our wedding, two years after we first met. The smell of Catholic Church pews and incense filled my nose. How happy I was in that moment! Meeting her, marrying her, were some of the rare moments the darkness did not own me. I loved Jaclyn, but she would be better off without me.

This was it.

Fade to black.

Then, as if I were dreaming, I felt my body fall to the floor, my ribs bouncing off the tub. I coughed, taking in oxygen. Jaclyn gasped. "No! No! You are not doing this."

She untied the belt from my neck and stood in the doorway, crying. I tried to reattach the belt, to finish the job. She begged me to stop.

I pulled the wedding ring off my hand. It had only been there for a month. I threw it at her and yelled, "It's over; you do not want to be near me. It's for your own good."

I collapsed.

Jaclyn sobbed.

Moments earlier, my body was becoming numb, the actual life slowly choking out of me. And now, on the floor, I felt blood rushing to my hands, feet, and eyes. My skin rippled with sensation. The tile grit smelled like dirt, and the cleaning supplies under the sink reeked of bleach. In this instant, looking up at her, that's when I wanted to live.

I thought of the moments when I felt most alive, like when I built a tire swing with my dad in the backyard and flew to the top of the branch of my family's towering pecan tree. Or when I won a big wrestling match in the sixth grade and my coach told me he couldn't believe I beat my opponent. Or that time in college I jumped off a cliff into an open aquifer. But none of these happy moments made me feel more alive than when I saw Jaclyn for the first time.

Now, I was alive and she was standing over me, but all I felt was despair.

What had I done?

I don't remember going to bed that night, but I awoke with a sore throat, red marks on my neck, and Jaclyn by my side, stroking my forehead.

"I am going to get help," I said, looking into her bloodshot eyes. She must not have slept at all as she sat up watching me. "I want to spend the rest of my life with you."

We embraced. We cried.

"I'm sorry."

The date was June 24, 2007, more than two years after I had come back from Iraq, and I couldn't see the road ahead or the significance of hitting rock bottom on this date. All I knew was that I wanted to hold Jaclyn's hand.

Forever.

And I would never fail her again.*

---

* From my medical records: "He had a suicide attempt…on the anniversary of a very close call with an RPG in Iraq. His wife intervened."

DISCOVERY

CHAPTER 1

TASTE

IT'S 0600 IN Mosul, Iraq, in the early summer of 2004, and I'm eager to open a package sitting at the foot of my bunk. Mail call is always special; a letter from home can shift your "sick of this shit" attitude to the will to survive another day. This box was, how should I put this...illegal.

"We can't buy alcohol in Iraq," I had written my friend back home weeks ago. "Because of our general orders. I need you to sneak whiskey in the mail to pass the MP's inspections. Here's what you do: get a bottle of regular Listerine, dump it, and refill it with Jim Beam or Jack Daniel's. It's pretty much the same color. They won't know the difference!"

Four weeks later, my friend sent the package. I had picked it up the night before and listened to the beautiful sloshing inside the bottle. I knew sweet, precious whiskey awaited me. But I couldn't open it yet. I had to wait for tomorrow, when I had the day off.

Today, a long day of patrols and raids awaited my camera,

M16A2, and me. I laced up my boots, slid on my body armor, strapped on my Kevlar, counted my rounds, and attached a D-ring to my camera, cinching it to my body armor strap. I touched the package and said, “Tonight, I’m gonna sip ya.” I hopped out the door with a smile on my face. Soon there would be whiskey. But first, patrols.

If you saw me walking in Iraq, you would likely do a double take. A camera swayed back and forth as I gripped my weapon. Was I a soldier? Media? I was both. I was an army photojournalist, a staff sergeant, whose job was to document the war. Some photos were classified, used to brief generals, and some were used in the media. I floated from unit to unit, knocking down doors, getting shot at, and documenting it all. On this day, I was attached to an infantry platoon, a fifth Group Special Forces team, and a squad of Iraqi military, following up intel on potential insurgent hideouts.

This raid was somewhat unusual in that American forces were in an observer role and the Iraqis led all the grunt stuff. Typically, when Iraqi forces were by our side, American forces mapped the routes and led the assaults. This time, the Iraqi soldiers created the mission plan and we followed up on intelligence about enemy forces. This was similar to how we trained stateside, where the NCOs and officers observed us execute our own missions. Only this was real, and we’d be knocking down doors and taking prisoners or engaging in combat with the Iraqi soldiers in front. The mission brief said our target was military-aged men with weapons and information on insurgent activity. In other words, we were looking for lower-ranking and middle-management members of terrorist cells to rat on their bosses.

Special Forces walked side-by-side with the Iraqis, whose uniforms mimicked ours. Regular Iraqi army wore green and black battle dress uniforms; this outfit wore the same desert camo with the pants neatly tucked in their boots. They walked like us, too, even held their weapons the same way—with their trigger finger across the firing area but not on the trigger.

For the first house, I stood behind a concrete barrier, photographing the Iraqis kick down the door as they screamed in Arabic. A woman and child ran out with their hands up. The Iraqis drew weapons on them both, shouting. The situation escalated, and a Special Forces soldier and an interpreter strolled in, not with their weapons at ready, and talked to the lead Iraqi soldier. I don't know what was said, but he patted the Iraqi on the back and we went to the next house.

Here, we found weapons. Not a full cache, but a couple of AK-47s and several full magazines. Nobody was home, though; they must have been tipped off that we were coming.

In fact, of the dozen or so homes we raided, we found many AKs, but only women and children inside the buildings, leaving the commanders convinced that an Iraqi had leaked our mission beforehand.

Nonetheless, for twelve hours, the sun radiated on my neck and through my body armor while Iraq's superheated concrete seared my boots. The weatherman said it was ninety-six degrees, but it felt even hotter. Sweat traveled down my spine and up my calves and met in the middle.

When I returned to the base, I jumped into the shower, my dog tags suctioned tight to my chest. All I could think about was the package and how good that whiskey would feel on my lips. I changed into my PTs—army speak for athletic gear—and went to chow, where our Turkish cooks whipped up an incredible roast beef and carrots dish that I inhaled, washing it down with two cartons of milk. I was so ready for the whiskey.

Or so I thought.

After a brief conversation in the barracks with my buddies, my eyelids felt heavy. Day off tomorrow or not, right now I was more interested in sleep than whiskey. I laid my head on a folded OD Green wool blanket and closed my eyes with my M16 across my chest. Just as my eyes were shutting and I found a comfortable position, an all-too-familiar whistle from overhead came closer. Closer. And closer. My bunkmate, Jopek, jumped up and yelled, "Minnick, bunker…now!" Jopek jetted out the door, but I was slow to move.

The whistle grew closer.

I reached for my body armor, trying to sling it over my shoulder, but it was stuck. My elbow poked out with my hand simply stuck in the body armor. In my haste to put on the armor, my watch had snagged.

Closer.

"Minnick, hurry your ass up!" Jopek screamed.

An explosion pulsated through the base. The mortar was close, so close it rocked my living quarters. Many soldiers had been killed by these mortar attacks while they were sleeping in their bunks or walking to the latrine. They were no joke.

I threw the body armor and ripped my watch off.

Jopek returned. "Damn, that was close."

"Yeah, it was." And I definitely was not going back to bed now.

I presumed another mortar would soon follow the first. "Fuck it," I said to Jopek. "Want a whiskey?"

"Huh?"

"Yeah, that care package I got is whiskey."

"Well, duh, let's drink that shit," he said. "I'll grab the smokes."

I drew my pocketknife and slit the masking tape, cracked open the box, and pulled out a beautiful Listerine bottle. The childproof closure had swelled, likely from the Iraqi heat pressuring the alcohol content. Air released, sounding like a small balloon deflating, as I cracked it open. Sure enough, it smelled like whiskey. Just before we stepped outside of our living quarters, into the gravel alleyway between our neighbors, I poured two fingers into Jopek's metal canteen cup and he lit a cigar while I drank straight from the jug.

"Damn, that burns," I said. "And it's so damn good."

Jopek tilted his cup, the metal ridges clinking against his teeth. "That's good shit."

We sat just outside our living quarters, wearing army-issued athletic wear and flip-flops. My head thrown back, the whiskey down my throat tickling my belly, I looked up at the stars, wondering if they looked the same back home. As an Army National Guardsman, a citizen-soldier, I had left the exciting world of forestry communications in Milwaukee, where I wrote scientific and marketing articles about how to manage tracts of pine and oak. It was my first job after graduating from Oklahoma State in 2001 with a degree in agricultural communications, and I loved it. I traveled the country meeting with foresters and writing about their biodiversity programs to keep quail, turkey, deer, and more populated in private lands, negotiate power line rights of way, and manage large timber tracts. Whiskey in hand, I dreamed of being back in the southeastern forests, analyzing how to rid the area of kudzu.

The minute a soldier enters a war zone, they begin pondering returning home. For me, with the spirits taking hold, I wondered if my job would expand into new territories, such as European forestry communications, and whether I would fall in love. All my buddies received love letters from girlfriends and wives, while I longed for the embrace of somebody I cared about. At twenty-four, I simply had not found the right person yet.

That night, Jopek and I drained the bottle just below the Listerine branded tagline on the label and I slept in until 7:00 a.m. the next day. No hangover or regret, but little did I know that my chosen bootlegged elixir would soon replace my forestry gig as my dream job and would provide the motivation for me to live in the most unusual circumstances.

But, most importantly, whiskey would turn out to be the drink of choice for the woman of my dreams.

Sometime in December 2004, I was told we were going home, leaving Iraq after a year in country. But it wasn't like we got this good news and drove straight to the airport. Nope. Our ship-out date moved back from January 1 to January 10 to February. As we finally sat in the airfield getting ready to depart, I feared I was about to become like one of those retired cops in the 1980s movies, who either gets pulled back into duty or is killed at the very last minute. Fortunately, my fears of a rocket, suicide bomb, or a random stray bullet didn't come to fruition and I boarded an outbound plane to New Jersey, where I took my boots off and touched the ground.

Some people kissed the ground; I wanted to feel my pinky toes in the stiff cold. I knew this was stupid, but I just had to feel the soil, frozen or not, and connect with my home, the country I fought for.

From New Jersey, we quickly transported to Fort McCoy, Wisconsin, where we out-processed for a few days. That entailed filling out reams of paperwork for our security clearance, combat pay, benefits, and medical records. We were briefed on what we could talk about and when we were expected to return to duty. But not once did somebody say: "You know, you're gonna be messed up for a while."

If I could go back to that moment, when my commander said, "Dismissed. Enjoy civilian life," I would have stopped my twenty-five-year-old self and went straight to the veterans hospital. But I didn't know how deeply the war had affected me until I looked in the mirror some days later.

I genuinely thought I'd be my old self—gregarious and interested in other people's conversations. But the old me had faded, maybe even died, in Iraq. I looked in the mirror and saw a shadow of the man I used to be.

I tried meeting new people but quickly realized all my conversations—whether in bars, coffee shops, laundromats, or gas stations—felt desperate and forced. Would this be me forever?

I knew isolation would only grow the darkness within me, so I forced myself to interact with people. But in-person dating wasn't the right fit, so I gave online dating a try, starting trials on Match, OkCupid, and eHarmony. For the first month, there were a few phone calls, first dates, and a lot of attempts to find something in another person that made me smile. It simply wasn't happening. I closed my eyes at night, thinking I would die alone, and the only chapter of my life anybody would know was my tour in Iraq.

My cousin Ryan, an MMA fighter, was the only person keeping me sane. He lived with me in a Milwaukee apartment and offered the strangest suggestion.

"You've been only dating people from Wisconsin," he said.

"So?" I replied. I mean, I had moved to Wisconsin after graduating from Oklahoma State for my sweet forestry gig. I absolutely loved it, but I will admit that Ryan had a point. Many women I dated laughed at my Okie drawl.

"Dude, you're a hick from Oklahoma. You need to find people who can relate to you."

Following his advice, I expanded my eHarmony parameters to nationwide, and within a day, eHarmony emailed me the "best match" for me in the entire country.

Jaclyn was a nursing student in Louisville, Kentucky, and her profile picture made my heart jump. She wore a black wool jacket with thin white checkered lines and her hands were hidden in her pockets. Her brown eyes sparkled as a gust of wind caught her jet-black hair. I clicked "connect" and waited for her to accept.

Was my profile strong enough?

My main photo was of me in uniform. Should I have picked something else? Or would she like my wry grin?

I fretted for the next several hours, contemplating this young nursing student regarding me, wondering if I was worth a click. I hadn't felt butterflies in my belly like this, well, possibly ever. Was

I so lonely that a warm face and pretty eyes could stop me in my tracks? I went back and forth, questioning whether I should have even reached out to her. Fortunately, she accepted before I could withdraw the request.

I wrote to her every day for a week. Jaclyn replied with many LOLs—I made her laugh, an easier feat via messaging than in person. We spoke on the phone, and a month later, I stood in the Milwaukee airport holding a "Manbreaker" sign.

Where should I take her for our first date? Jaclyn was cultured; I was not.

I grew up in Jones, a little town in central Oklahoma with no stop lights, plenty of railroad tracks, and farmland on all sides. A tall pecan tree centered my backyard, and I played in a creek, shot BB guns, and got into all sorts of trouble with my bicycle gang buddies. Although we weren't poor, we didn't have much, and Dad was known for buying junk cars just to see if he could fix them, often cleaning out a radiator or carburetor in the sink and leaving it overnight on the kitchen table. Mom once threw a can of green beans at Dad for dirtying her kitchen with car parts. Food-wise, we were pretty simple. I recall Grandpa's cornbread, Mom's coconut brownies, known as "Hello Dollies," and eating a ton of Hamburger Helper.

Needless to say, the post-Iraq me was an unsophisticated kid who had no taste in clothes, food, or the arts. So, naturally, I took the daughter of a doctor and former playwright to the pizza joint, Pizza Man, next to my apartment. It was an odd name for a restaurant, but the pie was spectacular.

We sat down in a booth and Jaclyn ordered a Maker's Mark on the rocks. Maker's Mark? On the rocks? In 2005, I loved bourbon. I mean, I loved drinking bourbon straight from the bottle and falling down the stairs later. But the way she caressed this glass, the way she smelled it, the way she sipped it—was unlike any way I had ever seen bourbon consumed.

I ordered Pinot Noir, because I had just watched the movie *Sideways* and, well, I needed to impress this brilliant, beautiful woman.

Then she ordered a salad.

"I will take an arugula salad with balsamic vinaigrette," Jaclyn told the waiter.

Okay, time out. *What the hell is balsamic vinaigrette?* Hand to a hot stove, I had no idea. The waiter looked down at me, holding his notepad and fidgeting with his apron.

"Sir?" he said. I wanted a salad, but I had already forgotten the words that had just come out of Jaclyn's mouth. Should I get ranch dressing? Blue cheese? No. I don't want to look pedestrian. That's when it clicked. "I'll have the same," I said.

And then the salad appeared. I was, at least, familiar with arugula, but the little black puddles all over my greens were completely foreign to me. I am by no means afraid of new food. I was at the forefront of the 1990s sushi buffet revolution in Oklahoma, and I taught line cooks how to perfectly grill onions when I worked at a burger joint at Oklahoma State. But still I panicked, fearing Jaclyn would judge me for not knowing or understanding this balsamic thing. Still, even as my anxiety rose, Jaclyn's presence calmed me. It's as if she could look at me and completely quell all fear. It was absolutely remarkable.

Jaclyn held her fork in her right hand, cut the salad with her left, slipped food on the fork and moved the fork to her left hand, placing it in her mouth. What in the hell was that? In the span of fifteen minutes, this woman opened my eyes about how to sip bourbon, a new salad dressing, and an intimidating style of eating I had never seen before. If I could, I would have gotten on a plane back to Iraq out of fear of screwing up this date.

Breathe. Just breathe.

I couldn't even begin to eat with my left hand, so I ate the way I always have. I jabbed my fork, poking the arugula to no avail. I slid the fork under the balsamic-drenched green and moved it to my mouth in one motion. It fell on my shirt. Great. Just great. Not only was I an uneducated food person, but I was also apparently a slob. Thankfully, Jaclyn didn't notice or acknowledge the stain on my shirt. Eventually, the salad ended up in my mouth.

"Wow," I said loudly. "This is amazing."

Jaclyn smiled, nodded her head, and simply said, "I know, right? So good."

The rush of flavors in my mouth was second only to the butterflies I felt about this woman. But the balsamic vinaigrette moment shaped every meal I ate after that day, and it became a catalyst for the few moments of joy I experienced during my early Iraq War struggles. I didn't realize it at the moment, but tasting this exquisite salad dressing paused my war anxiety. The relief came in the moments when my mind shifted to what was on my tongue, and for a split second I wasn't thinking about the time I nearly died or the friends I had lost in the war. Looking back years later, I saw that exploring the sense of taste helped me feel whole when I was utterly broken.

Who knew?

My therapist did.

I kept the promise I made to Jaclyn the night I tried to commit suicide and sought help right away—therapy.

As I pulled into the VA hospital parking lot, I surveyed the other VA patients and wondered if they showed my destiny: elderly men gingerly walking with gauze patches over their eyes, ears, and parts of their faces. Some rolled out in wheelchairs. And most quickly lit up cigarettes the minute they were right next to the "no smoking" sign, reminding me of soldiers smoking in the army who often cited the phrase: "Smoke 'em if you got 'em." As these veterans exited the building, men in suits carrying briefcases rushed in, likely eager to sell their drugs or surgical devices to the hospital.

This observation may have played a role in me not finding a parking spot. I'd later learn that no matter the VA, no matter the city, parking is always an issue. And many of these World War II vets with limited mobility had to travel the length of a football field to find their car.

By the time I parked, I was five minutes late.

Elevators made me uncomfortable, so I took the stairs to the basement, where the PTSD treatment center was manned by a large security guard.

"Can I help you?" he asked.

I wanted to turn around. To leave.

"Yessir, um, I have an appointment," I said.

"That way," he said, pointing toward the door.

Ah yes, your typical doctor's office waiting room. Cold white tile floors. Stacks of magazines nobody read. And the office attendant talking about her life as the rest of us waited in fear of what lay down the dimly lit hallway with a flickering overhead fluorescent.

"Mr. Minnick," a lady standing at the door called.

She stood no taller than my shoulder with short, dirty blond hair and glasses. She held a green folder as thick as a book. Was that my chart?

I walked toward her, extended my hand for a shake. But she didn't return the handshake. Instead she smiled and said, "I'm Betty,[†] your therapist. Follow me." Why didn't she shake my hand?

I could hear, almost *feel*, the fluorescent lights humming as we walked past offices. Hers was the last one on the far right. As she opened her creaking door, part of me wondered if this wasn't some experiment or an organ harvesting center. Somehow, I found the idea of an unlicensed doctor cutting out my kidneys comedic.

Fortunately, Betty's office contained just a couple of chairs, a desk, stacks of books, and a dozen yellow sticky notes on her computer.

I sat down in an ice-cold metal chair with the overhead light beaming down. An air conditioner thumped.

Betty looked at her chart, looked at me, and after the usual "any thoughts of harming yourself or others" therapy check-in, just went straight into it.

"Tell me about yourself."

I had tried therapy a couple times since coming home and it

† Betty is not my therapist's real name. She requested that if I ever write about her to not use her name.

hadn't worked. Within the first twenty minutes of a session, the therapists wanted to prescribe me an antidepressant. While I wasn't opposed to medication, I also wanted to know what the hell was happening to me. I hoped this time was different and that I could fix myself, go back to the old me.

I poured my heart out to Betty. Told her about the nightmares, the flashbacks, and every little thing that turned me into a hot mess.

During our first few sessions, I felt relief. Just talking to somebody who didn't want to medicate me was therapeutic, and I genuinely thought therapy's sole role was pouring your heart out. But Betty was about to teach me how much work really goes into war trauma recovery. It's not just talking, and it involves homework.

"I want to focus on a single traumatic event. The one that comes up a lot," she said. "I want you to write about that event. Describe every single detail. How you felt in every moment."

Betty was referencing June 24, 2004, the day I almost died in Mosul, Iraq. June 24, 2007, also happens to be the date of my suicide attempt. I soon learned trauma anniversaries frequently lead to reliving the trauma and creating new negative life events.

In the exposure therapy exercise, I wrote about this incident every single day for three months, with the goal of its grip lessening each time I wrote about it. In our sessions, Betty made me read it out loud:

I am leaving the battle update brief when we get word that insurgents bombed several police stations in Mosul. And higher-ups wanted documentation of the car bombs. I joined a small team and photographed the craters, piles of scrap from the car explosions and the body parts. I am numb to seeing charred body parts, but seeing them still doesn't feel good.

As we are leaving one of the bombing sites, we receive an order to go to a mosque, where insurgents are shooting at the Stryker battalion. "Have the photographer take a picture of them shooting from the mosque."

We arrived minutes later, the firefight fully engaged. Before the Strykers launch TOW missiles into the mosque all but ending the fight, I am able to capture an image of the enemy firing at us from a holy site, which is against the Geneva Conventions.

The battle over, my small team and I are still in the road leading up to the mosque, alone, vulnerable and away from the main fighting force. A white van pulls up to the grassy field, adjacent to our three humvees. Several men jump out, all carrying weapons. One had an RPG.

Bullets are flying everywhere. I can hear them zinging past my head. We return fire. Our .50 Cal gunner mows them down. I slink my camera to the slide and take a firing position with my M16. The RPG is fired. It's coming right toward me.

It looked like a baseball bat with a tail of fire. And in that instant, I just knew I was dead.

The RPG landed with me in the kill zone and bounced over me. It did not explode. It was a dud.

We killed all but one person, a wounded man in brown pants who limped away from the fight. The squad leader screamed to get back in the vehicles. As we drove, we were pelted with AK-47 rounds that could not penetrate the armor. I also realized my firing port was open. I had fired my weapon during the exchange.

Even though I've written hundreds of these therapy essays and recited the story in therapy and publicly, I still cannot write about or verbally recall the events of June 24, 2004, without deep emotions. The what-ifs never go away. I am not sure trauma victims ever lose that initial recognition of what happened to them. The difference is learning how to cope with what happened, so you don't fall further into the trauma hold.

After thirty or so exposure reading sessions, Betty stopped me in the middle of a reading, asking how it felt to read a certain line and what my belief was in relation to how I felt. She dissected June 24, allowing my brain to process each moment. Why didn't I die? Why did they have to shoot at us? Why were they there? Did I shoot somebody? Why did so many people have to die? How? Why?

When these questions run through our minds, in private or public moments, we fill the unanswerable void with the worst possible scenarios: *I don't deserve to be alive. That mission was because of me, to take pictures; I risked everybody's lives. What was the point of it? Nobody cares.*

These beliefs took me down the dark path of fear, a suicide attempt, and unrelenting anger that could have put me in jail. The questions or beliefs in my head sparked a feeling in the moment that, in any given split second, it could be the end of my life.

"Trauma is like an onion," Betty told me. "The foundation trauma is in the center. And your new traumas layer over it. So we need to peel away at each one of these beliefs before they lead to new traumas."

Betty handed me a single piece of paper—an ABC worksheet,

which was so named for its model of (A) activating events, (B) beliefs and (C) emotional and behavioral consequences. The worksheets continued the work of prying into my mind to examine the beliefs that made me angry or sad. This helped me process what happened, my belief about it, and whether that belief holds up to facts. Every time an incident derailed me, I filled out a worksheet. An argument with Jaclyn. A speech about the war by President Bush. Helicopters. Buildings. White vans. Pieces of garbage. Anything that reminded me of Iraq. Anytime I was triggered, I filled out a worksheet. I also used the worksheets for life situations.

What happened? A car cut me off.
What's your feeling? This person has it in for me.
What belief is this associated with? Anger.
Is this belief based in fact? No.
What can you tell yourself the next time this happens?
The car was in a hurry and just rushing in traffic. The driver was not intentionally trying to attack me.

Over two years, I filled out so many worksheets that my mind began to automatically process the moment in real time, in my head. Eventually, an Iraq War political discussion could be playing on the TV in the background and I wouldn't start seeing red. I transformed the thought *I was sent to Iraq to fight an oil war* to *I served my country and cannot control what our leaders do*. This distinction, for me, was the difference between slamming my fist on a restaurant table and calmly carrying on with my meal during potentially triggering moments.

I still could not attend concerts because of the overwhelming anxiety crowds caused and did not enjoy sports like I once did. The only things that truly brought me joy were a good meal and spending time with Jaclyn. Every second I spent with her, my anxiety deteriorated, but early in our relationship I ignored how happy she made me. In fact, I nearly ruined this happiness before it even truly began. When our relationship had grown to the next level, she wanted me to move to Kentucky to be closer to her. I was clearly done with Wisconsin, ready to move on to the next phase of my life. But instead of going with what my heart truly wanted—to be with her—I told Jaclyn I wanted to move to New Mexico to live with my college buddy, Shawn.

I believe some men possess this awful trait: We act like a petulant child or an untamed bronco when facing true love and make decisions against our own best interests, because we don't want to admit we've been "claimed."

Suffice it to say, my marriage to Jaclyn almost didn't happen, simply because I was an idiot. When I told her about the move to New Mexico, she replied, "Well, then, you're sending me a very clear message." And then silence, which sent a thousand spears into my heart, knowing I was on the verge of screwing up the best thing to ever happen to me. I decided to move to Kentucky right there and then.

But as I packed up my car for the move, I wondered: *Had I made this decision out of love or fear of losing her? Was it the same thing?*

When I saw the "Welcome to Kentucky" sign on the I-65 bridge, I knew I had moved for love. Not fear.

Her love opened my life to new doors and possibilities. I am who I am and where I am today because Manbreaker broke me in a good way.

Jaclyn said yes to me on May 25, 2007, and we embarked on a life journey together consisting of good food, silly adult cartoons, travel abroad, and the need to hear each other's voice. She worked nights as an ER psychiatric nurse and would later pursue her doctorate in nursing practice, while supporting me through both my PTSD struggles and low-income profession as a writer. Even though we didn't have much money, we never argued over finances. And I often called her during a shift, just to hear her voice and cope with some Iraq-related trigger or nightmare.

Of course, I couldn't strap Jaclyn to me to help me deal with every moment of everyday life. Thus, my coping tools helped me survive, and Betty was just beginning to give me the tools to become a happy person.

"Have you ever heard of aromatherapy?" she asked about two years into my therapy journey.

"Yes, of course, that's what they sell at my wife's yoga studio. Well, that and crystals," I replied, wondering if we were about to go down some sort of New Age road.

"Well, it's not exactly that. But I think you can use your other senses to help ground yourself, especially since you're becoming such a foodie... Whenever you feel the trigger warnings, close your eyes and take in the smells," Betty said. "Imagine where they come from and what are they, and process those thoughts."

I come from a long line of great smellers. I first recognized this family trait when I was about twelve and my mom called out the smell of burnt popcorn in a movie theater parking lot while we were still in the car. As we walked into the theater, the place reeked of overcooked popcorn. This natural talent, though, was as much a curse as a gift. When a kid farted in class, I was the first to smell it and always got blamed, because of the class loudmouth's classic "the smeller is the feller" detective work. And there's no escaping the stench of a New York City cab driver who hasn't bathed in a week or a fermenting trash room in an apartment building. Ugh, that stink!

I also nosed essential oils that calmed me. A little lavender or eucalyptus under my nose relaxed my shoulders, eased all tension, and brought me peace.

Aromatherapy made sense in theory, but I seriously considered looking for a new therapist when Betty handed me a bag of barbecue potato chips. She instructed me to take a chip and slowly bite. She said to think about how it feels on the tongue, how the salt separates from the barbecue, about what part of the tongue it's hitting. "Where does it crunch? Be very, very specific about it," Betty asked.

Was she insane? How could eating a chip help me?

I grabbed the bottom of my chair and rocked back and forth, contemplating whether I was ready for this. Then, I wondered: *What am I afraid of? It's a friggin' chip!*

I placed the chip on my tongue, closed my eyes, and crunched. I was alone with it, thinking about how the saltiness separated on my tongue from the sweetness. The flavors populated all over my tongue. I felt the crunch push the chip under my gums, along the back of my tongue, and onto the roof of my palate. I felt every single detail of this chip, and my tongue was lighting up in much the same way it did when I had first tasted balsamic vinaigrette on my first date with Jaclyn.

I really tasted a chip for the first time.

Oh sure, I had placed handfuls of Lays in my mouth, washing them down with a cold beer, usually while watching a game on TV. But had I ever really stopped and thought about the chip?

"Wow," I told Betty. "That was amazing."

I left this therapy session with my mind racing. All I could think about was how my tongue had perceived the chip. Could I apply this intense concentration and sensation to other things?

When I tasted bourbon for the first time using this technique, I closed my eyes and let my tongue pulsate on the sides, middle, and front instead of just swallowing or trying to evade the sensation of the alcohol. As I did so, a cadre of flavors blossomed within seconds, and suddenly the everyday bourbon Henry McKenna turned into the most complex thing I had ever tasted.

I also noticed how I felt when tasting fine foods and how Jaclyn introduced me to fare that tingled my tongue. In a matter of a couple years, I went from the generic gelatin can of tomato soup that didn't expire for five years to sprinkling basil leaves over top of Whole Foods's freshly made soup. When I sipped this soup or crunched a cold piece of chipotle-dusted jicama, my soul's darkness lit up, offering joy and a search for this new person developing. With every nip of smoked paprika, cumin, or fine wine, I felt honest-to-goodness change in my inner being.

While I still loved sports, I started to pick cooking shows over the World Series on TV and chose distillery and wine tours over going to football games.

What was happening?

I couldn't exactly describe what this taste discovery had done to me; I just knew I liked it.

And when I love something, I turn it into work. What's the old saying? If you love what you do, you'll never work a day in your life.

CHAPTER 2
TO KENTUCKY

BEFORE MARRIAGE, BEFORE my taste mindfulness exercise, I needed a job.

Back in 2005, you looked for a job in the newspaper. There were some job-searching websites available, but I still felt the need to circle the two-inch "help wanted" ad in red pen. Perhaps there's something romantic about that.

With a pocket full of coins, I walked to the newspaper stands a block from Jaclyn's condo in downtown Louisville directly above the Spaghetti Factory. I popped a quarter in the newspaper stand's slot and it rolled right out. I tried again. And again. In a fit of rage, I kicked the rusted hunk of metal and glass, and the lid tumbled down with a thud. Apparently, it didn't need quarters. Free paper. I felt silly as I grabbed the tabloid-shaped weekly and flipped to the advertisements.

I needed a job. This paper seemed to do quite well with advertisements for strip clubs, music halls, and people selling bongs. Not what I was looking for, I thought, but a tiny ad caught my eye—"restaurant trade editor." Since my balsamic vinaigrette moment, I had explored other vinaigrettes, such as champagne raspberry, and fallen in love with diced garlic on pepperoni pizza accompanied by, of course, Pinot Noir.

I applied for the restaurant trade editor job, and the interview featured two incredibly different people—Joe Grove, the former editor of the *LEO*, a free Louisville newspaper, and Paul Barron, the publisher of a new magazine called *Fast Casual*.

"We need somebody to cover the business of fast-casual restaurants like Panera Bread and Starbucks," said Paul, who was a fan of Oklahoma University, the rival of my alma mater. "And even a Poke can do that."

Joe said, "You'll report directly to me, but the job is yours."

I honestly didn't talk much about my skill set in the interview. They read my past forestry works and loved my military background. The job was mine for a whopping $35,000 a year, and I was elated.

I covered the fast-food industry. Or what the "industry" called *quick-service* or sometimes *fast-casual*, which was still being defined then. I investigated companies, especially the publicly traded ones, broke news on limited time offerings, such as the return of the McRib, and interviewed major corporate CEOs, who taught me a thing or two about how to be pricks. I'll never forget asking Chipotle CEO and founder Steve Ells about why he used Tabasco sauce in his restaurants instead of making his own hot sauce. Chipotle competitors like Moe's Southwest Grill and Baja Fresh had created unique custom-branded sauces, so I thought it was a fair question. Ells was so angered by my question it was as if I had punched his dog. He wrapped up the interview shortly after the query, grabbed my digital camera, and pointed to the only image I had taken. “This one will work,” he said as he marched out of the conference room.

I was always on the hunt for a juicy scoop or the next big trend. I once received a tip about Panera Bread testing wine service in a few locations. Serving alcohol in a fast-casual concept is commonplace today, but in 2006 there were many questions about the legality and ethics of it. Could you serve alcohol in a drive-through? What if somebody wanted to take the wine to go? Is it responsible to serve alcohol in a place designed to turn around tables in thirty minutes? Could the fast-casual restaurants get actual licenses to sell alcohol?

As I looked into it, I found that the restaurants faced public pressure from churches and a little more scrutiny from the local cops. After all, wherever alcohol is served, some slick kid has a fake ID. Then, there were these strange laws, such as you couldn’t sell wine on Sundays in some states, even in restaurants, and a store worker must pour you the wine in others. The alcohol laws fascinated me and would be a source of lifelong intrigue.

In May 2006, my first alcohol article, “To Wine or Not To Wine,” was published in *Fast Casual* magazine. Little did I know that this short piece planted the first seed in what would become my career covering booze. I would spend the majority of my adult life unraveling oddities in the alcohol world. And it really did start with fast food.

I loved this job.

But I earned diddly-squat and managed a stable of freelance

writers, some of whom earned more than $100,000 a year. I was intrigued by the freelance life and knew managing my own schedule could pay dividends for my own mental health. I decided to make the jump.

I left my food editor job in December 2006, grabbed every restaurant, food, wine, and business trade magazine I could find in my previous employer's sales department, and pitched the magazine editors in hopes of finding new writing opportunities. Within a week, one replied with a simple question: "Since you live in Kentucky, could you write about the Kentucky Bourbon Trail? We are covering that for an upcoming issue." I said yes, and *Successful Meetings* published my first bourbon article several months later.

Within an hour of accepting this story, I wrote in my notepad, "Add bourbon to genres to cover." Truthfully, though, my bourbon curiosity had begun with Jaclyn ordering Maker's Mark on our first date.

So when I moved to Kentucky from Milwaukee, shortly after returning home from Iraq, I began learning from bartenders, the gatekeepers to whiskey knowledge. And it all started at a downtown Louisville restaurant bar called Bistro 301.

The sticky floor leading up to the bar didn't stop me from sitting down. I was thirsty. And a slight hint of sunlight broke through a sliver of a window and beamed right onto many brown-colored liquor bottles. All bourbon.

As I sat down, my elbows splashed tiny puddles of bleach-water on the long, lacquered bar. "What bourbon should I get?" I asked the bartender.

In 2006, while I had come a long way since bootlegging Jim Beam in Listerine bottles to Mosul, Iraq, I knew little about bourbon, relying on professionals to guide me. In a deep smoker's voice, the bartender said: "How about some Weller 12?" I had heard of Weller but wouldn't know it from Jack Daniel's.

"Pour me whatever bourbon you recommend," I said. The bartender reached into the well, bottles clinked, and he showed me one whose label read "Weller" in an old-fashioned script. It looked cheap.

Still, I nodded my head.

"So this is the best pour for your money," the bartender said, tilting the bottle into my glass for the special—$4 shots. I kicked it back, feeling the Weller 12-year-old rush down my throat with a slight tingle.

The bartender asked, "Well, what brings you to town?"

I raised my hand and pointed at my barren ring finger. I had yet to propose to Jaclyn but would soon. "Moved here for a woman," I said. "Now, tell me about this bourbon."

"Ever heard of Pappy Van Winkle?"

"No," I said.

He grabbed a bottle from the backbar. Its label featured an old man smoking a cigar. "This is Pappy 23. The best thing in bourbon. That Weller is the same recipe." I would later learn that both Pappy and Weller come from a style of bourbon called "wheaters" or "wheated bourbon," in which wheat is used as the flavor grain over the more typical rye. However, Pappy ages longer than Weller, giving it a deeper caramel flavor. He popped the cork off the Pappy, poured a thimble-sized nip into a shot glass, and pushed it toward me. "On the house. Welcome to Kentucky."

Before my immersion in the industry, I didn't really know how to sip bourbon, but I tried to mimic Jaclyn on our first date with her eyes making love to Maker's Mark. I caressed the warm glass rim, looked at its lush brown color, smelled what seemed like candied caramel, and kicked back that glass as if I were on the balcony of the Oklahoma State Delta Chi Fraternity house.

I cringed. Oh, holy burn, that hurt on the way down. It was as if somebody had lit a match in my throat.

The bartender laughed. Looking back on that moment, I'm more than embarrassed I slammed a bourbon that would later auction for $40,000 a bottle. In my defense, however, I was three years away from my groundbreaking training—the moment that sealed my fate as a taster. I was in the minor leagues at this point. Heck, I wasn't even in the minors; I was a junior high backup catcher with bad knees.

Bistro 301 became my early bourbon classroom. I learned the differences between rye and bourbon, the meaning of a mash bill, and how Weller was a younger version of Pappy. I earned my bourbon chops here and turned those lessons into freelance writing pitches. I was a sponge and parlayed my bar talks into deeper, more meaningful lessons with distillers, who, as it turns out, are brilliant educators.

In college, I struggled in chemistry. But when distillers talked about turning corn into bourbon, I absorbed every iota. I couldn't name more than five element symbols from the periodic table, but through distillers, I learned how yeast ate sugar and created alcohol as waste, how heat separated the alcohol from solids and condensed vapors into the spirit, and that toasting and charring a barrel changes the wood's chemical composition. Just like wood imparts flavor in barbecue, so do a barrel's wood sugars give bourbon its sweeter base.

Perhaps most importantly, these distillers taught me their trade when I was in the most need of guidance. The internal wounds fresh from war, I still suffered from nightmares and flashbacks. As I learned in therapy, I needed a positive hobby to occupy my brain and help override the constant thought of war. Granted, no therapist would encourage a veteran to turn their attention to alcohol. And I genuinely hope my story doesn't become a crutch for alcoholics as they reach for their second bottle of the night. But learning about bourbon, how it's made and the history behind it, actually made me want to drink less. I savored it instead of downing it, and bourbon became a sanctuary from my war thoughts early in my career. I obsessed over its history, a deep dive into a niche American truth not taught in schools.

Early American settlers distilled grains for medicinal purposes and the occasional soiree. George Washington, a distiller himself, issued whiskey to his troops during the Revolutionary War and with the help of Alexander Hamilton, George Washington's Secretary of the Treasury, later imposed the whiskey tax that led to the Whiskey Rebellion in the early 1790s. Farmers moved west into Tennessee and Kentucky, founding distilleries along the Ohio River and near natural springs. They distilled corn and eventually stored it in new charred oak barrels, a type of whiskey later called *bourbon*, which President William Howard Taft codified in federal law in 1909. At the time, many companies bottled a colored neutral spirit or rum and called it bourbon, creating mass confusion over what was bourbon, which is why Taft felt the need to define all types of whiskey. Congress later etched the definition in stone in 1964 as a unique product of the United States. Thus, no country with a free trade agreement with the United States can label its whiskey bourbon even if it was made the same way as in Kentucky. Bourbon's geographical protection is the same as that for scotch, cognac, and champagne, which is why its uniquely American pedigree often makes bourbon a target in trade wars.

Presidents Washington, Thomas Jefferson, Abraham Lincoln, Ulysses S. Grant, Grover Cleveland, William McKinley, Taft, Franklin D. Roosevelt, John F. Kennedy, Barack Obama, and Donald Trump have all played historical roles in American whiskey. And that's not even counting the U.S. leaders meeting for a drink in closed-door discussions. Henry Clay, Kentucky statesman and runner-up in the 1832 presidential election, said he used bourbon "to lubricate the wheels of government."[1]

I attacked bourbon writing from every angle: science, history, production, tourism, why it's made, and even taxes. But, truthfully, the market wasn't ready for a full-time bourbon journalist, so I dabbled in bourbon where I could but mostly focused on wine, which offered a plethora of writing opportunities that bourbon simply did not.

I secured multiple writing gigs for magazines that sent me to wine country in Argentina, Chile, France, Italy, Portugal, Spain, and throughout the United States. But emotionally, I was still extremely vulnerable. Therapy had allowed me to survive in this new world, but triggers lurked at every turn and I would be tested many times over.

Wine media doesn't have many military veterans, so I was like an exotic creature walking in their presence. Fortunately, Betty gave me a unique grounding technique to help me through uncomfortable situations.

"When you are in a moment that you cannot process, your brain is being overwhelmed with whatever you are seeing and you can't stop and take a breath, find something to touch and focus on how it feels on your fingers. This will focus your brain on what you're touching instead of the overwhelming thoughts," she instructed.

Once, while on a press trip in a packed media bus winding across French roads, a California reporter cornered me in the back seat.

"So you were in Iraq?"

"Yes," I said.

"I mean, how. How could you do that? Don't get me wrong, I support the troops, but this war is totally unjust. We've committed war crimes; there were no weapons of mass destruction."

If this conversation had happened two years earlier, I am not sure how I would have responded. Likely with rage. But here I was in France, feeling pressure to be polite, with my heart beating faster and desperately wanting this man to go away. Other heads turned. Nearly half the reporters in the van were listening to the conversation, watching my reaction, as if they all had wanted to ask me the same questions. The soft voice of a National Geographic narrator likely echoed in their heads: "As the twenty-nine-year-old

Iraq War soldier is cornered, he surveys the room and considers the patented crazy veteran bull rush that could result in him leaving this bus in a straitjacket. But the young man takes a deep breath…"

I felt their eyes upon me. My anxiety climbed up to my throat. I tried to process the moment using my cognitive skills: *How do I feel? What's my belief? Is it based on fact or fiction?* With every answer, I felt poked, prodded, and pushed. My ABC worksheet skills did not work here. That's when I recalled my grounding exercise. "Touch something and think about how it feels," Betty had said.

I reached into my pocket and felt a U.S. quarter. I slowly caressed the ridges and the indentation of President Washington's head, and tried to make out the year it was printed. My mind concentrated solely on the quarter, ignoring the stares upon me. My body calmed. This trick likely saved me from a panic attack in that van.

"Yeah, look, I was just a low guy soldier and got my schooling paid for, and I am trying to move on from that part of my life," I said.

The heads turned, likely disappointed with my answer, and the California reporter looked at me with a dismayed expression. I really needed people to see me as somebody other than a veteran. I was not ashamed of my service, but I was trying to build a new life and the further I could move away from the Iraq conversations the better my life could become. Betty had also told me, "You cannot change people's beliefs; you can only change how you feel." Can you imagine a world where everyone followed Betty's advice?

Back in France, with my hand on the quarter in my pocket, I asked the California reporter to tell me about limestone's importance in wine. He was a veteran wine writer and knew far more about the category than anybody on the bus. Just as he was about to turn his back to me, his bushy eyebrows raised, transforming from the curious protester to the professor. He detailed the importance of limestone soils for soil drainage. "There's a reason Louisiana cannot grow grapes well—when it rains, the water stays in the soil. Limestone also provides minerals to the vines."

In bourbon, limestone filters out unwanted minerals from springs, while in wine, it helps with drainage and provides minerals. With every media bus ride and every conversation with drinks experts, I absorbed the information like a sponge, digging deeper. And, truthfully, this curiosity moved me one step farther from the memories of trauma, because I was always seeking answers instead of reacting to something that made me hurt.

I think I was meant to be in this fascinating beverage world, one that covered how things were made.

Because I had studied agricultural communications at Oklahoma State, I had a decent understanding of the soil chemistries for growing corn, grapes, and oak, allowing me a different angle than the typical bubblegum marketing crap often seen in drinks journalism. I traveled with master sommeliers, like Isa Bal of the Fat Duck in London and Paolo Barbieri of Alex in Las Vegas, observing how these brilliant tasters perceive wine.

While we were together in France, I watched Isa taste a red wine blind. He swirled the dark, fleshy liquid, its legs dripping down the glass, and the moment the whirlpool slowed he brought the wine to his nose. Moving the glass at all angles and tilting his head, Isa blurted, "Right bank Bordeaux." Completely connected to the glass, oblivious to the people watching him, he nosed again, this time a little farther away: "Saint Emilion." Everyone at the small table looked at him in awe; the French waiter nodded in agreement. Then, he sipped. "A Grand Cru Classé." At this point more people gathered around, watching Isa, who had won the Best Sommelier in Europe taste-off the year prior, and we all awaited his determination of this wine. "1990 Château Figeac," he said. The crowd went nuts. A couple of Frenchmen sighed. "Well, of course, he got that. Easy."

I watched Isa Ball with curiosity. Growing up in Oklahoma, where alcohol was frequently connected to the devil, and having a drunken grandfather who abused my father, I was curious about the idea of professional tasters. This offered me a new lens through which to view alcohol. Was it possible to taste and not become an alcoholic?

As I battled PTSD and fell in love with the alcohol industry, I asked my therapist whether I should cover alcohol. Because no matter what you tell yourself, the perception of others still can weigh heavily.

"Do you have a problem drinking it?"

"No," I said, thinking about it. But there were a few moments of drinking too much and doing dumb shit. "I mean in college, I definitely drank too much and fell down stairs and got in some fights. In the army, I may have urinated on a first sergeant accidentally while slamming beers. But I was drinking to drink. In these tasting settings, nobody is really drinking for intoxication in either wine or bourbon. It's a sip and a conversation, breaking down what they are tasting. I have never seen anybody intoxicated like I did on a random Tuesday in college and the military."

"Okay," Betty said, "but keep an eye on it. If you find yourself drinking to cope with a situation or feeling that you 'need' a drink, you'll want to address it."

But that never happened. The more I was around alcohol and spirits professionals, the less I wanted to drink beer or take a shot. I desired knowledge, not oblivion.

With bourbon, master distillers flexed their Glencairn in the sunlight, describing the color as "russet with purple hues." At first, I called bullshit. Then, I lifted my glass to a window and there it was, a shimmering deep russet reflecting purple. "In bourbon, describing what you're tasting is still relatively new," Chris Morris, master distiller for Woodford Reserve, told me in 2008. "We didn't start tasting notes until the 1990s." I definitely entered the field of bourbon writing during the beginning of a new frontier, which intrigued me even more about the subject.

I also discovered a passion for the history of drinking, diving into books such as *Wine & War* and devouring anything Chuck Cowdery wrote on bourbon. A former communications rep for Jim Beam and Brown-Forman, Chuck left the corporate bourbon writing profession in the early 1990s and produced and directed a bourbon documentary, *Made and Bottled in Kentucky*, that aired on PBS. He also created the *Bourbon Country Reader*, a monthly newsletter, and the first major blog covering bourbon. Chuck's book *Bourbon, Straight* and his blog works debunked many myths in American whiskey and romanticized the true stories and history of the spirit I loved. Chuck was inducted into the Kentucky Bourbon Hall of Fame in 2009, and his writing was actually used in court cases about bourbon. Chuck built the American whiskey writing profession, and I idolized his no-bullshit style of writing, constantly calling out brands and their questionable marketing.

I met Chuck for the first time in Canada on a Canadian whiskey trip, where my skills for PTSD recovery were truly tested. Like on the French wine trip, this one featured a curious reporter, who asked if I had killed somebody. No worksheet in the world can prepare you for that question.

We were in a fancy hotel that Queen Elizabeth once stayed in and drinking Canadian Mist Manhattans. "So did you?" the writer asked. I turned white as a ghost and stuttered, "Um, uh," before the leader of the trip started talking and saved me. As he shared the itinerary, I touched a quarter, closed my eyes, and imagined the ridges on its edge, slowly rubbing my thumb over George Washington's raised head. I focused every thought on that quarter, taking my mind off the "did you kill anybody" reporter guy.

That technique saved me many other times, while aromatherapy and taste mindfulness purged any leftover anxiety and triggers. It was a constant battle to keep my PTSD at bay, but I had tools to survive and a new hobby that was becoming my profession. And I realized how unique my situation was.

One day after a therapy session, I poured two fingers of my favorite daily bourbon—Henry McKenna—into a brandy snifter and raised it to analyze the color. Even early in my career, I loved looking at bourbon, noticing how some brands are darker due to more age in the barrel. This one also had slight purple hues, likely from some sort of reflection in my upstairs office. I swirled it around, brought it to my nose, and smelled it with my mouth slightly open—a technique taught to me by master sommelier Isa

Ball. My lips touched the glass, slightly tilting it back, and a wave of bourbon rushed onto my tongue.

I closed my eyes and focused on how the bourbon felt. What part of the tongue did it resonate? I tasted again, focusing the second time on the most prominent part of the tongue it populated. Henry McKenna felt powerful on the middle of my tongue and soft on the sides. As it tingled, I wondered out loud, "What does that taste like?" The flavor reminded me of something I couldn't quite put my finger on.

Cars drove by. A UPS man rang the doorbell. It was surprisingly loud for a Tuesday afternoon in my neighborhood. But I was not distracted. I was solely focused on my tongue. I tasted a third time, a thimbleful, and that's when the flavor hit me. "It's Grandpa's cornbread with butter and honey," I said, and jumped up and down. In a way, I am thankful nobody saw this gleeful, sophomoric kid doing dance moves that would trend on social media now for all the wrong reasons. But this is the moment a new me was born.

Life breathed in every fiber of my being. The slightest touch of a particular bourbon sent shock waves through my system. And this discovery could not have come at a better time.

While my career as a wine and spirits journalist was taking off, my skill set was limited to reporting, which was fine, but I envied renowned wine critics and bestselling authors Karen MacNeil and Robert Parker of the wine world, who delivered well-crafted tasting notes. My bourbon writer hero Chuck Cowdery said, "There's a difference between having a good palate and actually writing tasting notes." My goal was to have a great palate and to tap into the barbecue potato chip exercise to explain what I perceived. Taste mindfulness meant to truly connect my brain to my palate and thoroughly dissect everything I tasted.

I mapped my tongue, realizing I found sweetness on the tip, savory in the middle, bitterness in the middle back and the sides, and spiciness in the far back. And I tasted, focusing on what part of the tongue it resonated. Tasted again, focusing on those particular spots, and determined what came to mind. I found many notes taking me back to my grandma's kitchen or my school cafeteria (which was not always a good thing). As my library of taste grew, so did the tasting notes I could find, such as that wonderful slice of marzipan I devoured in a Saint Emilion café. I mapped my tongue, examining where I tasted particular flavors, taking taste mindfulness to another level.

I was reprogramming my brain to forward-think about my taste buds instead of Iraq. With each bite, sip, and food discovery, my consciousness placed June 24, 2004, the snipers and car bombs, farther in the rearview mirror. The more I actively thought about my taste buds, the less I thought about my trauma. I learned to focus on the things I enjoyed over the horrors I had endured.

When we hurt, a taste can make us feel whole again, bringing us back to the core of who we are. A good sip or bite can lead to a great conversation, laughs, and happy memories.

Or a taste can take you down a path you never expected. And in my case, an obsession to find the greatest bourbon ever made.

CHAPTER 3
OBSESSION

IT WAS 2010, three years since my suicide attempt, and I was at a key turning point in my career. Therapy taught me to stop the what-ifs and wondering if I would ever be the same person I had been before the war. A psychiatrist, not Betty, said: "You have to play the cards you're dealt." And even though I spent little time with this doctor and am not a poker player, that saying stuck. I stopped trying to be the former me, a pre-Iraq kid with no scars, and started to believe that overcoming adversity would make me a better person.

I built around the positives in my life—Jaclyn and bourbon.

Our marriage was a voyage of travel and food. We savored all tasty bites, from a Nathan's hot dog to a $600 dinner at Alex in the Wynn Las Vegas. With every meal, glorious conversation ensued over the absolutely ridiculous, fusing our own language into conversations from the likes of *Squidbillies*—"What you mean I gotta go to work on a Wednesday?"—and *Aqua Teen Hunger*

Force—"Tonight…you." Is there a better marital talk than one that nobody else understands or that makes the couple laugh? No, I say, but our dark humor sure draws attention.

Perhaps no story tells this better than when Jaclyn and I reserved our favorite table at our favorite restaurant, Corbett's, an ultra–fine-dining restaurant we could barely afford. A former dairy farm from the 1800s adjacent to a Costco parking lot, Corbett's was located in a two-story white siding former house with a limestone wall basement and was an island of fine dining fare in the Louisville area filled with fast food. Every bite from Corbett's brought me closer to Jaclyn. I felt the tingles over the food and our laughter.

One night, at Table 2, I took a small bite of pan-fried pheasant drizzled in truffle sauce and said out loud in my deep Southern preacher voice, "Now, praise, Jesus. Oh, Lord, oh my, oh my, aren't you tender. And don't you feel good going down my belly!" Jaclyn covered her mouth to stop herself from spitting out her drink, and the elderly lady next us dropped her jaw, looking at me. No doubt, she wanted to react as my grandma would if she heard me, and slap me upside the head with a flyswatter.

I also caught the sommelier's ear.

"Southern preacher tonight, Fred?" asked sommelier Troy Ritchie, refilling my water.

I laughed, taking another sip of Pinot Noir, likely an Argyle or Elk Cove. Now was about the time Troy started steering my palate toward dessert drinks. I often tingled for ice wine or port. But tonight, with the Southern voice fresh on my tongue, I had a hankering for bourbon.

"I have a nice picolit from Italy, Fred," he said.

"Oh, yes, that's super sweet. Maybe too sweet," I said, back to my normal Okie drawl.

"Are you thinking sherry? Or a port?" he asked, referring to a couple fortified wine favorites of mine.

"Hmmm. How about a bourbon?" I asked.

"Oh, you want to switch it up," he said. The somm handed me the bourbon list, and I picked 1792 for $7. Served in a squatty brandy snifter, the bourbon was layered in bananas Foster and cinnamon Red Hots candy notes. We didn't live far away from the restaurant, so we walked home and chatted about my choice of bourbon.

"1792, huh?" Jaclyn said.

"I know, I was just feeling it. I also just met the 1792 distiller, Greg Davis. Cool dude," I said.

We walked under the stars on a perfect Kentucky night, cut through the woods between our house and Corbett's, stopped under a large oak tree, and lay down and listened to the cars pass in a distance.

"You know, I think I am going to leave wine entirely and focus on bourbon," I told Jaclyn.

"You definitely love the stuff and are going to all the distilleries. I think it's an awesome idea, but do you have enough magazines that will pay you for bourbon work?"

Therein lay the rub of bourbon writing: I had garnered all the steady writing gigs possible for a freelance writer. But that was minuscule in comparison to wine or even knitting. Bourbon was a niche, albeit one that constituted a mighty legion of connoisseurs eager to learn.

"I think I could write a bourbon book," I said. This was just months after my first book, *Camera Boy*, had been published.

"Are you sure you want to go through that again?" she asked, referring to the rejection letters I had initially received from publishers. She was right to be hesitant. As I forged ahead and shopped my bourbon history book proposal over the next several months, I was told I was a nobody, that I had no audience, and that nobody cared about bourbon. That book did not come to fruition.

But this rejection only fueled my resolve and made me want to dig deeper into bourbon, learn more, and tell the story to the world. I sold magazine stories to *Costco Connection* and *Wine Enthusiast* and even picked up a few speaking/tasting gigs. Every chance I had, I talked bourbon.

While I still covered wine, and thoroughly enjoyed it, perhaps the greatest impact the wine world had on my foreseeable future was its fashion sense. Italian and French winemakers wore ascots, which I had fallen in love with as a kid. I watched *The Love Boat* and *Murder, She Wrote* in my youth, and many cool characters wore ascots. I could never find them in department stores.

While covering the Friuli wine region in northern Italy, I met an ascot-wearing curmudgeon, Bill Marsano, the former wine editor of United Airlines' *Hemispheres*. In his mid-sixties, Bill ignored the winemakers, even falling asleep when one led a tasting, and asked wine owners hard questions the rest of the writers dared not. He was a badass, and I instantly looked up to him.

I also took Jaclyn on this trip, and boy, did Bill fancy her! When I introduced myself to Bill, looking at his bright yellow ascot, he avoided me altogether and reached his hand toward Jaclyn. "Who is this beautiful young lady?" he said, caressing the top of her hand and meeting her eyes. Jaclyn blushed. Over the course of the trip, Bill flirted with my wife at wine tastings, over dinner, on hiking trips, and on the bus. Now, I didn't feel threatened, and Jaclyn said it was "cute."

I eventually cornered Bill and told him about my ascot love. He brushed me off and went on to scold a winemaker for improper marketing of a white wine.

When we returned home from that trip, a padded manila envelope was on our porch. It contained three ascots. They were from Bill, whose note said: "Please tell your beautiful wife I said hello." I don't think I have ever laughed so hard in my life.

Ascots aside, though, I knew my wine writing days were numbered.

Even though I received significant notoriety for my writings covering the controversy in the French wine region Saint Emilion, I gifted bottles of bourbon to winemakers and spent as much time educating colleagues on American whiskey as I did listening to them talk about wine. Wine had become a way to pay the bills; bourbon was the passion burning within. I wasn't sure when it would happen, but I knew I would eventually leave wine to entirely focus on bourbon.[‡]

I would soon make a fascinating discovery that would put me one step closer to bourbon exclusivity.

‡ When I made the decision to leave wine entirely, I was nominated for the world's best wine writer award in the under thirty-five category. We were in London in 2012 and surrounded by wine royalty, like Jancis Robinson, and all I could think about was bourbon people. That's when I knew it was time to focus on bourbon.

When the Brown-Forman publicist invited me to a Woodford Reserve trip with other bourbon writers, I was in the middle of a PTSD relapse.

On June 24, 2010, the anniversary of the RPG and three years since my suicide attempt, I awoke in the middle of the night under duress. Even though I was clearly in my own bed, I could feel the Iraqi heat on my brow and smell the asphalt from the Iraq highway. I was in a cold sweat, screaming, thinking I had just been fired upon. I had worked so hard to find coping skills and was in the middle of a burgeoning freelance whiskey writer career, and still PTSD had its meat hooks in me. Only this time, I didn't feel anger.

I was afraid.

"Bean, are you okay?" Jaclyn asked, using her nickname for me.

"No," I said, shaking.

She held me tight until I stopped trembling, but my mind raced with the episode that nearly took me from her before we had even met. Jaclyn was now a mental-health professional, and she knew how to ground me. But my depression and agoraphobia often surfaced, and I feared leaving home and was terrified of being on a bus with a group of inquisitive journalists on my upcoming trip. I didn't think I could withstand another confrontation like I had in France.

I was about to turn down the Woodford Reserve opportunity when Jaclyn simply asked, "Why?"

"Because I don't want to."

"You want to avoid your career?"

"No," I said, looking down, because I knew where this was going.

"You are trying to build a career in a new industry. You have to make decisions that build toward your goals. Avoiding lets the trauma win."

I know, I know. This was one of many of Jaclyn's pep talks that pushed me to where I needed to go. I kissed her on the cheek, stroked her hair, and said, "I don't know where I would be without you."

A couple of weeks later, I met the publicist and fellow journalists at a new hotel in Louisville called the 21c, which had an unusual number of penises passing off as art. Even at its front desk, naked cherubs stood over the concierge. In the hallways, penises. Basement, penises. Large, small, medium. Penises were everywhere. And in the men's bathroom, at the urinal, a one-way mirror made it seem like somebody was looking at your tallywhacker. Whoever designed this hotel definitely had male genitalia on the brain. And whatever PTSD was on my mind escaped with the gonads.

Come to find out, the hotel proprietor was a member of the same Brown family that owns Woodford Reserve and Jack Daniel's, among other brands. Steve Wilson is an eccentric fella who bronze molded his penis into a statue that you can stare at in a private dining room in the hotel restaurant. I'd later learn Wilson was a fan of art of all kinds and loved pushing creative boundaries that made people feel uncomfortable. Some years later, a good friend had to rush me out of the hotel when I nearly fell into pure rage after looking at 21c's featured art display—a bust of Osama bin Laden. Shock value has its place, I suppose.

Obviously, on this press trip, the penises were noticed by all.

"Have you ever seen that many penises hanging on the wall?" a colleague asked on the bus ride to Woodford County. I laughed and shook my head.

"Were those statues of naked children?" I asked.

"No, they were cherubs, a form of an angel," somebody said.

"Okay," I said, "weird."

As I looked upon the limestone cut roadside walls, I chuckled, thinking about how just a few weeks ago, I didn't want to go on this trip. And now I was making friends over conversations about art and absorbing the beauty of the short road trip.

I-64 cuts through the heart of Kentucky, from Louisville to Lexington, and is a geological wonder. From the 1950s to the 1970s, crews used dynamite and machines to slice through the hills, placing roads in the middle of tall, exposed limestone walls. Growing up in Oklahoma, I had never seen rock so beautiful. The Sooner State rivers were also red from the mud. But in Kentucky, the streams were a glistening blue or clear, with the fish near the bottom as visible as if they were an inch from the surface.

Kentucky also has something else in abundance—thoroughbreds. Upon exiting the highway, we saw horse farms lining both sides of the road. These majestic animals galloped along double-sided black fences in pastures so greenish-blue I could barely believe it. You hear about the Bluegrass State nickname, but you cannot fully comprehend its inspiration until you see a Kentucky Derby contender trotting in a field of sweet grass.

But as beautiful as this sight was, I couldn't help but notice the squalor next to these estates housing animals for the Sport of Kings. Next to $3 million horse farms stood dilapidated trailers with clotheslines of dingy shirts blowing in the wind, cars up on blocks, and empty toddler swimming pools. How could there be such income disparity between two properties so close together?

So much wealth and poverty in a short drive. *What is going on in this state?* I wondered. By the time we entered Woodford Reserve, the visible wealth disparity and what it must mean for this community had me deeply troubled.

I needed a bourbon.

A short, slender man with blondish-red hair and glasses greeted us as we got off the bus. He reached out his hand. "I'm Chris Morris, master distiller of Woodford Reserve. This is the home of James C. Crow and where modern bourbon was born." I had met Chris before at an industry cocktail event in 2008, but I had never been to his distillery, and I certainly hadn't heard of Woodford being the birthplace of modern bourbon or where James C. Crow distilled. I had heard Crow mentioned before, but I hadn't realized how significant he was until Chris touted him.

Looking around, I saw I was surrounded by the beautiful stone I had fallen in love with on the drive. Large limestone warehouses bordered the Woodford Reserve campus. The sounds of barrels thumping into one another echoed from a distance, while the smell of wood and mash filled the air—a combination of a lumberyard, butterscotch, and brown-sugar butter melting on hot oatmeal. I was in awe.

Chris walked us past the visitor center to a narrow flight of stairs sliced into a steep hill. If one had too much to drink, I imagined these uneven steps could lead to quite the tumble. Shrubs and ash trees bordered the sidewalks leading to the warehouses and fermentation room. The building's rock facade, cool to the touch, was so sharp I could cut myself if I touched it at the wrong angle. But I felt a warmth inside. It was as if I belonged here, and the stone calmed my leftover anxiety.

This place was special.

We entered a large open room with three cypress wooden tanks banded together with what looked like steel ropes. Inside them was a yellow mash, boiling and bubbling. It looked like the Malt-O-Meal my momma made me as a kid.

"This bubbling you see is caused by the yeast," Chris said. "We mill the grains into a flour, then cook them to convert the starch into sugar. From there, we add yeast, which is a single-celled organism that feeds on sugar and produces alcohol as its waste." Or as an Irish distiller once told me, "Yeast pisses alcohol."

Chris continued: "Now, anybody here eat sourdough bread?"

We all raised our hands.

"Good," he said, "we use a technique like making sourdough bread in these fermenters. We sour the mash to avoid bacterial infestations."

Essentially, when the distillation equipment turns the alcohol from the fermenters into liquor, the remaining mash, or the solids, drop to the bottom. That leftover fermented grain or backset is pumped into the new batch of mash, and it balances the pH level as fermentation is just beginning. If mash falls below 3.7 pH, it becomes acidic, increases the risk of contamination, and hurts the yeast, resulting in off-putting flavors.

"This sour mashing technique built the bourbon industry in the 1800s, and it started right here at the Woodford Reserve distillery," Chris said. "Dr. James C. Crow was the distiller here in the 1800s and introduced this technique to the industry."

The site of today's Woodford Reserve was built in 1812 by farmer-distiller Elijah Pepper, who chose it because of its access to a natural spring and nearby Glenn's Creek. When Elijah died, his son, Oscar, took over the distillery, and Chris said that's when the father of modern bourbon entered the picture. Oscar Pepper recruited and hired Dr. James C. Crow, a Scottish doctor, in the 1830s for his chemistry background. Dr. Crow would come to modernize the bourbon industry, applying a scientific process that used to be done purely by feel and intuition.

Chris described Dr. Crow as if he were a god among men, or at the very least the patron saint of distillers. "Dr. Crow was the greatest distiller of the nineteenth century," he said.

As he spoke to our group, Chris leaned over large cypress tanks with a yellow liquid, beating, pulsating, and swirling. I wondered if they were similar tanks to what Crow had used.

Chris walked us down narrow halls supported by thick wood beams from the 1800s into another warehouse with three shimmering copper pot stills, the cistern room where barrels were filled and that held the bottling lines. This place felt like a romantic stroll back in time, and I imagined Dr. Crow rolling barrels and fixing bad mashes in this very building. This man I had barely heard of was the godfather of bourbon production, a Benjamin Franklin of sorts, an inventor who had pioneered an industry still alive and well today.

Who was he? If he was the founder of the modern bourbon industry, why wasn't his name more widely known? And why was this place called Woodford Reserve and not Dr. James C. Crow's Magical Sour Mash Time? On the bus back to the penis place, my mind focused only on Dr. Crow.

I traveled to the local library the next day, expecting to find a biography on Crow but didn't find one. Instead, a *Spirits* magazine article from April 1935, titled "Jim Crow's Formula," offered a peek into the man I had become instantly fixated on. "To James Crow, who lived from 1789 to 1856, many authorities give credit as the original discoverer of the exceptional quality of limestone water which made Kentucky the ideal whiskey state. Known as 'Old Jim Crow,' he began making whiskey on Glenn's Creek on McCracken Turnpike in Franklin County sometime around 1850 with a partner named Oscar Pepper… Half their production was named 'Crow' and the other half 'Pepper,'" the unnamed author wrote.[1]

The article described Crow as a physician and surgeon, a graduate of medicine and surgery from Edinburgh, Scotland, as well as a philosopher, and listed his whiskey recipes, which are still used in modern bourbon making: 75 percent to 80 percent corn, 8 percent to 10 percent rye, and 12 percent to 15 percent barley malt. The article went into greater scientific detail about how Crow made whiskey, publishing his cooking and mashing temperatures, but didn't provide much more information about Dr. Crow than what master distiller Chris Morris had already offered.

I kept searching and found an encyclopedia entry about Dr. James C. Crow with similar biographical highlights. I pieced together what little I could of Crow from a handful of bourbon history books, but even these were sparse and didn't tell much more than what Chris had mentioned.

Perhaps the greatest detail I discovered was the existence of a modern bottom-shelf whiskey brand named after him—Old Crow, which I had thought was named after the bird. The discovery of Old Crow rocked me. Here I was, wanting to write a bourbon book, and I knew so little about this historic bourbon. The brand was considered the hallmark of bourbon in the 1800s, so much so that companies sued each other all the way to the Supreme Court for the rights to the Old Crow trademark. W. A. Gaines made the brand famous, but it was National Distillers that took Old Crow to the promise land in the mid-1900s. And for some reason, National Distillers sold Old Crow to Jim Beam in 1987. Bourbon historian Mike Veach told me Jim Beam stripped Old Crow of its heritage and relegated it to the bottom shelf to promote its brands like Booker's and Knob Creek. "Somebody at Jim Beam should be in prison for what they did to Old Crow. This was criminal," Veach told me when I first started looking into the brand.

While I was mesmerized by this Old Crow saga, becoming fixated on what happened to it, I realized I was not ready to write a bourbon history book.

Could I actually write a history if I didn't even know about this brand? Until this point, I had spent my time studying brands that sold well or had a recognizable figure to tell their story. I realized there were so many brands that no longer existed or didn't have a spokesperson. In a humbling moment, I knew the publishers had been right to reject my bourbon history proposal; I was not the right author at the right time.

So, like all good bourbon stories, I expanded my research into the liquor store and went directly to the aisle with Old Crow, where it was on the bottom shelf for $8. The screw-cap bottle had a sandpaper-feel label with a crow and notations that it was 80 proof and three years old. It felt cheap because it was. When home, I poured a dram. Its straw-like color told me it was young. The longer bourbon sits in the barrel, the darker it gets. Straw color is an indication of a two- to three-year-old bourbon. I brought it to my nose, and it smelled like rubbing alcohol and corn. Who wants to drink something that smells like that? I guess that's the drawback of being a taster—you must taste the bad with the good. When I put Old Crow to my lips, well, it was awful. It's as if somebody took gristmill sweepings and mixed them with the whiskey. At this point in my career, I don't think I had tasted a worse bourbon.

But this lackluster bourbon donning the Old Crow name only made me want to learn more. Who was James C. Crow? And how did this bourbon savant's namesake brand become rotgut swill? Over the summer of 2010, I went to the library several times seeking these answers.

On my last visit, I left the library wondering how a man so accomplished and admired as James C. Crow could have no written, detailed history about his life. I found newspaper ads referring to Crow's 1800s-era toil resulting in the "best whiskey ever made," and discovered President Grant fancied himself an Old Crow fan. Mid-twentieth-century advertisements told the story of famous people falling in love with Crow whiskey. Old Crow had been the drink of choice for Daniel Webster, Andrew Jackson, Henry Clay, Hunter S. Thompson, and John Wayne.

So how did Old Crow go from being the preferred bourbon of Mark Twain to $3 shots with a pickled egg at a grungy strip club? And why had Dr. Crow's life never been chronicled?

Weeks and months after my first Woodford Reserve visit, I kept turning those questions over in my mind. I was still a green reporter in the beverage space, but I looked for Crow clues as I expanded my reach and learned more about the industry. If I really wanted to know more about James C. Crow, I reckoned I should start with tasting Old Crow from back when it was good. But during this time of Kentucky bourbon, you had to "know a guy" to get a pour of something so old. And I knew just the place.

I found it incredibly odd that the beating heart of bourbon—Louisville, Kentucky—had only one bourbon-themed restaurant. But thank goodness Jason Brauner risked his retirement to start Bourbons Bistro in 2005, because our first meeting changed everything.

It was November 2010, five months after the Woodford Reserve trek that would forever change my career. I felt I was still a bourbon industry outsider and needed help breaking through the good ole boys network of Kentucky bourbon.[§] I had met Jason at a Kentucky Derby party and thought Bourbons Bistro would make for a great article. So I set up an appointment to interview him.

Right off Frankfort Avenue in Louisville at Bourbons Bistro, Jason, a shorter stout fella, squeezed through a tight gate and walked me to the restaurant's side patio, where a brick outdoor fireplace crackled. It was cold, so I warmed my hands over the fire. Jason fetched broken Louisville Slugger bats and tossed them into the coals to keep the fire going. He took the discarded, broken bats from the Louisville Slugger factory for this very purpose—to keep us warm. As he tossed them in the flames, Jason looked at

§ This is an interesting moment for me. I believe many will call it "impostor syndrome." I didn't want to spend much time on the "feeling" for the sake of getting to the whiskey, but at that time, in that moment, I did not feel worthy of being there. I would later learn people thought much differently of me than I thought of myself…in a good way. So impostor syndrome is right.

me, likely wondering, *Who is this kid in an ascot? What does he know about bourbon? Is he worthy?* He stroked his chin as the fire crackled, ambers flying. I must have passed the initial assessment because he said, "Why don't you come with me?"

We walked up a flight of rickety stairs. I dragged my hand on the 1920s-era exterior brick. The grittiness calmed me and took my focus off the real possibility of the stairs collapsing. He opened a door, pine tar sticky to the touch, and we walked into a room cut right out of a catalog. Beautiful exposed brick, shimmering tan wood floors, and what looked to be a new bar under construction. And in the corner, just before a small set of stairs, Jason's office awaited us.

I had never seen a room quite like this. It was large, about five hundred square feet, seemingly every inch covered in bottles of whiskey. The desk, his chair, the cabinet, the floor, and some boxes of bottles were stacked atop one another. Whiskey was everywhere, likely four hundred bottles.

As a newbie spirits writer, I had studied old bottles, read the whiskey greats—Chuck Cowdery, Mike Veach, and Michael Jackson (the beer and whiskey writer, not the singer). But I had never heard of the brands of the bottles I saw stacked around me—Fortuna, Old Lewis, and Jean Roberts.

"How did you get all this?" I asked.

And this is the part of the story that can be a little, well, complicated.

See, when the Twenty-First Amendment was ratified on December 5, 1933, to repeal the prohibition of alcohol, the federal government had little code or framework to allow the sale of booze across the country. After all, for the past thirteen years, federal agents had raided distillers, bootleggers, and speakeasies, and the federal laws were written to prevent the sale of alcohol. Instead of going back to how the industry had been structured prior to Prohibition, allowing alcohol manufacturers to sell directly to liquor stores and restaurants, the feds punted the majority of commerce power to the states, and a three-tier system was born.[2]

Each state and its municipalities created their own tax code, zoning restrictions, and morality laws. One example of this kind of law was the practice of not allowing alcohol to be sold on Election Day, which held in Kentucky until 2013.

From a business perspective, American distillers and importers of foreign spirits worked directly with each individual state, selling product to licensed distributors, who in turn sold product to liquor licensees, who then sold to customers. Failure to follow this general format would lead to a suspended alcohol license for the distiller, distributor, or liquor store, but the laws varied greatly between states. And in some states, such as Virginia and Pennsylvania, the state governments bypassed the private businesses entirely and created their own liquor store system. Those were known as monopoly states. Jumping into the liquor business in 1935, no doubt, had to be a learning curve, with every state acting as its own individual entity.

Even today, new entrants frequently pull their hair out, trying to treat the alcohol industry like, say, the car business or appliance sales. But this three-tier system prevents online shipping in most states and keeps the flow of commerce similar to how it has been since the 1930s—distiller to distributor to retailer or restaurant/bar.

That's why, when I saw all of Jason's rare bottles, I knew he didn't buy them from the liquor store down the street and there was no distributor offering them for sale. While many laws would eventually loosen, such as when Kentucky passed the Vintage Spirits Law in 2018, which allowed restaurant owners like Jason to buy directly from consumers instead of distributors, there was no way he could have bought them under the three-tier system in 2010. Of course, we were in his office and not in the official bar. Still, at this meeting, he took a big risk showing a reporter these likely illegally purchased bottles from people's estate sales, homes, and "on eBay, where you can still get this," he said to me, pulling down a tall ceramic bottle that wouldn't even fit on most liquor store shelves.[3]

The tan decanter was shaped like a court jester's face. A line of text at the bottom read *Old Crow. 10 Years Old.* Jason told me it was called an Old Crow Chess Piece. "It's from the 1960s," Jason said. "They never made this again."

Developed by a former spirits conglomerate, National Distillers, at a time when bourbon faced a critical challenge with vodka's rise in popularity, Jason told me, this forty-year-old decanter represented one of bourbon's last offensive strategies to capture new consumers. In the late 1960s, young drinkers turned their backs on the alcohol their parents and grandparents traditionally drank and flocked to white spirits such as vodka and gin. Vodka didn't even have a U.S. federal definition until 1958, but it was cheaper to make than bourbon. Plus, consumers loved its mixing potential and the fact you could drink three martinis during lunch and not smell it on your breath. It certainly didn't hurt that James Bond sipped martinis.

Bourbon distillers tried to compete by lowering proof points from the popular 100 to 86, promoting mixing it like vodka, and even creating a new type of whiskey—Light Whiskey[4]—to taste more like vodka. None of it worked. At that point in history, people wanted vodka, not bourbon.

So if people did not want to drink bourbon, marketers hoped that putting the booze in fancy packages could garner interest. This approach developed into an industry-wide decanter strategy that distillers hoped would appeal to the upper echelon drinkers in country clubs and complementary markets. Jim Beam partnered with organizations such as the PGA, banks, Ducks Unlimited, and car companies to create specialized porcelain vessels purchased by grandmas to place on their fireplace mantels. This decorative aspect, I believe, is what made Jim Beam so popular. Beam's most famous decanter was used as Jeannie's bottle on the hit show *I Dream of Jeannie*. Michter's, a dying Pennsylvania brand, sold King Tut tributes for $50, telling the press the decanter business was giving their company a spark. Distillers marketed decanters depicting Elvis, golf clubs, fiddles, old men fishing, and rockets. They each chose a unique co-branding interest, hoping these enthusiasts would become fans of the brand through the sheer power of marketing.

Old Crow's Chessman line tapped into one of the greatest American curiosities of the time—phenom Brooklynite Bobby Fischer, who won the World Chess Championship in 1972, just three years after the Chessmen were released. Fischer, a temperamental kid and improbable chess genius, commanded the sports pages, receiving placement above the New York Yankees and Dallas

Cowboys in some newspapers as he defeated chess masters with skill and ease.

Thanks to Fischer's popularity, chess clubs across the country regularly met and held tournaments, creating a marketing opportunity for Old Crow's parent company, National Distillers. Its New York advertising agency, Lennen and Newell, positioned these multicolored full chess pieces and felt chessboards as a gift "fit for a king." Sold as set for $400, the chess pieces were sought out by "collectors and chess buffs."[5]

National Distillers was certainly not thinking of the bourbon consumer as its marketing target and cared more about the Kansas City Chess Open than bars and liquor stores. Wherever prominent Americans played chess, an Old Crow set would be strategically displayed nearby. Perhaps this is why, more than forty years later, these unopened bottles were still available—nobody drank the bourbon inside. The twentieth-century buyers only cared about the novelty of the chess set. But that was a good thing for me, as Jason was about to open the bottle.

He slowly twisted the top, breaking a long red piece of tape known as the "tax strip," and slowly pulled the decanter's head. "This bottle is fifty years old," he said, pouring two fingers into my Glencairn. "But bourbon doesn't age in the bottle like wine. Its aging stops when it leaves the barrel."

I swirled the glass, watching the legs drip up and down, bringing it to my nose and taking in the aroma. My neck hairs stood up. Hand on the good book, they actually stood up! The aroma reminded me of the French bakeries I had visited in cognac. So many confectionery aromas! Was that a macaroon? Marzipan?

Religieuse? I raised the glass to my lips and let the wave of velvety, creamy goodness drench my tongue, dropping down my jawline like melted butter. If there are fifty types of caramel, all fifty were in this bourbon.

I tasted it a second time, closing my eyes and focusing on every inch of my tongue as it lit up like a city of streetlamps, covered in so many sweet, savory, and spicy notes that I could not comprehend its intensity. This bourbon was made in a different time, distilled in 1959 and bottled at the height of the Vietnam War in barrels made from first-growth trees. I was connected in palate and history. It was divine.

This was the beginning of my spiritual bourbon journey. The Old Crow Chessman honored the name it held. When I first learned about Dr. Crow, this complex bourbon is what I imagined his legacy tasting like. I left Bourbons Bistro with the taste of Old Crow still in my mouth; even to this day, I can close my eyes and go back to this moment. But I couldn't help but wonder: *How had Old Crow gone from that sublime bourbon to the rotgut cheap crap it is today?*

I knew enough even then to understand that whiskey marketing is filled with folklore, half-truths, and downright lies, all in the quest of selling bourbon. The saying "It's an acquired taste" came from whiskey marketers selling bad juice, because they knew the more a person drank, the less taste mattered. And the bourbon industry crowned a Baptist minister, Elijah Craig, as the so-called father of bourbon with a tall tale of him discovering charred barrels in a barn fire. Despite many distillers having stronger and more credible claims to the title of bourbon creator, Craig received it because he was a minister and many hoped his profession would quell the temperance women for pushing for another Prohibition in the 1950s.

So if the bourbon industry could lie about so many things, could it have made up Crow's story? And why had this iconic distiller's legacy since been turned into swill bourbon?

My thirst for knowing Crow would take a long time to quench. But I needed this quest.

Three years before I tasted the vintage Old Crow, I had fastened a belt around my neck, wondering if I should end it all. The Iraq War damaged me, and I could barely hold a job, sleep, or walk a city block without fearing snipers would take my head off. I couldn't keep living this way.

With that taste of Old Crow for the first time, using the taste mindfulness exercise, it was like my palate completed an equation I had been seeking an answer to since Iraq.

I became obsessed with this whiskey, this brand, and the man behind it in a time when I needed to focus on something other than my trauma. Around this time, I also received the greatest news a husband could ever wish for.

Jaclyn sat me down at our dinner table, beaming with joy from ear to ear. She grabbed my hand and smiled. "We're pregnant."

In a few short months, I defeated trauma fears, found a whiskey obsession, and learned I would become a dad. I was living the dream. But was it too good to be true?

CHAPTER 4

FINDING CROW

HIS LEFT ARM leaning against a bulging whiskey barrel, James C. Crow looks directly into the camera with raised bushy black eyebrows, a gray beard, and the only smile in an 1850 Oscar Pepper (later Labrot & Graham) distillery group photo. The rest of the crew is straight-faced, with hands folded or tucked inside their jackets. Crow is dressed formally but appears the opposite. He is perched on a low stool or stump, dressed in a buttoned-up vest and black coat that matches his trousers, a white shirt, and bow tie. But he seems laid back; his hands are pushed deeply in his pant pockets, and he wears the smirk of a prankster or a fella who knows something the others don't.

Of course, that was just my interpretation. As I looked at this photo for the first time in the special collections archives at the University of Louisville, I allowed for the possibility of being wrong. After all, the grainy photo was 150 years old and reprinted in the 1935 magazine I was viewing. Could a smudge on the original negative have caused the smirk? There was also the possibility, of course, that the man in this picture wasn't Crow at all. In their mid-1900s era advertisements, Old Crow marketers depicted him as more of a Victorian-looking man with thinner eyebrows, no beard, and a wider cranium than that of the man in this photo.

In late 2010, I was a spirits author on the rise, ambitious to tell stories nobody had researched, and my personal life included an awesome wife, two cats, and a dog. Most importantly, I was about to be a dad. I couldn't wait to push my kid in a swing and read a book to him or her. On our long list of baby names, I penciled in *James* as an option for a boy name. But I definitely needed to learn more about the ole Scottish chap if I were to name my kid after him.

Every time I ventured into researching Crow's past, I found the same general details: Dr. James C. Crow was a Scottish immigrant who attended medical school at the medical college in Edinburgh. He introduced sour mash fermentation and the saccharometer to the bourbon industry. Crow was heralded everywhere for revolutionizing bourbon, despite the fact that there didn't seem to be much information available about him. I suspected there was something more to his story.

As I progressed in my alcohol education, I began to understand why Crow's accomplishments were buried, and why high school history classes never taught the fact that our first president, George Washington, was once a prominent distiller. Or that Thomas Jefferson believed whiskey production to be a key effort in growing the American farmer's acreage, repealing a federal whiskey tax to help farmers sell their grains to distillers. And President Taft's PR team never once tried to change his "stuck in the bathtub" narrative to "this is the president who defined bourbon."¶ This huge element of our national history is hidden, in short, because so many people have drinking problems.

The U.S. educational system and the general populace have downplayed accomplishments and history related to alcohol because of alcohol abuse and drunk driving. In fact, from the 1930s to today, dozens of campaigns led by surgeons general and universities have offered teachers strategies for teaching kids about the dangers of alcohol. One case study often used to hammer home their point was Zap, North Dakota, a small town that had more than three hundred drunken incidents among teenagers in 1969. Marian Wettrick, an associate director for the Pennsylvania Office of Mental Health, said in 1969, "Two-thirds of the people over 15 years of age use alcohol and most do so without the guidance or assistance in learning how to protect themselves against its dangers. The problem is that society does not frown on the use of alcohol as a tension reducing device and therefore fails to discourage a type of drinking that leads to alcoholism."[1]

The truth is, she was right. Coping with your problems through alcohol can lead to drinking far too much, which can lead to a whole host of additional problems. But does that completely negate how whiskey helped build this country? I don't blame schoolteachers for avoiding intoxicating histories. If you've ever seen a drunkard fall down a flight of stairs or lost a friend in a drunk driving accident, it's easy to reject any positive elements of the industry.

¶ After multiple lawsuits and queries into the Department of Agriculture over the legal definition of whiskey, because the Pure Food and Drug Act of 1906 was vague, President Taft wrote the federal definitions for American whiskey types in 1909. Known as the "Taft Decision," it became the first federal code of definitions in American spirits.

Even the spirits industry tempered its advancements in marketing alcohol after Prohibition, which ended in 1933, implementing self-imposed bans on radio advertising until the 1950s and television until 1996. In the 1990s, old-timers feared any type of marketing that portrayed alcohol as positive would lead to a new legion of dry leaders trying to ban alcohol.

Another reason for the lack of information about Crow could be that more researchers had studied salt and potatoes than bourbon, at the point my research began. So I chalked up the lack of history on Crow as both a preventive strategy against a new Carry Nation, the axe-wielding temperance woman of the pre-Prohibition era, and the fact that there were just not enough people interested in researching his legacy.

To find out anything new about Crow, I would need to go deep and dig into places people had never looked before. And the first clue of his life? His burial plot, which I found in a folder at the Woodford County Historical Society. The plot description stood alone in the folder but was one of many descriptions for plots at the Versailles Cemetery: "James Crow was born in Scotland year 17–89 [*sic*]. Came to Frankfort KY year 18–25 [*sic*]. In the same year was employed by Col. Willis Field at his farm on the Mortonsville Road, where he was engaged in Mr. Field Whiskey business. He invented [*sic*] that famous brand Old Crow whiskey. Later was employed by Eliga [*sic*] Peper Sr. James Crow was a fine chemist and owned the finest chemist equipment in the country at that time."[2]

Almost all accounts of Crow's life noted his chemistry prowess. "The intimate knowledge displayed by Mr. Crow with the requirements of the distillery business was truly surprising. Whatever he did in connection with it was well done. It unquestionably arose from that studying medicine he had devoted considerable attention to investigating the truths of chemistry, and he was very proficient in many of its uses as applied to art and useful manufactures. The great success and reputation scheduled by him as practical distiller can be attributed to his knowledge of that science," Crow's friend wrote on December 9, 1870, fourteen years after Crow's death, signed simply as "E. J. S."[3]

Crow's approach to chemistry essentially introduced measuring devices for fermentation that ensured he distilled beer that wasn't layered in bacterial infestations. He also perfected the sour mashing technique, allowing it to become the most common form of bourbon fermentation. While sour mash had been around for at least two decades when Crow entered Kentucky in 1835,[4] Crow adjusted the simple souring technique to allow it to scale. After the mash or beer is distilled, many solids drop to the bottom. This is the leftover beer or backset from the first distillation. Crow would start a new fermentation batch and add the backset, which would sour the total fermentation and prevent bacteria from taking over the yeast. Early on, this technique was called the "Crow way," and other distillers referred to his scientific instruments as "those sticks" that helped "get more whiskey out of the grain."[5]

Sour mash eventually became one of American whiskey's most noted marketing terms and appears on modern labels for whiskeys such as Jack Daniel's and Michter's. In fact, the production style for the vast majority of American whiskeys can be linked to the sour mash technique that Crow made mainstream.

One big reason Crow's sour mash technique took off was that bad whiskey was simply a fact of life at the time. His whiskey was much cleaner than others on the market because he avoided fermenting and distilling large chunks of bacteria that would ruin entire batches.

The lack of regulations, standard techniques, and understanding of chemistry back then was a hazard to whiskey drinkers. If you bought a jug of whiskey in the United States in 1840, you might have gotten a fine helping of kerosene mixed with a little prune juice for darkening. Or perhaps tobacco spit? Maybe you craved good ole tree bark floating in your glass.

Distillers sold barrels of whiskey to wholesalers, store owners, taverns, druggists, and middlemen known as rectifiers, who adulterated the spirit to increase the volume and, in some cases, make it taste better. Unlike today, distillers did not bottle their own whiskey; the rectifiers did the bottling. This practice lasted well into the late 1800s and would lead to significant legislation, such as the Bottled in Bond Act of 1897 and Pure Food and Drug Act of 1906, to curtail the unwanted floaties, deathly additives, and false medicinal claims rampant in the nineteenth century. But in Crow's lifetime (1789–1856), whiskey was a never-ending risk-taking venture of deathly concoctions and flat-out gross.

To be fair, many wholesalers bottled or placed whiskey in jugs and sold it as they received it or added benign enhancers like cinnamon sticks to make the whiskey more drinkable. It just wasn't enough. Much of the whiskey entering the market made people sick, likely because it contained poison. In fact, early American governance over alcohol was often motivated by "bad whiskey" causing sickness.[6] One of the leading arguments that convinced America to pass alcohol prohibition was that alcohol often killed people without giving warning. These drinking deaths were lumped into the country's far greater concern: morality and drinking were tied to brothel-visiting adulterers and every other sin.

American whiskey needed a savior, somebody who could reliably manufacture a product that wouldn't cause you to go blind or worse. And that savior appeared to be Crow.

I have never tasted something that James Crow made himself, but I imagine a long, lingering mouthfeel, completely entrenching my tongue and dropping down my jawline like melted butter. His corn and malt recipe, aged in oak up to twelve years,[7] brings a thick caramel chew, savory-and-sweet vanilla curd, grapefruit, and burned honey. Of course, back in the 1830s to 1850s, when Crow was alive and actively making whiskey, there were no professional tasters publishing books of tasting notes. But the retailers of the day sure had choice words for Crow. Advertisements referred to Crow Whisky as "celebrated"[8] and "unequaled."[9] Charleston's F. W. Wagener & Co. advertised in all caps: "IT IS THE BEST WHISKEY MADE."

From what I've been able to find, it didn't matter where he worked; Crow always labeled his whiskey with his name. Crow worked as a distiller for Captain Zachariah Henry, Orlando Payne, Thomas Edwards, Willis Field, and James E. Pepper at the Oscar Pepper Distillery and Labrot & Graham Distillery. Inside these distillers' stone warehouses sat his barrels that his nephew and future revenue gauger, the person collecting alcohol taxes, said were branded C-R-O-W. "I was a boy and was there around the distillery, and old man Crow would take a piece of chalk and would make the letters, and then he had a gouge that he would gouge it out with C-R-O-W," said Richard H. Whittington in court proceedings determining the use of the Old Crow trademark in the late 1800s.[10]

With a steel point, Crow etched his name and traced it in chalk deep in the barrelhead's steel and wood, solidifying his brand.

When the 1857 Louisville fire engulfed much of the town, including the famous Galt House hotel on the Ohio River, store owner John Raine lost 230 barrels of 12-year-old Old Crow whiskey, for which Raine told the *Louisville Courier* somebody had offered him $5 per gallon. The average market value for a gallon of whiskey then was 25¢. Perhaps Raine's barrels were so valuable because they were truly made by James Crow.[11]

Before bribing voters with drink was outlawed in 1948, Kentuckian Joseph C. S. Blackburn offered his constituents what he called "genuine Crow whiskey" he had kept around for a special occasion. While campaigning for the state house in 1871, Blackburn promised: "As you drink that, sir, I want you to remember that you are helping to destroy the most precious heirloom of my family. It is the last bit of genuine Crow whiskey in the world. Observe, sir, that you do not need to gulp down a tumbler of water after swallowing the liquor to keep it from burning your gullet. On the contrary, you know instinctively that to drink water with it would be a crime. All I ask of you is to remember that you are getting something in this liquor that all the money of an Indian prince cannot buy. Drink it, sir, and give your soul up to the Lord. Then if you can vote for Ed Marshall I cannot complain, because it will be the Lord's act!"[12]

Blackburn would go on to win his first race as a politician and would later become a congressman and senator. In 1907, President Theodore Roosevelt appointed him the governor of the Panama Canal Zone, making him one of the most influential politicians from Kentucky at the time. Did Old Crow make Blackburn's journey possible?

After Crow's death in 1856 and well into the twentieth century, more colorful stories circulated about Crow whiskey. Some of these tales may be about whiskey Crow himself made, such as a rumor about the barrels of Crow being a Union-army favorite during the Civil War. Or a tale of Jayhawker Colonel James Montgomery listing Old Crow in his Battle of Olustee supplies and generals trying to oust then-General Grant for drinking too much of it.

Alexander McClure's 1901 book, *Abe Lincoln's Yarns and Stories*, shed light on his friends' interest in Grant's drinking prowess. A group of army officers ratted to Lincoln about Grant's excessive drinking, and McClure observed:

> Lincoln was not a man of impulse and did nothing upon the spur of moment action with him was the result of deliberation and study... He judged men by their performances and not speech...
>
> So Grant gets drunk does he, queried Lincoln, addressing himself to one of the particularly active detractors of the soldier who at that period inflicting heavy damage upon the Confederates. 'Yes he does and I can prove it,' was the reply.
>
> Well returned Lincoln with the faintest suspicion of a twinkle in his eye. 'You needn't waste your time getting proof you

> just find out to oblige me what brand of whiskey Grant drinks because I want to send a barrel of it to each one of my generals.'[13]

Historians later agreed that Old Crow was Grant's brand of choice, while Grant biographers objected. Meanwhile, the owners of the Old Crow brand in the twentieth century heralded Grant as a regular drinker of the product.[14] Like many old stories of the alcohol industry, the truth is impossible to prove.

And there's no better way to understand bourbon truth from fiction than in the courtroom documents of old. Fortunately, bourbon distillers love suing each other, and that gives us historians a chance to find out what really happened.

When I first looked into *W.A. Gaines & Co. v. Hellman Distilling Co.*, I had no idea what I would discover. This case decided who had the rights to use the Old Crow brand after a dispute arose between the Hellman family of St. Louis and W. A. Gaines & Co., a company named after its founder William A. Gaines and that was originally named Gaines, Berry & Co. before Gaines bought out his partners Hiram Berry and Edmond Taylor Jr. Filed in 1906, this case would establish precedent in the courts for trademark law and play a role in the legal definition of bourbon in the United States, which is today: "Whiskey produced in the U.S. at not exceeding 80 percent alcohol by volume (160 proof) from a fermented mash of not less than 51 percent corn and stored at not more than 62.5 percent alcohol by volume (125 proof) in charred new oak containers."[15]

As I read the arguments between the Hellman family company, which was blending neutral spirit into the whiskey it labeled Old

Crow, and Gaines, who claimed to follow Crow's method exactly, I couldn't help but wonder if Crow ever imagined that his techniques and name would spark a Supreme Court case. After Crow's death in 1856, many whiskey dealers, including Hellman, bought as many barrels of Crow's whiskey as they could, thinking that doing so would allow them to claim ownership of the brand. But as they sold through the whiskey that had been made by Crow, their own concoctions replaced the iconic juice while they kept using the Crow name. In 1867, W. A. Gaines & Co. adopted and commercially applied the words *Old Crow* as a trademark for the whiskey it distilled, and the legal battles began.

Gaines claimed it made whiskey the same way Crow did and accused Hellman of selling a blended whiskey under the Crow name in the 1880s. The bulk of the case was dedicated to proving that Gaines actually made genuine Old Crow the same way James Crow had, and thus should get to keep using the name.

William W. Darnell, a distiller, malter, and farmer, testified that all the whiskey made at the Oscar Pepper Distillery was Old Crow and that he was positive the whiskey made there at the time of testimony was the same as when James Crow was alive.

Part of the trial transcript reads:

Question: I understood you to state a little while ago that the words Old Crow meant whiskey made by James Crow?

Darnell: All the whiskey made there at the distillery was called Crow whiskey because Old Crow learned this n*gger man of Oscar Pepper how to still; that's how it came.

Question: What negro man do you refer to?

Answer: ...I believe his name was Albert.

Question: Do you know by what formula that negro man made whiskey, of your own knowledge?

Answer: It was run just the same as Old Crow run it, put in tubs and dumped it the next day, they all ran that way then.

I've seen enslaved people listed in tax records, and I've held wanted posters for runaway slaves. While I know this is how people talked back then, nothing can prepare you for looking at a historical text and seeing such hurtful language. I still get sick to my stomach knowing that slavery existed. How could we, as a nation, have treated people this way? I in no way condone the testimony, but I also believe it's important to view history from the people of their time's words. And in this testimony, we discovered a human being, a person who's relegated to a racial slur, was entrusted with carrying on the Old Crow legacy. James Crow instructed Albert how to make the whiskey that became the preferred drink of presidents.

When I read the testimony, I immediately scanned the rest of the case looking for confirmation of Albert's position as Crow's apprentice. I found that confirmation from Crow's nephew. Whittington's testimony confirmed the apprentice's name was Albert and added the name of another former enslaved person who worked with Crow—Dick. "They would draw the slop and pack it to these small tubs and always put in ten buckets to the tub, then they had a vat they would empty these tubs in the next day,"

Whittington said. "They have a different process of mashing now, and they get more whiskey out of the grain. He just mashed it with those sticks."[16]

As I read this for the first time, my heart raced. As an industry historically run by white men, the whiskey world knew nothing about Albert or Dick. I searched for more information on them to no avail. An application from the Woodford Reserve to become designated as a historical landmark notes that twelve enslaved people worked on the distillery site, and a 2013 archaeological dig discovered evidence of slave quarters, but no names were mentioned and I never found any more evidence of Albert's life. That said, according to Crow's nephew, every barrel of Old Crow after James C. Crow's passing was made by Albert, a former enslaved person, making his contributions as important in American whiskey as those of another former enslaved person—Nearest Green, who taught Jack Daniel how to distill.

But unlike Green and Jack Daniel's friendship story, which has been told on Jack Daniel tours and in Jack Daniel history books, and is now the subject of a bestselling book, documentary, and two iconic whiskeys, Albert's story has been lost to history, only briefly mentioned in testimony. I hope that one day I, or another researcher, am able to tell Albert's story so he may be properly remembered. For now, his life remains a mystery.

When I first cracked open these lawsuits, I didn't expect to find Albert and found myself derailed from my original research. Still, these cases definitely shed light on Old Crow whiskey, how it was made, and how valuable it was for the industry (more on that later). But after learning about Albert, I seemed to care more about the human aspect of Crow. Did Crow have kids? Why did he leave Scotland, especially if he was a doctor and presumably relatively successful?

Who was Crow, really?

Over the decade, I would hire researchers, dig deep into whiskey history, and spend a hefty chunk of time, energy, and money relentlessly pursuing my quest to learn more about James C. Crow. What I found could change whiskey history. Forever.

But little did I know that seeing the information on Crow's life was really a way of hiding from mine.

Jaclyn's tummy protruded out of her thin blue shirt, her brown eyes twinkling. "Want to feel?" she asked as we prepared for our first ultrasound visit. I rubbed my hand along her smooth belly, bumping up against her belly ring, wondering out loud, "Do you need to take out the belly ring? Is that gonna hurt the baby?" I'd later learn that new-dad anxiety will find hazards in a room of nothing.

"No, silly, the belly ring isn't going to hurt the baby."

We were preggers, around twelve weeks, and told everybody. My parents. Hers. Her brother. Neighbors. We were so excited that I could barely contain myself on our way to the ultrasound.

I wore my favorite shirt, a Cutter & Buck plaid turquoise, and my lucky Irish cap. I also brought my Nikon D2X, eager to snap photos of Jaclyn's face as she saw our baby for the first time.

The doctor's waiting room was filled with parenting magazines and the soft sounds of Lionel Richie. It smelled like potpourri had a baby with rubbing alcohol—by far one of the strangest smells I can recall. A lady holding a clipboard greeted us and walked us into a cold room.

Jaclyn changed into a hospital gown and lay on the adjustable bed. The doctor entered the room, and his appearance threw me for a loop. I don't know what I expected the person who'd show me the heartbeat of my kid to look like, but I wasn't expecting arms so hairy that you could braid a quilt with them.

"This is a little cold," he said, squeezing a near-empty tube of K-Y Jelly on Jaclyn's belly and spreading it around with the ultrasound knob. He moved it around and looked at the screen as the vibrating sonar sounds hummed. I stood back and snapped photos. I'd never seen Jaclyn smile so big.

I looked at the screen and saw what looked like a plum. Was that the baby? The doctor kept moving the ultrasound wand around Jaclyn's belly. Jaclyn's posture changed. She raised her shoulders, looking at the doctor. Jaclyn, a nurse, knew this world; I had no idea. But I knew my wife. Was something wrong? I held her hand. The doctor put the ultrasound device down and grabbed a larger handheld tool. "Okay, so we couldn't find the heartbeat on this, but that could just mean the baby is playing hard to get. Let's try a transvaginal ultrasound."

The glee in my wife's face turned to one of discomfort as the doctor moved the probe, looking for the baby.

I gripped Jaclyn's hand tightly and looked into her eyes. She was scared. I didn't know what to do or say. I tried to muster a smile and say something comforting. But I just stood there with my camera slung over my shoulder, holding her hand, looking at her face and then the screen.

The doctor stepped away, took off his gloves, and turned off the screen.

"There's no heartbeat."

He went on talking. About what? I don't know. My entire body became numb. I felt my soul trying to climb up into my tear ducts. I wanted to scream in sorrow. But I had to be strong in this moment. Jaclyn lay flat on a table, knowing that our baby angel would soon pass through her body. Whatever I felt had to be a fraction of the pain she was feeling.

I just held her hand and didn't let go.

The next three months were a dark, depressing hole that made my Iraq War pain feel like Little League Tee Ball compared to Major League Baseball. My body went through the motions. I tried all the coping skills I had learned in therapy and nothing worked. The dull, aching feeling of loss persisted. And the trigger that hurt the most was one that made me happy for somebody else—seeing family, friends, and strangers out in the world with their own babies. We would soon have another miscarriage, and Jaclyn worried that she was doing something wrong, that it was her fault she couldn't carry the babies to term. And no matter how much I told her this was not true and that we would keep trying, she felt it deep in her soul. I helped the only way I knew how—by providing good food and drink and never leaving her side.

This woman had seen me through my worst of times. I had to be there for her now.

I cooked most nights, starting the evening off with a gin cocktail or rum drink, and switching up the fare with delicious proteins. One day it would be a thick and juicy New York strip pan seared in butter and olive oil, served with wine-reduced portabella mushrooms and al dente carrots or green beans. The next, I'd buy a chicken from a farmer down the road and either bake or pan fry it, serving it with risotto topped with thinly cut and sautéed garlic and parmesan. And we drank the best wine.

On days I didn't cook, I took her to our favorite restaurant, Corbett's, sitting at Table 2 with our backs against the window, looking toward the kitchen. Corbett's menu rotated, but we lived for the sea salt baguette that, to this day, remains the best bread I've ever had. Here, I ordered everything from pheasant and quail to oxtail soup to Portuguese stew. Jaclyn, more of a creature of habit, almost always ordered scallops. We drank wine with the meals and bourbon afterward.

We went to couples therapy and it helped, but these dinners at home and at restaurants are really what got us through the pain of losing two babies. We smiled and never let our love slip away. All over a good meal.

But we both buried our heads into work to cope as well. Jaclyn entered the University of Tennessee's doctoral program in nursing, while I chased a ghost.

CHAPTER 5

WHO WAS JAMES C. CROW? THE TRUTH

THE JOURNEY INTO discovering who James C. Crow truly was begins in Bardstown, Kentucky, a quaint small town that boasts roughly three million barrels of bourbon, more than any other place in the country. I began my research at the Oscar Getz Museum of Bourbon History, named after the former bourbon executive and author Oscar Getz.

Inside an old redbrick church, the museum offers glimpses of bourbon history, with thin copper stills, displays of Old Crow advertising campaigns featuring a bird dressed in a tuxedo, and Prohibition-era bourbon crates that unfortunately display swastikas. While the good executives at Frankfort Distillers chose this swastika logo before Hitler took power and certainly didn't intend to offend anybody then or in the future, I still cannot look at that symbol without feeling pain in my stomach.

Sadly, the swastika crates weren't the only cringe artifact hanging in the museum. There was a Four Roses ad showcasing two farmers sitting on bales of hay and laying down money for a cockfight. I would venture to say two chickens gutting themselves is second only to horse racing for the original bourbon distiller's sport of choice. Muscular roosters became hallmarks for bourbon marketing in the 1800s, leading to Chicken Cock commanding massive sales in the later part of the century.

As I walked up the narrow stairs to the archive room, I wondered whether Crow played the ponies or watched chickens fight. Would I learn these personal details?

In my short stint researching whiskey, I discovered all sorts of interesting drinking facts and personal histories of the distillers through wills, lawsuits, and old books. One of the more interesting finds was that Jacob Beam, the first of the iconic bourbon family, had a father-in-law who didn't care much for him, refusing to put his wife in the will if they married. Would I find a comparable string to pull on Crow?

When the door swung open to the archive room, a laser-like beam of sunlight hit me right in the eyes. The small, closet space was crowded with a couple of filing cabinets, bottle-filled shelves, and a hand-crank window that seemingly scooped every ray from the sun and injected it right into the room. Once my eyes adjusted, I simply stood in awe of the bottles. An old Rip Van Winkle decanter, Old Lewis, vintage Jim Beam decanters, several Old Crows, and so many brands I had never heard of. They stood there on the shelf absorbing sunlight (an awful way to store whiskey, by the way), their fill levels inching below the label neck area.

Alas, I was not here for the bourbon. I needed to research. I opened the middle file drawer and felt something rattling inside.

A stack of papers was sloppily draped over a broken picture frame. Glass shards covered the bottom of the drawer. And the papers were just blank construction paper that a kid would use to draw.

I opened the next drawer and found a few newspaper clippings, trademark filings, and journal notes. They were fascinating because they showed the pen of a person who managed distilleries and didn't spin marketing webs, but there was no information about Crow. Same in the next drawer, and the next.

Finally, I found a single folder labeled *Old Crow*, which held a single sheet of paper. The paper contained a partial recipe for Old Grand-Dad, one of Old Crow's sister brands under the National Distillers' portfolio.

My first stop on my research trip was a bust.

Next stop, the Kentucky Historical Society, a beacon of archival professionalism. Near the Kentucky state capitol, these archives contained Abraham Lincoln family papers, documents related to every prominent moment in Kentucky history, and a ton of distillery history, usually from company archives. And while I found a ton of information about companies that used Old Crow trademarks after Crow's passing, nothing shed light on the man or his life. I found this to be particularly odd since this archives contained family bibles and letters from other historical distillers.

I had one more major shot: the University of Louisville Special Collections, perhaps the strictest archive I have ever visited (and I've thumbed through papers at the Smithsonian, National Archives of Ireland, and the Library of Congress). No pens, jackets, bags, or anything heavy that could tear a piece of paper are allowed inside. To view some items, white gloves must be worn to avoid passing human oils onto the parchment. The archivists did allow me to bring a camera set up on a tripod to snap pictures—with a watermark over the paper, of course.

"What are you looking for?" the attendant asked.

"I am looking for particular items on Dr. James C. Crow, who was a..."

"Oh, the distiller," she interrupted, "yes, we have several boxes of his material from a researcher in the 1990s."

Was this it? Was this the jackpot I'd been waiting for? And who was this researcher in the 1990s?

She delivered box after box after box to my desk. There must have been twelve cardboard containers filled with letters, newspaper clippings, contracts, and distillery procedure guides. Finally, here was the information I was looking for! I looked over my shoulder, as if somebody might steal these documents and beat me to whatever nuggets were within. I lifted the cardboard lid from the first box, smelled a whiff of stale air, and uncovered the truth that had already been mostly unraveled by one of Kentucky's preeminent researchers—Samuel Thomas, a renowned Kentucky historian who wrote twenty-one books.

From what I could gather from his correspondence, it seemed that Jack Daniel's parent company Brown-Forman had employed Thomas to learn everything he could about the site of the future Woodford Reserve distillery, including Crow's involvement. If the researchers could prove Crow implemented new whiskey techniques, it would no doubt go a long way for their National Historic Landmark application, because the federal review board looks for significant events within the request and creating new American whiskey styles would definitely hit that mark.

Thomas passed away in 2012, around the time I was researching Crow, but his thorough archives were a testament to his professionalism and craft to preserving history. I was honored to touch the very letters he penned.

Thomas started with the archives of the University of Edinburgh, which was mentioned in an 1897 *Woodford Sun* article as the medical school from which Crow had graduated. Within two letters to archivists in Scotland, Thomas made a groundbreaking discovery that challenged the most widely believed information about Crow—James C. Crow never attended Edinburgh Medical School, let alone graduated from its program. I can only imagine how Thomas felt as he uncovered this information. Was his heart racing like mine? Did he feel the bourbon industry's legends crumbling with a simple stroke of a pen?

But that wasn't all. As it turned out, the librarian found a hidden factoid in the same time period of Crow living in the area.

"Since receiving your letter of 21 February, and being able to think a little, when one cannot do too well on the telephone, it has dawned on me that James Crow could be an anglicization or Americanicsation [*sic*] of the good old vernacular Scottish name Craw, and we actually do have a James Craw in matriculation indexes studying medicine in the sessions 1804–5, 1805–6 and 1806–7," wrote Mrs. Jo Currie, assistant librarian of the special collections at the University of Edinburgh. "This was only three years of a four-year MD course, and he did not graduate. We know nothing else about him..."[1]

Currie theorized on the possibility that Craw may have joined the army or navy, which, at the time, would have allowed a three-year medical student to practice. She also said it was possible he completed his medical degree elsewhere. But, most importantly, Currie confirmed that Craw would have most certainly studied distillation and chemistry techniques while at Edinburgh.

Was it possible that James C. Crow changed his name? While not nearly as earth-shattering as Crow not being a doctor, Crow actually being Craw changes the history books quite a bit. If it's true, though, he certainly wouldn't have been the only prominent whiskey player to have changed his surname. The Beam family was originally the Boehms.

Names aside, Currie had more research to provide Thomas. She wrote:

> The plot thickens, and I am getting interested in James Craw myself! After posting my letter today, I looked up Craw in the Edinburgh Street Directory of 1805–1806 and found John Craw WS living in the Canongate opposite of Queensbury House. A WS is a prestigious kind of solicitor—a writer to the Signet. So because there is a published list of WSS, I looked at it and found that John Craw, admitted WS in 1795 was the son of John Craw Writer (i.e., solicitor) in Haddington. The Canongate John Craw, WS married Margaret Hardie, daughter of John Hardie, brewer in St. Anne's Yard, Edinburgh, Bailie of Hollywood. John Craw WS died 23 March 1816 aged 44 and was buried in Holyrood Abbey.

> There were only 3 Craws in the Street Directory for 1805–6—one was s silver smith, one a bookbinder, and one a WS. If James Craw was the son of the WS, then the maternal grandfather was a brewer. But John Craw WS if 44 in 1816 is too young to be the father of a man born in 1789, and James Craw was our medical student could not matriculate before the age of 15.
>
> I leave you to speculate on all these things…

After this letter, I believe Thomas moved on from researching Crow's medical history. He wrote to Currie on June 2, 1995: "All of this leaves us not able to explain Crow's often remarked medical education. Maybe that has been exaggerated and perhaps he had only limited exposure to the university or to a member of its faculty. Could there have been another college of medicine and surgery in Edinburgh at the same period?"[2]

Alas, nothing Currie supplied nor Thomas found confirmed Crow went to another medical school.

As I looked at these papers for the first time, beads of sweat formed on my forehead. I was in total disbelief, angry even, that I had been hero-worshipping a man based on a total lie. Or was it?

I needed to find out who James C. Crow really was or it would drive me nuts, like a retired detective reflecting on the one big case he never solved. Thomas did leave another important bread crumb in his files: he discovered there was a James Christopher Crow born in West Fenton in 1789.

A thorough genealogy report revealed James Christopher Crow was born on June 11, 1787, at West Fenton Farm in the parish of Dirleton, Edinburghshire (now Midlothian) to father William Crow, a tenant farmer, and mother Catherine Earby.[3]

Once a prosperous woodlands area, West Fenton became farmland as the Scottish population grew. Today, the area, which lies about thirteen miles east of Edinburgh, is littered with farmsteads and tourist cottages. Tiny ponds and waving weeds are scattered throughout the small area that supported twenty farmers at the time of Crow's birth, growing five hundred acres of wheat, eight hundred acres of barley, twelve hundred acres of oats, and much more.[4] Being as grain rich as it was, the area's insurance records are especially good. And that's where we find our wee baby Crow listed as an infant on August 28, 1789.[5]

The Scottish economy was blossoming in the 1790s and early 1800s, with textiles and agriculture paving the way for a prosperous industrial period. Crow would have grown up in a rich and fertile parish that paid farmworkers "nine bolls of oats, two bolls of barley, two bolls of pease, a cow maintained summer and winter; and if they sow and stack the grain, one firlot of wheat, and a pair of shoes."6 The area would have been rich in tradition and Scottish culture, but it's likely that these country inspirations did not connect with our future distiller, as his father, William, was born and raised in Jamaica to tenet farmers, moving to Scotland sometime later. James had an older brother, George, and a sister, Elizabeth.

As a teenager, James worked for George's company, Crow and Wood, as a corn merchant, in Leith. Leith was also a hotbed for wine and spirits sales then. Perhaps this tickled his fancy on drink?

I imagined a young Crow being curious of the world's ways, tipping back a Scottish punch in a gray coat and complaining about taxes. Then again, that would have been risky, to speak against the king, especially since his family was in debt.

We sadly learn more about James through his father's death paperwork. In the Testament Dative for William Crow, the executor, a "James C. Crow," signed with an educated hand, with a curled *J* and swoosh-like loop on the top of his *C*. Unlike the other historical finds on this man, his signature, the one verified thing he touched, barely moved me. Even with years of research, I still am slightly somber when reviewing wills and testaments. Somebody died. And James C. Crow had to validate the life of his father's legacy with the stroke of a pen.

At eighteen years old, James C. Crow, listed as a corn merchant apprentice, managed his father's nearly $90,000 (in today's value) estate in 1805. Sadly, most of his father's assets would go to the government. Prior to his death, William Crow's assets were being seized. On July 10, 1804, The Lords of Council and Session issued the following petition against him: "That the estates, real and personal, of William Crow, formerly merchant in Leith, were sequestered by your Lordships."

William Crow's bad luck followed his sons. The Lords began looking into the family company, Crow and Wood, issuing summons to the firm's creditors in 1807, and would seize all its assets in 1812. This paints a far different picture than that of James C. Crow coming to America as a licensed doctor, eager to use chemistry knowledge to help America.

I suppose the falsehood of Crow's profession isn't the first time the whiskey industry has led us astray with a fraudulent tale. After all, Elijah Craig allegedly invented bourbon after a barn fire miraculously charred the insides of the barrels. Craig was a Baptist minister, and his story was cooked up after Prohibition, likely to thwart the religious communities' objections to bourbon again. And then there were the unscrupulous whiskey salesmen who claimed their products cured cancer and helped you to live to well into your 160s. Whiskey history is often one giant fairy tale and sometimes a concocted lie.

But the fact is Crow changed the whiskey world with his chemistry techniques. There's far too much testimony and personal written accounts from the time for that element of his biography to be false. And the idea that his technique garnered more yield is consistent with how a good sour mash operation works today. So I went back to the drawing board, ruling out medical school and trying to determine how Crow learned to distill in the first place.

That's when I discovered that Crow's neighbor Rennie is confirmed to have attended medical school and took classes under Joseph Black, a renowned chemistry professor known for discovering magnesium. In the Thomas correspondence with Scottish librarians, they said Black and his later replacement, T. C. Hope, essentially consulted for commercial brewing operations, lending their chemistry expertise to local brewers. "In this subject, at least, Edinburgh University was not an ivory tower," Currie wrote.

Because of that information, my leading theory about how Crow learned chemistry is that he worked with his neighbor Rennie to brew beer and distill whiskey. Rennie passed on his knowledge to James, who took it with him to New York, where he moved to for unknown reasons and married a woman named Eliza sometime around 1810.[7]

James and Eliza had a daughter, Catherine Crow, in 1812 in New York, and learning about her was the last piece of evidence I needed to convince me that James Crow from Leith, Scotland, was our guy. I had considered it possible that James C. Crow may not have survived the voyage to America or died in New York or Philadelphia, and somebody stole his identity before relocating to Kentucky. But James and Eliza's daughter was proof that this was indeed the same James C. Crow, the corn merchant, son of William Crow, who lived in Leith. Based on the traditional Scottish Protestant naming convention, daughter Catherine is honoring her paternal grandmother, Catherine Earby, James C. Crow's mother. While that name is common enough, it was all I needed to close the case that I was tracing the right guy.

As for what happens next in Crow's life, before moving to Kentucky, the long-held theory is that he lived in New York, which we know to be true from his marriage, and Philadelphia, where his brother operated a merchant business similar to their father's. At least, that's what had been published in past newspaper and magazine articles. But there's a clue that James Crow may have actually been in Kentucky long before we previously thought.

Still an undeveloped state in the early 1800s, Kentucky was an early battleground in the American war on Natives. One of six hundred men sent to fight the tribes, volunteer John Allen wrote in 1812 that during his journey into Frankfort, Kentucky, which neighbors Woodford County, a James Crow "contributed so largely to our comfort," giving Allen's company provisions, corn, and bacon.[8]

Was that our guy? If only the soldier said Crow gave them whiskey, then we would know, right?

There's another record that presents an interesting possibility.

An 1816 Port of Buffalo manifest places a "J. Crow" on a Lake Erie ship to Detroit with furs, steel, pork, household goods, and a lot of whiskey.[9] Was this James C. Crow?

When I took into account the 1870 published letter from his friend "E. J. S." that states Crow's New York firm, not named, had valuable cargo lost and cost him financial ruin, I began to wonder if Crow was transporting whiskey from New York City to Buffalo to Detroit. If so, Crow most certainly would have been selling Pennsylvania and New York ryes, and it would explain why he gravitated toward Kentucky. After all, if you're in the whiskey business, Kentucky is the American mecca. Nonetheless, after the collapse of the New York business, E. J. S. writes: "He was compelled, as he said, to start anew once more, and look about him for some new field of enterprise in which to earn a livelihood for himself and his family."[10] And while I want to connect E. J. S.'s cargo anecdote to the Buffalo ship, I must take into account that in his same article he said Eliza was of the famous Knickerbocker family, which I found no evidence of, and that Crow moved to Kentucky in 1825. But Versailles Post Office records put him there in 1820.[11]

In addition to E. J. S.'s inconsistencies with records, I also had to take into consideration that Crow may have been a fibber, telling false stories to people just to look good or feel better about himself. I didn't want to believe this, especially with E. J. S.'s personal context to Crow, "whose reputation and sterling character extended to a host of friends and acquaintances throughout the state," which showed the affection he had for Crow. And truthfully, I loved reading: "The passing away of this good man recalls to the recollection the many virtues that distinguished him while yet with us; and his kindly influence and acts of benevolence associate his memory with all that is pure and noble. Surely the memory of the just is blessed, and in kind remembrance of Mr. Crow these slight reminiscences are gratefully revived as a humble tribute to the memory of a truly good man… E. J. S."

So James C. Crow was a great man. Loved by his peers. I had to throw out the conman theory. Even if he had lied about being a doctor or marrying into a rich New York family, he clearly was a good person or at least he found a way to be a good person.

I so badly want to travel back in time and witness a baby-faced twenty-something James Crow schlepping barrels of whiskey on a ship or pouring a soldier a dram before battle. I'd love to see him interacting with neighbors or helping a kid learn how to read.

Alas, time travel doesn't exist. Yet. All I have to track my bourbon hero are letters and government records.

In 1826, Crow appears in the Woodford County tax records for the first time, which adds credence to the 1897 *Woodford Sun* article noting that he first worked for Willis Fields on Grier's Creek in the 1820s in Woodford County and would later work for Zachariah Henry on Glenn's Creek, Oscar Pepper, and the Johnston Distillery. He appears in the 1830 and 1850 census. And on December 3, 1839, Shelah Bailey published the following: "Notice is hereby given to Mr. James Crow, who left two horses with me in August last, to keep for him, that unless he comes or sends some person duly authorized, and takes said horses away, I shall, on the 3d [*sic*] Monday in January next, sell said horses in the town of Frankfort to pay myself for keeping them."[12]

While I found no legally binding issues to signal money troubles for Crow, James C. Crow died "almost penniless"[13] at the Johnston Distillery and was buried there in 1856. He was later moved to the Versailles Cemetery, where his wife and daughter would eventually join him.

As I studied his life, I cared less about the whiskey James C. Crow made and more about the kind of man he was. My heart ached, knowing James's bloodline stopped with Catherine, who never had children, and that his name just became a commodity for future millionaires. I imagined James running around with his little Catherine, looking for rabbits, playing hide-and-seek. Teaching her to tie knots and ride a horse.

Of course, I wasn't really thinking about James C. Crow at all. I was fantasizing what it must be like to be a father. Would I ever become one?

With a belly full of bourbon, I stared at Guy Fieri's face plastered on a frying pan inside his Times Square restaurant. My friend, author Damon Brown, was standing there laughing, definitely influenced by the bourbon. "Who puts their face on a pan?" he said, doubling over. We were in town for the American Society of Journalists and Authors conference, both of us figuring out ways to survive the freelance writing world and become authors that people wanted to read. Neither of us would admit it, but we were likely a little jealous of the massive brand Guy had built. I vowed that if I ever made it, I wouldn't put myself on a frying pan.

At that moment, Jaclyn called.

She was with her mom and almost never calls me when they are together. I felt it in my bones: Something was wrong.

"Baby, everything okay?" I answered.

Jaclyn sniffed. "Bean?"

"Yes," I replied, afraid something had happened. Had she been in a car accident? Was her mom okay? Had one of our cats escaped? Suddenly, I felt completely sober.

"I am pregnant," she said, starting to sob. A wave of joy dropped from my head to my toes.

"What?"

"Yeah, baby, I'm pregnant."

It had been a couple years since our last miscarriage, and I instantly knew this one was different. This baby was strong; the bourbon in my gut told me so.

After the first trimester, we told everyone and were showered with love, gifts, and more. But as we prepared for our first child, I ventured down a path I never expected: the natural birth cult. Jaclyn and I became obsessed with a natural birth, to the point of hiring a doula and watching every documentary about avoiding medication during labor and delivery.

According to everything we were hearing, hospitals were evil. Epidurals the devil. Ricki Lake's *The Business of Being Born* documentary discussed how American women went from home births to having babies with midwives to doctors to about one in three now giving birth via "unnecessary" C-section. Speaking to pregnant women everywhere: "Remember this, for it is as true as true gets: Your body is not a lemon. You are not a machine. The Creator is not a careless mechanic. Human female bodies have the same potential to give birth as well as aardvarks, lions, rhinoceroses, elephants, moose, and water buffalo. Even if it has not been your habit throughout your life so far, I recommend that you learn to think positively about your body."

According to Lake, drugs like Pitocin and Cytotec would lead to all sorts of problems for the baby and mother, so Jaclyn, who now was a doctor of nursing practice from the University of Tennessee, and I believed a natural birth would be the best for us. And then we listened to women who had natural births and how amazing they were, how connected they felt to the baby. I wanted that for Jaclyn.

That documentary and real-life women's stories had a profound effect on us, leading me to one day protest on public streets about women's breastfeeding rights. Looking back, I am a little surprised we didn't start living outside and sleeping next to a campfire. From the outside, we probably seemed a little strange.

About five months into the pregnancy, Jaclyn's parents had us over for dinner. We had her dad's famous coq au vin, matching its slight smoke with a green pepper–centric Chilean Carmenère. We talked about the state of the world, cribs, toys, and our potential baby names. When it came time for aperitifs, Jaclyn's dad, Charles, and I stepped out onto the porch.

Charles was a radiologist and very likely the most intelligent person I had ever met. Wise and thoughtful, he never shared an overarching opinion or found ways to circumvent me as a husband. He was a great father-in-law. But his demeanor at this porch meeting was different. Shoulders forward and his bald crown wrinkled, Charles seemed tense, eager to ask me something.

"So Anne tells me you're planning to have a natural birth," he said.

Oh, boy, I instantly knew I was in trouble. His years of practicing medicine had likely prejudiced him against home births, I thought. And he probably advocated for doctors to pump women full of drugs prior to labor. But I had watched a Ricki Lake documentary, making me as intelligent as Dr. Google. Rebuttal, here I come!

"Well, you know, Charles, we..."

"You know, there's a lot that can happen in birth. Best to be at a hospital. Not at home," he interrupted.

"Well, as for home birth, we are looking into it and Jaclyn's not sure she wants to do it at home or if it's even legal in Kentucky. But we are looking at a midwife commune in Eastern Kentucky..."

Charles raised an eyebrow and lit a cigarette. In our six years of marriage, I had never seen Jaclyn's dad smoke. I had heard he smoked, but he never once lit up around the family. He smoked when he went to the post office or on one of his nature walks, but never ever did he smoke at his house. I took this as a grave sign that he was about to filet me with words. There was nothing Ricki Lake could do in this moment. With one puff of smoke, I was toast.

"Yeah, you don't want to do that."

I dared not refute him or do anything to continue the discussion. We sparred; I lost without so much as landing a point. I looked in the living room, and Jaclyn was engaged in a similar discussion with her mother. That's when I realized her parents had planned the discussion in advance. And I've always wondered if Charles's lighting the cigarette was a planned tactic, because it worked.

When we returned home that night, Jaclyn and I agreed to have the natural birth in a hospital. Our doula suggested we go across the river to have the baby in Indiana instead of Kentucky, where doctors often dismiss "natural birth plans."

When we visited the hospital in Jeffersonville, Indiana, its staff were recruiting us like we were college athletes deciding the fate of its football program. Past patients, now veteran mothers of toddlers, shared how beautiful their births were, and all I could do was nod. I was in support mode. If this hospital was where Jaclyn wanted our child to be born, that's where we were having it.

The pregnancy was almost spiritual. Jaclyn grew and glowed, with a healthy diet of mortadella and white American cheddar keeping her going. Whatever she craved, she got. But I honestly can't think of anything weird like pickles and ice cream; her diet was just protein and calcium rich.

We took birth classes, practicing what to do during contractions. I downloaded apps, practiced the route to the hospital, and read natural birth books. I was ready to be by her side when the time came. I even had a plan for if we had a quick birth and I needed to deliver the baby myself. I imagined waking up to Jaclyn in labor with the crown of the head already showing. I'd instruct Jaclyn to squat and push while I readied my soft hands for the catch. The paramedics would walk in just as I cut the cord.

Yeah, that was wishful thinking.

When Jaclyn went into labor a couple weeks late, she started throwing up.

"Nobody ever throws up in labor," our doula had once said to us.

Well, Jaclyn was hurling up her guts as if the baby were squeezing her stomach dry. She couldn't stand for more than a minute, and the contractions were getting closer and closer together. By the time the doula, Angela, arrived, Jaclyn had sweated through her clothes and was hovering over the toilet.

Angela helped Jaclyn into the car and followed us to the hospital. With one hand, I held Jaclyn's. The other hand was firmly on the steering wheel, and my foot pressed so hard into the floorboard my arch nearly cramped as I sped 105 miles per hour to the hospital.

Jaclyn puked within minutes of being admitted, and the nurses pulled up our birthing plan. I wanted to tweet at Ricki Lake to let her know our natural birth was about to begin. Looking back, I am glad I didn't.

The doula and nurses spent the next few hours rubbing Jaclyn's back and feet, placing cold rags on her head, and doing all they could to keep her comfortable. But she kept puking, leading one nurse to tell me, "This is a first for me. Never had a puker while giving birth."

I was a nervous wreck, pacing back and forth and trying to make sense of how two hours had turned to four to six and then eight. Why wasn't the baby coming? All the while, the hospital sounds were making me weary: the beeping, doctor pages, nurses thumbing through charts, and the families chatting in the lobby. It was overwhelming me. Yet I reminded myself that I needed to suck it up. I was tired? So what? The love of my life was in absolute, bone-stretching pain and continued to refuse any medication to assist with the birth.

I looked into Jaclyn's soft brown eyes. "Are you okay?"

"Yes," she said, crunching on ice chips.

"Do you want to get something for the pain or to aid the baby?"

"No. Do you think I should?"

"Baby, we wanted this natural birth plan, but you do what you feel should be done."

The head midwife was in her early forties and had delivered hundreds, if not a thousand, babies in natural births. She said we should continue to monitor the dilation and the baby's and mom's vitals.

For twenty-four hours, Jaclyn endured contractions, no sleep, nausea, and little dilation progress, and refused to take any medication. I cannot even begin to imagine the amount of pain she was willing to endure to experience a natural birth. But everything changed when the machine's vital sounds went from a steady beep to a beat the pace of a drum. Nurses ran in to reposition Jaclyn, and the midwife pulled me aside immediately.

"The baby's D-cells are dropping and we have to do an emergency C-section now. We have already called the doctor. He is on his way."

The words hit me like a brick to the head. I couldn't breathe. The only thing I felt was the need to hold Jaclyn's hand. "We're sorry, but you cannot be in prep."

Jaclyn was going to have to do this alone.

It all happened so fast that I didn't even notice the tears running down my cheeks or the doula's hand squeezing mine. The nurses could no longer speak to me; they were like NASCAR pit crewman moving in short bursts and ignoring all else around them. *Was my wife in danger? Was the baby?*

One of Jaclyn's greatest fears was that she would die in

childbirth. Angela tried to reassure me. "This is the best emergency C-section team in the area," she said. "Jaclyn is in great hands."

But the baby? My precious baby boy that I had yet to hold. His heart rate was dropping? Was he okay? Was he still alive? I feared the thought of Jaclyn having to hold a stillborn child and me not being there to bear the pain with her.

"Mr. Minnick, your wife can see you now," a nurse said about thirty minutes after I saw Jaclyn hauled away. I wore itchy hospital garb that smelled like rubbing alcohol.

She walked me into the room where Jaclyn was laid up, legs splayed out and a tarp separating her and the doctors. Jaclyn requested Frank Sinatra as background music. She reported that she was numb and was definitely feeling the effects of the medication. I held her hand as the doctor sliced her open. "He's holding the cord," he said with a chuckle.

The cord had wrapped around the baby's neck, and he had managed to move his hand in between and get just enough space, like a grappler fighting off a choke. When they pulled the baby out, he did not cry but checked out the room to see what was going on. Jaclyn saw him for a split second before they kicked me out and began sewing her up.

I took my shirt off and pressed his head against my chest, all the while looking at her and hoping she was okay. I wanted to be here in the moment with my son, but all I could think about was Jaclyn and how she was feeling. Then, I looked down at my little rascal and there he was. His head was huge, rounded with an enormous brain, and big eyes that were still murky from the fluid. He wiggled so much I could barely hold him.

After they carted Jaclyn back to the room, the baby and I came to see her so she could hold him for the first time. We had yet to name him, and I decided that I'd let her decide from the many names we had in the running. Kaymen was the front runner, but Oliver, Oscar, Edwin, Samuel, and James were all possibilities. His wiggle and toughness made me think he was an Oscar, which sounded like a fighter's name.

As Jaclyn held him for the first time, she said, "He looks like an Oscar."

"I know! He is an Oscar," I replied.

Jaclyn smiled, still under the meds' influence, having gone through God knows how much pain, and now she was with our boy, Oscar, for the first time. The glow, energy, spiritual feeling, or whatever you want to call it, of that room was so extraordinary and special that I hoped I could experience it again one day. Then, without hesitation, Jaclyn asked, "Hey, did you bring any bourbon? Maybe the Booker's?"

I did bring bourbon, including Old Forester Birthday Bourbon, which felt right to crack open. Therein is the perfect moment of my family's life. At every turn, bourbon was there in a supporting role.

THE HUNT

CHAPTER 6

FAME AND ILLEGAL ACTIVITY

JACLYN'S HEAD RESTED on a pillow, and her feet stuck out from under the covers. Oscar slept by her side in the bassinet. I lifted the blanket to examine Jaclyn's C-section scar. The emergency surgery left her with a gaping wound that I had to clean and pack every day. She could sit up a bit in bed, but I had to bring her food, Oscar, and help her walk during those first few weeks.

She nursed our baby boy and fought an infection.

The wound healed three-quarters of the way along the incision but then stopped like a stuck zipper, and I funneled gauze string inside with surgical swabs, packing the wound tight and sealing the half-dollar-size hole with medical bandages. Everything was sterilized. I wore gloves and joked with Jaclyn that I should have become a nurse. But while I did the best I could and maintained a clean environment, she was not getting better.

The love of my life had just gone through a traumatic delivery and now faced new frightening concerns. I took her to the doctor and my fears became reality.

"Look," the wound care doctor said, "this is going to turn into sepsis if it doesn't clear up. We will need to do surgery if it's not better in a week."

That night, as both Jaclyn and Oscar slept, I held her hand and teared up as I silently prayed. "Please do not let her go through this and help her heal, Lord." I made the sign of the cross and fell asleep. Two days later, her wound had fully healed, and I never told her about my prayer or how I cried that night in fear of the pain and agony she would endure in surgery.

She had to return to work at the hospital almost as soon as she was better, and we enrolled Oscar in day care. It didn't feel right.

Is this how new families are supposed to work?

The mother gets three months with the baby before her work puts her back into the rotation? And the partner shouldn't even take more than a week off?

I didn't quite understand society's need to push work so hard on a family with a newborn. That is, until I saw the hospital bills. Even though insurance covered most of the costs, we were still on the hook for several thousand dollars. And the mortgage wasn't taking a break because we had a baby.

Then, there was my competitive instinct, an overwhelming worry that somebody would replace me at my job, fueling me to get back to work. At this point in my life, I had never worked harder, writing for as many publications as I could and promoting my work to any radio station, magazine writer, or TV station that would listen.

My byline was at the top of all the major whiskey publications, and my first whiskey book, *Whiskey Women*, had been published two months before Oscar was born. *Whiskey Women* was the first book on how women impacted all whiskey types. I don't know why it took so long for somebody to write, but I spent a couple years in archives around the world digging up anecdotes about women like Jane Corrigan, the owner of Bushmills, who were not mentioned in the typical whiskey histories or promoted by the brands they once made or owned. In 2013, the media loved a good untold story in women's history. I was on a mission to tell the world about whiskey and the women who made it. But something happened that I neither planned nor prepared for—people started to recognize me from my TV appearances promoting the book.

On multiple occasions, people came up to me at the store and asked, "Are you that whiskey guy?" I smiled and picked up bread, cereal, or whatever I was shopping for, and kept on. But I won't lie, it felt good, as if the simple hello was a pat on the back for my work. At industry trade events where I spoke about the history of whiskey or led a tasting for bartenders, people stood in long lines with my book in hand or tasting mats or random pieces of paper for me to sign.

"I want to thank you for writing this book," a young bartender told me, as she clutched her copy of *Whiskey Women*. When I signed it, I noticed how tattered and torn it was, how she had flagged pages and highlighted text. This hit me right in the feels—it's every author's dream to connect with somebody like this.

People asked for photos with me and bought my book for holiday gifts. And my magazine writing was in high gear as well. I was now breaking news and covering bourbon at the highest level. People appreciated it when I called out brands for lying about their histories or when I took them to task for bad business moves.

During this time, large distillers such as Heaven Hill and Jim Beam were feeling intense pressure from consumers. They simply did not have enough product to keep up with the growing demand for bourbon. They all attempted ways to satisfy supply requirements, such as making the whiskey non–age stated. To many consumers, seeing language such as "nine years old" on the label is a sign of quality; legally, it's also a guarantee that the youngest barrel in the batch is nine years old. If the distiller eliminates the age statement, it can fill the same brand with four-year-old juice, which is lower quality. Another common method to stretch product was lowering the proof, which is the measurement of alcohol strength—the higher in proof, the more potent it is. Maker's Mark famously lowered its proof from 90 to 84, allowing it to get an extra bottle for every one hundred and just barely meet its demand. I covered this change in 2013, interviewing the Samuels family and reporting on the consumer reactions, garnering all sorts of accolades for my journalistic-style coverage of the controversial decision. Eight days after the proof drop, Maker's Mark returned to the original proof, leading people (including me) to buy the 84-proof bottles until they cleared the shelf, assuming they would become a collector's item. This left us all to wonder: Had it all just been a marketing ploy? Maker's Mark simply said it made a mistake but never fully explained what happened.

Nonetheless, every time a brand pursued one of these strategies, I covered it, and consumers thanked me for being a watchdog of sorts. For the bulk of my whiskey writing career, I overwhelmingly received thank-yous.

In the span of a very short time—three years since my taste mindfulness moment in therapy—I went from a virtual nobody to a notable author and one of the best known whiskey journalists in the world. It felt good to be recognized for my work. But of course, there's always the other side—the hate.

Criticism had never bothered me; I'm a writer, after all, and good editors bleed on our papers with red pens from the moment we start. So I had never cared about readers questioning my reviews or saying they flat-out didn't like something I wrote. What hurt were the memes and public commentary on my appearance, making jokes about my favorite necktie—the ascot, which I frequently wear—and the strangest false accusations about me. I guess this all came about because I was becoming a known face in the bourbon space, a public figure. In a Facebook group, a poster claimed they saw me demanding a discount at a liquor store because I was a famous whiskey writer, and another claimed I was writing positive reviews about my own books under a fake name. I'd later learn that somebody pretended to be me to get discounts and access to rare bottles at liquor stores. Sometime later after these false claims, a person tried to garner backstage access at the music festival I helped create—Bourbon & Beyond. During the event, my business partner Danny Wimmer received a radio call from security.

"Hey, there's a guy in a truck says he's Fred Minnick," security called out.

"That's impossible; Fred's with me," Danny replied, and then sprinted toward the truck, whose driver hit the gas pedal so hard he threw gravel and burned his tires on the asphalt.

Why would anybody want to impersonate me?

When these public attacks first hit, I was also a new dad, vulnerable both emotionally and physically. Let's face it, I was operating on about two to four hours of sleep with Oscar bellowing all night to the tune of an alley cat. Perhaps I couldn't mentally process the attacks because I was so tired. I also wondered whether I was juggling too much, or whether I just needed to toughen up. I couldn't say, but I felt my grasp on the industry I loved weakening as other parts of my life became more important. I was a freelancer, after all, and there was no job guaranteed to me, no paid leave or vacation for me to use to take care of my family. I either covered the whiskey industry or I didn't.

So I tried to cover it the best I could at the time and still managed book signing events, a few of which my infant and awesome wife attended. Those were fun! But truthfully, I missed a lot, which is where I drew criticism from a few haters. I simply couldn't cover the industry at the same rate as I did without a newborn. And I missed perhaps the biggest story of my career.

In mid-January 2014, the Japanese spirits company Suntory acquired Jim Beam for $16 billion. It was the biggest news in the whiskey industry in some time, and outside of a small blog post, I really didn't cover it or provide any insight. I couldn't have done it even if I'd wanted to: I was so darn tired. But my lack of coverage drew criticism with one Twitter follower suggesting I hire somebody to change diapers so I could get back to covering whiskey. While it was likely meant as a joke, and he later deleted the

Tweet, the comment genuinely pissed me off. When I read this anonymous handle's commentary, I felt a rage I hadn't experienced since the height of my PTSD. And that rage quickly turned into depression.

A couple of weeks later, at the Bourbon Classic event, where whiskey industry leaders lead tastings and workshops—and one of my first moments away from my new family—I absolutely bombed my onstage appearance, often asking questions that didn't make any sense and speaking over my fellow panelists. I was awful, and a few attendees told me how badly I sucked.

That hurt. But at least they told me to my face.

On social media, people lambasted me.

While I intellectually understood that I had become a public figure and as such was open game, I felt small. Like a tiny pebble being kicked and kicked and kicked until finally it falls to the bottom of a stream, where it cannot be bothered.

I tried my therapy worksheets. I figured out the belief causing me to be so impacted by the negativity: *I want people to like me.* Such a simple thing, really. I wanted to be liked. Who doesn't?

I tried leaning into the academic pleasure of researching Old Crow, sorting through the papers at a historical society. I felt the coarse parchment on my fingertips and read the elaborate handwriting of an 1800s-era lawyer. But I could not focus. I constantly checked my phone to see if anybody was saying something about me on social media. I remember looking at the reflection of myself in the phone screen and wondering, *What is happening to me?*

My passion for whiskey, the desire to study Old Crow, dwindled with every negative comment.

I could not process what to tell myself when these people ripped me to shreds on social media. By March 2014, my Iraq War trauma was in-hand, but I had no successful coping mechanisms for people hating on me. The criticism of strangers on the internet did more damage to my soul than I could have ever predicted.

I wanted to quit.

I was thirty-five years old and still had GI Bill money remaining from my nine years of military service. I made plans to shift my career, to focus on the business side of things. What business? I didn't know, but in 2014, becoming a businessman meant going for an MBA. I applied to Bellarmine University and was scheduled for an interview.

When I walked into the MBA administration's office, a tall lanky fella with black hair and an all-American smile greeted me. "Turner Wathen, nice to meet you. I'm a big fan of your work," he said, extending his hand.

"Wathen, any relation to the famous whiskey family?"

"Yes, that's my family," he replied.

He proceeded to interview me about my background and what I could bring to the MBA program. After I rambled for a while, he stopped me.

"What are you doing?" he asked, honestly putting the fear of God in me. Had I said something I shouldn't have?

"I'm sorry?"

"Look, you're accepted into the program. But you don't need this. You're Fred friggin' Minnick. You are the most influential whiskey writer in Kentucky, and you just published the best whiskey book in a long time. What are you *doing*?"

I wanted to tell him that the haters had gotten to me, that I could no longer handle the public limelight, and that I was questioning every move I made. Instead, I said something I was a little less embarrassed about but that was also true.

"Well, I don't make much money. Books don't exactly make you rich," I said.

"Look, the money will come. You can do this MBA program, but I think it's a mistake. If you want my advice, stay the course and everything will turn out fine. You're too good to quit writing about whiskey."

That pep talk was the two in a "one–two" combo that saved my fledgling career. The first happened when I was researching *Whiskey Women* in 2010. I was in the office of Bill Samuels Jr., who is the equivalent of Steve Jobs in the whiskey world, to interview him for the book. The chairman of Maker's Mark, Bill is largely responsible for bourbon's current popularity. When he was promoting Maker's Mark in the 1970s and '80s, he also promoted Jim Beam, Wild Turkey, and Evan Williams in an effort to grow the entire category, not just his brand. Bill's unique marketing mind revolutionized how people thought about bourbon, bringing it out of the doldrums of country clubs and into the masses. But his greatest skill was reading people and knowing who would do well at a job.

"Can you tell me how the sale to Hiram Walker came about in the early 1980s?" I asked Bill, who rubbed his chin and looked around the office.

The sale happened, in part, because his mother, Marjorie Samuels, had been ill at the time. And she was to be prominently featured in *Whiskey Women*, because she created the concepts of Maker's Mark's distinctive packaging and essentially invented bourbon tourism in the 1960s. For this, she was inducted into the Kentucky Bourbon Hall of Fame posthumously. But I was trying to capture stories that had yet to be told, and there wasn't much information on the sale in the early 1980s. "Well, sure, I can tell you about Hiram Walker. But let me interrupt you for a minute," he said.

Much like that heart-stopping moment in my interview with Turner Wathen years later, I thought I had crossed a line with Bill. Was there some mysterious reason that Bill didn't want to talk about this? Instead, much to my surprise, he said, "I do not know what you are going to do, but you are going to change the industry."

While these comments from Samuels and Wathen were three years apart, my MBA interview helped me recollect what Bill had said and helped me carry on every time I read a naysayer's words. If these two had that much confidence in me, why couldn't I have the same?

I continued to battle the "why doesn't this person like me?" belief that would eventually find a way past the one–two Samuels-Wathen confidence combo and take me down again. When the haters got to me again, I was in Washington, DC, promoting my new book, *Bourbon Curious*, and saw an online comment from somebody I considered to be a friend making fun of my tasting notes to the tune of *The Lego Movie* song "Everything Is Awesome."

At the famous Jack Rose Dining Saloon, where we were having my book launch party, thousands of whiskeys line the walls. It's a whiskey lover's dream venue. My friend and the bar's bourbon manager, Jared Hyman, saw something was wrong with me. I slumped over a railing, my head in my hands.

"Fred, you okay?" he asked, putting his meaty paw on my shoulder.

"I don't—I don't get it, Jared," I replied. "Why are so many people attacking me? The hardest part is I actually considered some of them to be friends."

"I don't know what to tell you, bud, but you're only focusing on the people who attack you. Look at how many people are here to get a book from you," he said. "My advice is to focus on the good things."

No matter how hard I tried to focus on the positive, I always fell back into the same self-degrading belief system. If I was meant to stay in the whiskey industry, I genuinely needed to focus on how to prevent another PTSD episode.

I went to Betty.

"Where are they saying these things?" she asked.

"Reddit, Facebook, Twitter. You know, all the social media places," I said.

"I understand you have to be on there for your job. But how do you find their comments?"

"I look for them," I replied.

"So you're actively looking for people saying negative things about you that make you feel bad?"

"I guess so," I replied.

"Interesting. Have you ever thought about not looking at their comments, and definitely not going out of your way to see them?"

I suppose the best advice for dealing with haters or trolls is to ignore them. But who can truly do that? I mean, when you're tagged, emailed, and called awful things, you can't avoid the commentary. There's just no way. It's impossible, right?

But I decided to give her advice a try.

For a solid week, I avoided all social media that was not my own, meaning I didn't go onto pages to browse or read any comments that were not within my own threads. It worked, but I'd still get hate mail and people tagging me in negative comments. That's when I realized hiding from hate would never work, and that the core issue wasn't the people chastising me. It was me. I was letting the "people don't like me" belief hold me back.

I chose to feel sorry for myself when somebody gave negative feedback. I had never felt this way when an editor ripped my work. Why did I care about an anonymous person?

I would eventually realize that haters took the time to read my work, watch my videos, and attend my events, and were akin to the sports talk show caller who vocally bullies a quarterback but watches every game. Much like how I became obsessed with Old Crow, for a short period, I became fascinated with the human psyche, especially what possesses somebody to criticize a nonpolitical public figure on social media.

I studied Peyton Manning, Tom Brady, and my favorite heavy metal band—Metallica—to see how they reacted to negative online commentary. Peyton throws an interception: "I gotta do better." Tom Brady loses: "Need to get back to work." Somebody on Facebook says Metallica's guitarist Kirk Hammett looks like an old lady: they sell out another arena show.

How these greats dealt with haters helped me understand that we create our own story and that the people who criticize you can motivate you just as powerfully as they can tear you down. I flipped how I felt as soon as I realized this. Haters fueled me to write better, to become a better speaker, to explore new ways to discuss whiskey. They also lit a fire under me to dive deeper into the whiskey community, to try something new.

In many ways, I am so thankful for the people who ripped me to shreds, because they helped me understand who I truly was and why I definitely am meant to cover whiskey. I also grew to understand their position, a lot of which was fueled by jealousy. If I were them, I'd probably talk shit on me too. I drink, talk, and now buy whiskey for a living.

Who wouldn't want that job?

After the near collapse of my career, I realized another reason I had become such an easy target: I spent as much or more time in archives and libraries, looking for James Crow anecdotes and sorting through old newspaper clips for bourbon clues, than I did in bars with actual cool whiskey people. I realized I had isolated myself for reporting and historical fact-finding missions. I was not truly experiencing the modern whiskey movement; I merely told it.

"If you let people define who you are, you become what they say you are," Betty told me.

This sage advice became the battle cry for my professional life: *I am a whiskey writer, who seeks the unknown and ventures to taste*. I also vowed to get out more, to not fall into the rut of just focusing on history. This meant my brain was going to take a break from good ole James C. Crow for a minute and tell contemporary stories people wanted to read.

Does something taste good? Is it worth the price? That's what

90 percent of the whiskey lovers cared about, and I knew if I didn't pioneer new work in the tasting space, my writing would become irrelevant.

My professional tasting career was just beginning when Oscar was an infant. I regularly wrote reviews for *Tasting Panel* and *Whisky Magazine*, but it wasn't until I joined the San Francisco World Spirits Competition in 2013 that things truly began to take off.

I peeled away the secrecy of the spirits competition, detailing every aspect in my blog, and began describing bourbon with notes that had not been used before. While describing the flavor of marzipan in a single-barrel bourbon would draw criticism from those pesky haters, it was a direct result of those taste mindfulness exercises. I could just taste more than I used to, more than most people could, because of the time I had put into developing my palate and focusing deeply on the sense of taste.

With each tasting, I placed a small amount of whiskey on my tongue, closed my eyes, and focused on where the spirit felt most prominent. That first taste was solely to identify the part of the tongue the spirit lit up. I didn't think about flavor, I just wanted to see where it hit. With the second taste I concentrated on the part of the tongue I felt it most prominently on the first taste, and that's when my brain recalled flavors felt on that part of the tongue, and I began to define actual flavors. The notes rang through my head like a spelling bee champion reciting letters: banana, Chinese five spice, chestnut, dill, frankincense, ginger, lilac, pear, peppermint, raspberry—every flavor I had ever tasted rested in my brain, waiting for the right moment to be revealed in a whiskey.

I gravitated toward pleasurable taste experiences, such as fresh macaroons at a French bakery or my grandpa's cast iron skillet Jiffy cornbread. Within a year, my lexicon of tasting notes landed me the most prestigious reviewing slot in whiskey—*Whisky Advocate.*

I came home, filled with glee, to tell Jaclyn about my new gig.

"Bro, you are not going to believe this," I told Jaclyn in our specialized marital speak.

"Sup," she replied.

"Guess who is the new *Whisky Advocate* American whiskey reviewer?"

"Get on up in here."

I realized that if aliens visited our planet one time and listened to a random conversation between Jaclyn and me, they would think we are a species that could not survive, let alone tie their own shoes.

"Right? But I do have to go to work on a Wednesday," I said, referencing our favorite adult cartoon, *Squidbillies.*

We high-fived and went out to dinner somewhere fancy with a comfortable booth for Oscar to sleep in his car seat. I looked at him, his big blue eyes closed, and just watched him sleep. Out of nowhere, anxiety overtook me. *Was I making enough money? Would I be able to pay for Oscar's college? What if something happened to me?*

Even though it was a huge opportunity and an incredible honor, the additional *Whisky Advocate* work resulted in only slightly more money. Not a lot. And anyway, my whiskey review funds mostly went to buying more whiskey.

I earned about $55,000 in 2015, and whatever didn't go to bills fattened bootlegger pockets. I never cared about the modern bottles coveted by private jet owners; I sought the bottles from dead distillers, forgotten brands, and of course, my holy grail—vintage

Old Crow. With each bottle find, my whiskey knowledge and passion grew.

For my first vintage buy, I surveyed eBay and Craigslist, looking for affordable bottles, such as an Old Crow from the 1960s called "The Traveler." Designed to fit in the suit pocket of a businessman, it was meant to be carried onto planes and buses and enjoyed with your fellow passengers. When I found a bare-bones Craigslist listing for Old Crow Traveler, I reached out.

"Yes, I am inquiring about the Old Crow bottle you advertised."

"Cool. You with the ABC?"

I honestly did not know what the ABC was at that time. I later learned it meant Alcohol Board or Bureau of Control (or Commission). Every state is different, but most ABC agents can arrest you and throw you in jail for selling alcohol without a license. Since I didn't know what the seller was referring to, I merely said, "no."

He sent me PayPal instructions and said he'd mail the bottle to me. Fifty dollars and a good deal of bubble wrap later, I was the proud owner of a bottle meant for a 1960s banker. It had a leather strap securing a wooden cover over the cork to the narrow rectangular bottle. The label was tattered and torn, and it smelled like somebody had kept the bottle in a smoke-filled basement, which made me realize I should have asked the seller for more information before making the purchase. Where had it been stored? Who had owned it before? I could have also asked for pictures, but I was nervous.

Oscar was in his crib when the bottle arrived. He peeked at it and me, wondering if he could have a pull. "Not yet, buddy," I said.

I twisted the wooden topper and twisted the cap, exposing the whiskey to air for the first time in forty years. I remembered Jason Brauner, owner of Bourbons Bistro, telling me to let the oxygen get in there before you drink, because the whiskey will change as air opens it up. There was an actual chemical reaction occurring, and the proof would change from the top of the bottle to the bottom. Add water and that's another chemical reaction.

So I poured two fingers neat in a rocks glass and let it sit there for about twenty minutes. I sat down, raised the glass, and analyzed the color. It was so dark, far too dark for the supposed eight-year age and 86 proof. I swear it was darker than twenty-three-year-old Pappy, which is significant, because bourbon, which can only be aged in new charred oak, gets darker the longer it sits in the barrel. Why was this bourbon so dark?

I jotted down a reminder to investigate it later. But for now, I brought the glass to my nose, opened my mouth slightly to help my olfactory receptors process alcohol smells, and took a whiff.

"Holy Mother of God, this smells like a dirty basement," I said, disappointed.

Here I was thinking I was about to repeat my experience with the Old Crow Chess Piece and be reconnected with the greatest whiskey I had ever tasted. Instead, the aromas of mold, cigarette smoke, and green shag carpeting are what I got. But I had been there before. Sometimes a bad smell doesn't always translate into the flavor.

On a panel at the San Francisco World Spirits Competition, the holy grail for spirits tasters, a friend said he initially smelled "goat shit" in a whiskey and ended up voting for it for best in show.

Turns out, it was a Laphroaig, an Islay single malt, and barn smells in Laphroaig are quite common on the nose but never appear on the palate. It's just because of the way that whiskey is made—with peat. Anyway, I linked the Old Crow Traveler to my lips, allowing a thimble-sized amount of bourbon to hit my tongue and travel all over it, trying to figure out where I felt it most prominently. I would then taste again and focus on that singular most prominent spot to see if flavors appeared. And boy, did they ever. I tasted rust, dirt, mushrooms, bong water, and fifteen forms of bacteria I couldn't describe.

I was livid. Had the guy sold me a bad bottle?

I contacted him, and the email was returned to sender. I couldn't believe it. The dude had appeared online, asked if I was a cop, made some money, shipped me a bottle, and disappeared.

That's when I realized buying bourbon from internet strangers wasn't the best idea. At least not on Craigslist. So I went to a far more reputable place—eBay, where sellers had reviews and comments on their shipping. If somebody sold a bad bottle like Mr. ABC Asker, their reputation would soon be ruined among the community of anonymous bidders.

I hopped onto eBay, scrolled through the bottles, and found several Old Crow Chess Pieces. I couldn't tell if they were filled all the way or just being sold as decorative items. Either way, my $40 top bid for Old Crow was beaten, but my $40 bid on a 1970s bottle of Wild Turkey came through.

Now, Wild Turkey doesn't exactly have the same esteem as Pappy Van Winkle, but I'll be damned if I haven't always loved the flavor of it. The contemporary stuff is nutmeg forward with hints of cinnamon and sometimes a deep back-of-the-palate note of hatch chili. Would the 1970s vintage be as good?

This bottle arrived in a star foam tube and appeared just as it had in the eBay listing. A big-necked turkey glistened on the label and the words *Austin Nichols*, the parent company that would eventually sell to Pernod Ricard, were written in bold type. I was curious if there was anything different about this bottle than modern Turkey, so I drove to Lawrenceburg, Kentucky, to meet with master distiller Jimmy Russell, who made this and had worked for Wild Turkey for more than sixty years. His nickname is the "Buddha of Bourbon" for the way his belly protrudes, but he is a masterful distiller and a kind man who always waits in the visitor center to meet with fans.

Jimmy walked me into an aluminum-skinned warehouse, and I felt a cool breeze on this April day. It carried the aromas of all the barrels aging in here. Caramel, vanilla, and general bourbon smells filled my nose—oh, it was heavenly. I dragged my fingers across the barrels as I walked with Jimmy and his son, Eddie. They had a couple barrels pulled from the racks, where the bourbon rests, and wanted me to sample it with them. While I couldn't wait to do this, I also had to know about this bottle I bought!

"Is Wild Turkey the same today as it was in the 1970s?" I asked.

"Yessir," Jimmy said. "Same recipe."

"Same stills and barrel types?"

"Yessir."

"Same still and barrel entry proofs?" I asked, trying to identify any differences between the historical recipe and today's. When whiskey comes off the still, distillers proof it down with water. The legal limit to proof down to up until 1962 was 110, but distillers lobbied to change this to 125, because the higher the barrel entry proof, the more volume they could get out of the barrel when they went to bottling. Most of the distillers maintained 110, but as the old guard lost control to the accountants, the barrel entry proofs went up to 125.

"Well, I tried for as long as I could to keep Pernod Ricard from changing the barrel proof. I was able to only get them to change it just a couple proof points, but that's the only real change," Jimmy said.

Going into this Turkey tasting, I knew I was tasting something very similar to what I had in the 1970s bottle. Wild Turkey used the same yeast and recipe and even acquired the grains from the same farms as it had in the 1970s. If the barrel entry changed from 110 to 114, was that really enough of a difference in how it was made to create a flavor change? I saw this as an opportunity to compare two eras of the same product, both at 101 proof.

I poured the two different Wild Turkey genres and immediately noticed their smells couldn't have been more different. The 1970s: brown sugar, butter, cinnamon, autumn leaves, and sunflowers. The modern version: just nutmeg. While it smelled lovely, the contemporary was lacking the complexity on the nose that the vintage possessed.

Now for the taste. I took a small sip, allowing it to caress my tongue. The vintage hit my tongue like wet, soft butter, dripping down my jawline and covering every inch of my tongue. The modern version hit the mid-palate and slightly tickled the rest but was nowhere in the league of its predecessor. And from a flavor perspective, they were night and day, two different whiskeys leagues apart. The vintage presented that brown sugar–butter flavor, followed by clove, pepper, and so much more. The modern, while good, just couldn't hang, mustering only a single flavor that had the intensity of the vintage's many notes.

This research tasting led me to wonder: *If only the barrel entry proof had changed, why were the two vintages eons apart?*

I required more study to fully answer this, seeking out more Wild Turkey and repeating the tasting process. With every bottle, vintage Wild Turkey handily won over my palate. Was it the grains? The water? The yeast? The wood to make the barrels? Something was different, and I would unravel these details over the years. The mystery of bourbon never disappoints.

By the time I really started getting interested in buying vintage bourbon, eBay had discontinued its alcohol sales after several stores claiming to sell "collectible" alcohol bottles were caught selling vodka to thirteen-year-olds. This led to several undercover stings, parental outrage, and significant media coverage. eBay stated: "eBay will not allow our marketplace to be used as a way to circumvent laws regarding the sale of alcohol, particularly the illegal sale of alcohol to minors. We are beginning the process of removing listings of beer and spirits. We expect to allow these listings again after developing and implementing additional, reasonable requirements to support seller compliance with our policies and applicable laws. We will continue to allow listings by pre-approved, licensed wine sellers."[1]

This statement says a lot in one simple paragraph and brought forth an early lesson to my career: wine collectors will always be looked at differently than bourbon collectors. To the public eye, wine collectors are doctors, lawyers, and prestigious people. In almost all major markets, wine faces less scrutiny than spirits, because it's perceived to be more sophisticated and is lower in alcohol percentage. Bourbon was the biker bar drink, the working man's pour, and carried the devil's shadow from Prohibition. In some cultures, such as French and Italian, wine was not even considered alcohol, while whiskey faced the scrutiny of an intoxicant. These stereotypes, I believe, also led to regulations and the likes of eBay banning the resale of the product.

As a result, my cyber-buying experience was pretty much limited to underground Facebook groups. In 2016, Facebook was in its bourbon-selling glory. Famous bourbon lovers like Emeril Lagasse had proxies buy for them, while the chef Sean Brock, who would later write a foreword for my book *Bourbon*, almost single-handedly purchased all the product from an extinct distillery called Stitzel-Weller, once owned and operated by Pappy Van Winkle.

These self-policed bourbon secondary groups didn't have reviews or buyers and sellers. But they had open communication between members, shared spreadsheets, and maintained a general understanding similar to Fight Club: *You don't talk about these groups outside of these groups*. By the time I entered these sacred virtual marketplaces and was accepted by the members, Pennsylvania ABC cops had arrested people for attempting to sell bourbon online, so there was always a concern that selling on Facebook groups to the wrong person could lead to an arrest. But because this was all illegal, allegedly, we protected one another the old-fashioned way—by word of mouth.

In this underground world, we Google-sleuthed one another and analyzed each user profile. The admins also kept spreadsheets of sales and trades, and kicked people out for faulty shipping practices or buyers not paying in full.

The seller would post a picture of the bottle, along with some details on the provenance and the closing date of the auction. The bidders dropped their bids in the comments or offered the buy-it-now price. We were discouraged from using words and symbols that could get flagged by the Facebook police, such as dollar signs and alcohol types. So instead of *$15*, it was merely *15*, and rather than *whiskey*, it could be *whisk#y*, or no mention of the type of alcohol at all.

Then there were groups that attracted amateur historians who told stories about each bottle, the distillery, how it was made, and if the bottle was in a labor strike year or part of some grander moment. The years 2012 to 2016 were peak bourbon Facebook, with legions of bottles up for grabs and stories being told in vibrant online communities.

I won a few Old Crow 1960s to 1980s bottles for around $100 each, nabbed my beloved chess pieces for $180 to $220, and badly wished I had more money when a 1942 Old Crow bottle went for $750 in 2015. But I just couldn't swing it.

More than anything, I found the Facebook groups to be entertaining and educational.

It was here that I learned the weights of the Old Crow Chess Pieces drastically differed, with a King weighing 4.25 pounds completely full and 2.8 pounds empty, compared to the Light Pawn 5 at 3.8 pounds full and 2.14 pounds empty. Bottle collectors shared what the different tax stamps on bottles meant, and how to date whiskey simply by analyzing the stamp over the cork and pinpoint its exact retail origination with state tax stamps.

In a world that didn't teach alcohol education, total strangers were my greatest teachers in understanding true bourbon history. These enthusiasts, who totaled around two hundred thousand across all buyer and information groups, were the heartbeat of bourbon in this era. And the commercial brands followed the pricing of their bottles, often setting their own suggested retail price (SRP) based on how well a bottle sold on a Facebook secondary page.

I will never forget sitting down with Dave Pickerell, a former Maker's Mark master distiller who left the company in 2008 to embark on the greatest whiskey consultant career in history. He helped start more than one hundred distilleries and three hundred brands. Wearing a far-too-tight button-up shirt around his big belly and a panama hat, Dave sat for an interview with me about one of the brands he co-founded—WhistlePig—and the SRP of $500 for its latest line, Boss Hog.

"Why so much, Dave?" I asked.

"Well, Fred, it's either the people who make the whiskey get the money or one of the flippers is going to. Because this is rare and limited," he replied. He was referring to the people who buy a $40 bottle at a store and sell it on Facebook for significantly more.

After that conversation, I realized that all the bourbon pricing was going up in response to the growing demand. Michter's launched a limited edition Celebration for $5,000, while Heaven Hill, the king of value, increased Elijah Craig 18-year from $35 to around $200. "We are finally getting the value it deserves," the then-spokesperson for Heaven Hill, Larry Kass, told me. This was happening solely because of the companies watching the secondary groups and seeing people buying bourbon at the highest prices they had ever seen.

These Facebook groups were live data with the greatest pocket of bourbon lovers on the market. If only it could have lasted.

One frigid day in January 2015, I was driving Oscar to day care and tilted the rearview mirror to catch a glance at him. At just over one year old, the little nugget's big blue eyes looked out the window with the sort of fascination you can only dream of getting back from childhood. He absorbed everything in his mind and twitched, kicked, and pawed when he saw a bird on a rail or a dog in a yard. Every time I looked upon my child, my heart thumped deeper, richer, in my chest. Being a dad was everything.

Well, except for sleep. There was definitely not a lot of sleep happening in the Minnick household, with Oscar needing to be fed just about every hour. That boy was always hungry!

So when I saw cops surrounding his day care, I genuinely thought I was delusional from exhaustion. But as I drove closer, I knew something was wrong. Both entrances to La Petite Prospect were closed, officers stood outside their vehicles blocking vehicles from entering, and others were on foot searching a nearby ditch. I pulled up.

"Yessir, is there something wrong? My son goes to this day care," I asked.

"Yes. First, everybody's all right, but there's been a shooting."

Just minutes before, I had watched Oscar's eyes follow a bird. Now, I was in his day-care parking lot, experiencing a fear I hadn't felt since before he was born. *Was he safe?* Although he was sitting there in my car, I had so many questions. *Was the staff okay? They were wonderful and didn't deserve this stress. Why was there a shooter? What happened? Had he been arrested?*

The officer asked me to leave, and soon after, the day care messaged all the parents regarding the situation and explained how the workers had handled it safely and with professionalism. The area sheriff later told the media that a mother of a child was targeted in the parking lot. "After she dropped off her child, she was exiting the parking lot and she was approached by an individual. He walked up to her car, he was armed with a gun. He pointed the gun at her through the window," said Prospect Police Chief Jeff Sherrard.[2] The shooter's weapon misfired, and he tossed it in the ditch and ran. The officer later told me that it was a domestic dispute, and the assailant knew the mother's schedule and had been waiting for her at the day care.

I felt awful for the woman, the day-care staff, and every parent affiliated with the school. Jaclyn and I both cried, knowing school shootings are just one more stressor we have to deal with in this thing called parenthood.

That night, I read Oscar his favorite Grover book and watched him sleep for at least an hour. I never wanted to feel that fear again.

I also know how I can perseverate on fear, how a trauma of any sort can take you down a rabbit hole that you are not prepared for. So I sought escape through my greatest nonfamily joy of the time—the Facebook bourbon groups. But when I logged on that night to find my favorite group, it was gone.

Like, completely gone.

There was no admin notice of what had happened or a Facebook notification of my belonging to a banned group. It had just disappeared.

Over the next year, many Facebook groups with obvious bourbon names completely vanished. Admins changed many group names to avoid algorithm detection of anything alcohol-related. Meanwhile, some group investigators caught counterfeiters buying empty Pappy Van Winkle bottles on eBay, refilling them, and selling them in these groups. This led to all sorts of rumors about a Facebook-wide sting to stop counterfeiters. Was the FBI or another federal agency cracking down on the groups?

Another theory was that the distillery industry was secretly working with Facebook to root out groups that violated the selling of tobacco and alcohol policy, which didn't make sense to any of us, because of all the built-in publicity the brands received in these groups. We were not only building a marketplace, we were creating content that was far superior to anything else on the market. Facebook was everything to the bourbon geek.

By the time the Van Winkles admitted to me on stage at Bourbon & Beyond in 2019 that they had been secretly working with Facebook to shut down the secondary market, the groups were all but gone. A few were left, but the spirit of the community was on life support by 2017 and dead by 2018. The Van Winkles' rationale was people were profiting off their bottles who shouldn't have, and there were too many counterfeit bottles. While I disagreed with them and said I believed that the groups actually kept counterfeiters in check, it was inevitable that the Facebook secondary market would be attacked by somebody at some point. Those of us who scrolled Facebook posts, sitting on the couch in our underwear, had been living the dream with a wealth of information and bottles to buy at our fingertips. It was too good to last.

At this point, though, I had already secured the phone number of every major bootlegger in bourbon. Whatever I wanted, I could get, and sometimes I got an extra bottle in exchange for a signed book.

And although I tried not to allow my personal preferences to affect my scores and tasting notes, I soon learned it was impossible to hide my favorite budget bourbon. But in my defense, I tasted it blind.

Inside the Hotel Nikko in San Francisco on a breezy March day were the greatest spirits palates in the world. Founded by James Beard Award–winning writer Anthony Dias Blue, the San Francisco World Spirits Competition was the crème de la crème of booze judging palates. I rubbed elbows with the likes of James Beard Award–winning author David Wonderich and rum icon Martin Cate, and all of us wore white smocks as if we were working at the local pharmacy.

It was 2016, but the setup was no different than in any of the previous three years I had been judging this competition. White smock tasters sat in groups of three, four, and five at round tables. Each table had a captain. Mine was whiskey guru Steve Beal, a former master of whiskey for Diageo. Volunteers brought us flights of spirits, usually in increments of five or more. They told us the category and the proof, and said get to tasting. We tasted and rated each individual glass bronze, silver, or gold. Our table debated the individual spirit's merit and awarded it one of those three, or no medal at all.

Over the course of a weekend, a single judge could taste three hundred to five hundred spirits. So you may be asking: How do we not pass out drunk? Easy: We spit. Next to us are spit buckets. And believe me, we treat the people who dump those like royalty! But they do get to take home the bottles after the competition.

In between tastes, we'll nibble on Muenster cheese to coat the tongue, eat a raw almond sliver to bitter it up, and rinse with sparkling water.

It sounds taxing because it is. After tasting that much, your tongue feels like a cheese grater, but we are all trained to look for things in each glass and make selections accordingly. My taste mindfulness was well suited for spirits competition judging, allowing me to really focus on the different parts of my tongue.

In my first two years of judging San Francisco—2013 and 2014—two juggernauts won Best Bourbon: Pappy Van Winkle 15-year and a Four Roses private selection from Crown Liquors in Indianapolis. But 2015 was, at the time, the greatest upset in a major competition for American whiskey. I wrote of the eventual winner: "Glass No. 22 at 100 proof was complex and offered a unique structure that you could find in great scotch, where the whiskey just drops down your tongue and enchants your sensations with all of its wonder and glory." That glass contained regular-ole

9-year Knob Creek, which sold for about $30, whipping up on the Buffalo Trace Antique Collections and Pappy Van Winkles of the world.

After each San Francisco competition, I wrote a recap for my blog, which always got more views in a single day than my blog usually had in a month. The recaps were hotly debated on all social media, and the winning bottles increased in value in the secondary groups. When I blogged or wrote about a little-known brand like Weller 12-year-old for a magazine, it would subsequently become so popular that it would become hard to find. When Knob Creek won, it far outpaced its sales, to the point it had to change the age statement one year later so it could move the production process along faster and keep up with the higher level of demand.

Looking back, the market of bourbon drinkers often tasted bourbon and just said, "tastes like bourbon." People often didn't believe the tasting notes that I and others wrote, because notes of chocolate and marzipan just seemed too far-fetched to some. I think that's why, more than anything, people poked fun at my tasting notes. They simply didn't taste the same things as me. It didn't matter, though, because the people complaining about my notes still bought whatever I wrote about. Somebody on Facebook coined the term the *Minnick Effect*, and my brand became the guy who liked something and people rushed to buy it. Or if I didn't like it, they rushed to buy it to see if they agreed. This led to all sorts of people blaming me for "ruining bourbon," driving up demand for bottles people liked but could no longer find.

I mean, I was just one person, often just reporting details from public panels. And let's not forget, bourbon in general was booming. From the late Anthony Bourdain confessing his love for it on Twitter to nearly every hit TV show of the time—*Mad Men*, *Boardwalk Empire*, and *Justified*—it seemed like everyone in America was sipping bourbon.

But I never truly understood what other people went through when their favorite bourbon got popular until I screwed myself. I had been buying the vintage Old Crow Chess Pieces regularly at a rate of $40 to $200. And then, during one interview promoting my book *Bourbon Curious*, an Englishman asked a simple question, and my answer changed everything.

For the BBC segment "Business Matters," host Fergus Nicoll covered the growth of American whiskey and the white oak shortage in 2015. The segment was on the heels of the Verizon $4.4-billion acquisition of AOL; thus, a meaty news day in business. I talked about how smaller distillers such as Garrison Brothers in Texas and MB Roland in Western Kentucky were carving out nice competitive niches. And I gave an overview of foreign markets, such as Korea and China, and how Japanese companies owned Four Roses, Blanton's, and Jim Beam. The conversation was going smoothly in the lane of business. And then, like many interviewers before him, Fergus Nicoll asked the question everybody wanted to know.

"What's the best whiskey you've ever had?"

Now, I had been asked this question at least a thousand times and always answered, "Whatever you're buying me." This usually got a laugh, and the interviewer would move on. But this guy wooed me with his British accent and broke through my impenetrable fortress of bourbon secrecy.

"Oh, all categories, or just bourbon?" I asked.

"Let's be loyal and stick to bourbon," he replied.

Then I opened my big mouth and said, "Vintage Old Crow," revealing how this now bottom-shelf brand had once been the best of its day. But I couldn't stop there, with Fergus's seductive English voice waiting to ask me further questions. I had to please this guy.

"They had these special bottlings that were just phenomenal. This chess decanter set... It was by far the best bourbon I have ever put upon my lips."

He chuckled and said, "Fred Minnick, author of *Bourbon Curious*, with us from Louisville, Kentucky."

I hung up the phone, already regretting my comments and wondering if anybody notable had heard me reveal my all-time favorite bourbon. I convinced myself that nobody in bourbon listens to BBC Radio.

Boy, was I wrong.

Within a week, a BBC listener dropped a link to the episode into a Reddit thread, another did the same on Facebook, and before I knew it the news of the Chessman delight had spread into the secondary world.

Almost overnight, an Old Crow Chess Piece that used to sell for $40 now sold for $700. People who cleaned up their dead aunts' basements often found whole sets of the Chessmen. They googled the items and there my name was, atop the search rankings, with my big fat mouth spilling the beans about the brilliance of Old Crow. One by one, these random people found my email or direct messaged me on Facebook, offering to sell me the bottles.

You could cut the irony with a butter knife; I had ruined my own hobby. In my effort to promote a book, I killed my financial ability to buy my favorite bourbon of all time.

Fortunately, for me, the world of vintage spirits was about to change, and I'd soon use other people's money to seek out and buy Old Crow. And Jaclyn had a surprise for me that would require more income in the Minnick household.

CHAPTER 7

LEGIT–SORT OF

AFTER OSCAR WAS born, my events business blossomed. What went from a part-time job standing at a bar to sign a few books and talk about bourbon turned into an official role at the Kentucky Derby Museum, which hired me as its "Bourbon Authority." Corporations rented the museum and booked me for tastings. I spent my evenings teaching the likes of the Sikorsky helicopter company CEO and Humana chairman how to taste bourbon.

The best part of this gig was that everybody had a good time. And my attendees told their friends, who later hired me for their private tastings. The word got out, and I quickly became in demand not for my writing but for my ability to stand in front of a crowd and bullshit for an hour.

By 2015, hosting tastings put me so much in the public eye that I was talking to ten thousand people a year.

At one event, a couple of Los Angeles music festival promoters were in the audience. They approached me after I had interviewed master distillers on stage in front of a few hundred folks. We were at an after-party, with a packed bar, and I was, shall I say, enjoying myself. I honestly just wanted to relax. I wasn't in a bad mood or anything; I just was not prepared to interact with them.

A stout, short balding fella extended his hand. "Hey, nice job up there. I'm Damon and this is Clay." Clay, a couple inches taller than me, wore a ball cap, black pants, and an unbuttoned red flannel over a band T-shirt. I looked both of them up and down and wondered, *What the hell do these guys want?*

"I am with a company called Danny Wimmer Presents and we produce rock festivals around the country," Clay said, shaking my hand. I smelled cigarette smoke all over this guy. I already didn't want to talk to these fellas, and now my olfactory was one Parliament away from shutting down. But I tried to be cordial.

"Oh, nice to meet you."

"You were great up there. So we plan to produce a music festival in Louisville with a large whiskey presence..." *Okay,* I thought, *this guy's trying to pitch me on covering his festival and probably wants to turn bourbon into some sort of hipster thing. Here I was just wanting to hang with some friends, have a good time and this smoker guy is bugging me about his festival that I don't care about.*

Now, I'm not proud of this. I didn't want to talk to these guys, but that doesn't excuse what I did next.

"Go fuck yourself," I coldly said, turning my back to him and walking away.

I fully admit, I was a total jerk in that moment and had no intention of ever talking to them again. But Clay found my email and did not stop contacting me. Feeling bad for how I acted that night, I eventually set up a conference call with his boss, Danny Wimmer.

"Clay tells me you're a big deal in bourbon, and I really want to start a bourbon and music festival in Louisville. I need some help with our bourbon chops, because nobody trusts some LA music guys when it comes to bourbon," Wimmer said.

I turned him down. But then we had another call.

"Listen, I really want you to join the team to produce this festival. Just come to one of our shows, so you can see what it's all about. Our headliner is Metallica. Heard of them?"

Not only had I heard of Metallica, they were my favorite band. And I suddenly went from negotiating to thinking I was about to have the time of my life.

"Can I bring some friends?"

"Of course," Danny said.

So I took my cigar club buddies to Columbus, Ohio, for the Rock on the Range festival in 2017. We had all access backstage passes and were rubbing elbows with Les Claypool, lead singer of Primus, and Robert Trujillo, bass player for Metallica. When Metallica played, we stood at the sound booth, the absolute best place to hear music at a concert, and my buddy Mike Godfrey pulled me in close to whisper, "If you don't work with these guys, you're a fucking dumbass."

I shook hands with Danny Wimmer and Clay Busch, whom I'd later hire as my manager, and said, "I'm in."

From that point on, I was tied to the largest independent rock promoter in the country and co-founded the Bourbon & Beyond music festival, where I shared a stage with celebrity chefs Tom Colicchio and Graham Elliott, and musicians Stevie Nicks and Steve Miller Band. That first year was absolutely electrifying and catapulted my career to the next level. Suddenly, my name was in *Rolling Stone* magazine and I was doing press conferences with the Louisville mayor about how much tax revenue the twenty-thousand-a-day attendees brought in.

In January 2018, Wimmer and I were talking about the next festival.

"Do you like Sting?" he asked.

"Of course," I said.

"I think we are booking him for Bourbon."

In Louisville, the chatter about who was playing at the next festival was the hottest gossip in town, and I had actual insider knowledge not just for Wimmer's events but for all of them. I loved coming home and telling Jaclyn the juicy scoops of who was playing. She would love to learn about Sting, off the record, of course.

That day when I walked into the house, Oscar was playing with his trucks in the living room and Jaclyn stood in the middle of the kitchen. She looked nervous.

"I need to talk to you," Jaclyn said, pointing toward our bedroom. She walked into the room, sat on the bed, and cleared her throat, which translated into "Um, stop what you're doing and get in here." I slow-walked the few short feet to the master bedroom, assuming she just didn't want Oscar to hear bad news.

She sat on the edge of the bed, her hands folded and her toes barely touching the floor. She looked at me with trepidation, but her brown eyes were glowing.

"We're pregnant," she said, standing up.

I didn't know what to say. I stood there, dumbfounded.

"Are you upset?" she asked.

"Of course not," I said, holding her hands. "I am just shocked. We weren't even trying."

I immediately felt awful. *How could I say that? What was I thinking?*

Jaclyn simply said, "Oh," and walked away.

We had endured the most painful moments together when we lost our first two pregnancies and shared in the great joy of Oscar. But now, with my head so wrapped up in work—promoting a new book, writing a story, or preparing for an event—I wasn't there mentally. Did I want another child? Absolutely. Was I ready for that news at that moment? No, and that's the emotion I led with.

She left to have lunch with her mom, disappointed in my reaction. I tried to console her, to apologize for my lack of excitement. "It's okay," she said. But I knew that I had some work to do to make it right.

And that began, as it often did, with therapy and completing my cognitive behavior worksheets, which all pointed to the fact I didn't feel prepared for a second kid. Could we afford another child? Was I ready for the additional duties?

There was also the factor that the new baby's due date fell in September, bourbon heritage month, when I was usually full-throttle sipping bourbon with strangers and trading stories of distillers past. And of course, Bourbon & Beyond was smack in the middle of September. I had also resigned from all the magazines that had helped build my career, because I was soon going to announce that I was the founding editor-in-chief of the new *Bourbon+* magazine. I had also just joined Ryan Cecil and Kenny Coleman on the number one podcast on bourbon, Bourbon Pursuit, which was my first experiment with that new medium.

All of this helped me make a nice living, but I knew I would not be able to be as attentive to Jaclyn during the pregnancy as I had been before. My presence would be demanded by my business partners. Financially, too, I still felt I needed to do more, and I had a secret weapon up my sleeve that I felt could pay the bills. It just wasn't as clean as I'd like on the legal side.

In 2017, the Kentucky legislature passed the Vintage Spirits Law, joining North Carolina and Washington, DC, as the only areas that allowed an individual to sell alcohol without a license to liquor stores and bars. The bill became law in 2018, but it was littered with all sorts of stipulations, such as that the bottle sold must be out of distribution, meaning there was none left in the three-tier system, and the seller would have to show their license plate and driver's license to the buyer, a bar or retailer, who had to report the sales to the Alcohol Board of Control. The bill faced much backlash from wholesalers, who likely saw it as a threat to their livelihood.

"There are many tightly allocated products, and they're not available through a wholesaler very quickly. It happens every year," said Dan Meyer with Wine & Spirits Wholesalers of Kentucky, the lobbyist arm of the state's liquor wholesaler industry, in 2017. I published Dan's comments on my blog. "Somebody could purchase product, hoard it for a couple months, and sell it in January for $1,000 a bottle."[1]

There was also the fact that the federal government didn't approve of these state laws allowing non-licensed resellers to move product, but its disdain was much like the government's stance on states legalizing marijuana: just don't cross state lines where it's illegal and you're fine. This opened the door for me to start a new business that would not conflict with my journalistic ethics of covering the spirits industry. I could validate bottles for bars and liquor stores looking to build a vintage library. There were not many people who could look at a bottle and verify its label and authenticity, but I was one of them.

When I consulted with a lawyer about the legality of starting a vintage spirits consultancy, he was very clear: "Make the sellers come to you."

Sure, I'll do that, I said, and a week later I made an appointment to meet a towering, unfamiliar human in a grocery parking lot.[**]

With sweat dripping down my forehead, I opened the trunk of my 2001 Altima, grabbed a $30,000 cashier's check from my laptop bag, and handed it to the man who could have easily snapped me like a twig, taken my money, and left me to die. He took the check without looking at it and started handing over box after box filled with rare vintage bottles: a blueberry-and-fig laden 1945 Kentucky Tavern, black licorice-centric 1909 Old Overholt, and coveted 1938-distilled Weller, among several others. I inspected every bottle, wondering if it was an insult to the man. He stood there, arms folded, and looked at the clouds.

** This anecdote is slightly changed due to the fact that the seller is still active and requested I never mention his name or where we did business.

On the drive home I thought about how ridiculous it was that a hobbyist or spirits lover had to resort to meeting in parking lots to buy bottles. The wine industry had fancy auctions, but I was slumming around like a druggie seeking a score.

That said, this haul would make the client, Bardstown Bourbon Company, happy, even though I had yet to bring in the mother lode—an entire Chessman set.

Holding a Chessman, feeling the ridges around the eyes and the curvature of the nose, instantly took me back to the moment when I first tasted Old Crow. How glorious. It transcended all things bourbon and set me on a path to find more.

I thought about this when I shook hands with the seller of an entire chess set, whom I met from Facebook. About three months after my $30,000 parking lot transfer, I couldn't wait to hold one.

In her mid-twenties and around five feet tall, she carried box after box into the break room of Bardstown Bourbon Company, my client. I caressed the leather-like case, the size of a small rectangular TV speaker, feeling the tiny grooves on my fingers. Despite all the chess pieces I had purchased, this was the first time I had held the original packaging. When I opened it, a swoosh of air came out and you could smell the 1960s: shag carpet, cigarettes, and mom's favorite issue of *LIFE* magazine. Then, she pulled a thick clear bag from the box, which held the actual original chess mat that could have been mistaken for a rug. I rubbed the back of my hand across the felt and said, "Wow." I looked at David Mandell, then-president of Bardstown Bourbon, and he licked his lips and smiled. "We can bring in some chess masters and have them play in an exhibition match."

One of the most brilliant whiskey minds I've ever met, David hired me to build a vintage whiskey library that would become a cornerstone for the Kentucky Bourbon Trail, and these chess pieces would become the centerpiece inside the distillery's hidden library room. That was the hope, anyway.

The seller appeared fidgety as I weighed each chess piece, and I thought about our email exchange prior to this meeting. It was one of the lengthier negotiations I'd had, perhaps because the seller was not in the spirits business. When I asked about the weights of each bottle in email, she replied: "This set means a lot to me as it was gifted from a very close family member. This set is sentimental to me. I want to ensure it will be presented properly and respected. You may be a geek about the weight, but this set means more to me than you may understand."

That was the part of the vintage spirits I didn't like. Everybody has a story and a connection to the bottle, and they also have a price that will sever their connection. For this lady, it was $10,000 for the whole set, and 54¢ a gallon reimbursement for gas money contingent upon the majority of the decanters being full, and they were.

When David handed her the check, she folded it and said, "And the gas money?"

I'll never forget how strange I felt in that moment. I had just done the vintage deal of my career and confirmed the authenticity and weights of all decanters. I was on cloud nine and was able to get this young woman five figures she would not have received otherwise. Yet she was focused on gas money. I found it strange.

"Send us your mileage and we'll cut you a check," David said.

I never spoke with the lady again, but looking back, I think her fidgety nature and concern over gas money was likely due to guilt over selling the set. She revealed that a close family member had given her the Chessmen, and it had to be painful to watch me weigh each one. Would her family member disapprove?

Regardless, wherever she is, I hope she knows that those chess pieces have made countless people happy and are still basking in the fluorescent light of Bardstown Bourbon.

That said, not too long after this purchase, a plot twist was brought to my attention about these bottles. Unfortunately, the legitimate world of vintage sales was just like it had been in the illegal days.

No refunds.

Jim Beam decanters are among the most iconic bourbon packages of all time. Their most noted bottle boasted a fat bottom, slowly tapering to a topper that brought forth a mythical person on the TV show *I Dream of Jeannie*. Jim Beam reached deep into pop culture with this decanter in the 1960s and 1970s, at a time when bourbon was dying, and further rooted into the fabric of America by producing Corvette, hunting, golf, military-related, football team, and iconic figure decanters.

These fancy decanters flooded the collectible markets, saturating niche hobbyist genres and co-branded with the likes of Ducks Unlimited and the PGA. People flocked to these bottles, created collectible trading clubs in their respective markets, and then would try to sell them the old-fashioned way—through newspaper classified ads.

In my years of research, I've found more classified ads for Jim Beam decanters than anything else, because people used the decanters, which were beautiful, to decorate their homes. Even I, as a pre-bourbon career bachelor, had a few of them propped up on speakers behind a lava lamp.

So consider me intrigued when I was approached with a collection of Jim Beam decanters. But unlike the Old Crow decanters, I had little experience with them from an authentication perspective. I didn't have the weights, and since I couldn't see through the bottle, I had no idea how much was inside.

The fella who brought them had thinning reddish-blond hair, glasses, and a belly in the shape of an exercise ball.

"I have twenty-two of these decanters," he said, sweating.

"Okay," I said, looking at his forehead.

"Sorry, I sweat a lot," he replied.

I may have looked at him funny, but I really wanted to ask what was wrong. Had he stolen these bottles? Was he constipated? Before I could ask if he was all right, he offered, "I have a condition."

Okay, a condition. He's off the hook for hiding something, and I started to feel bad for thinking he may have stolen them. I handled each bottle. Some had leather straps, others fine cotton or wool on the exterior.

"Do you know if they are full?" I asked.

"Oh, yes, I am sure of it," he replied, his eyes open wide. "Well, let me leave you with this one, as a gift, to help you make up your mind on the set."

The bottle was the shape of a cardinal. I later cracked it, and the whiskey tasted like the inside of a leather couch. Scratch that. It tasted like Fruit Loops, plastic, a metal hanger, and the inside of a leather couch, which meant it was stored improperly and had likely collected mildew around the cork area. I nearly gagged. It would go down as one of the worst bourbons I ever tasted.

Were they all like this?

But I wasn't buying for me. I was buying for a client with the objective of bringing people to their bar to drink weird and rare stuff. The truth is, the bourbon economic phenomenon was more about storytelling and scarcity. The Jim Beam decanters answered the call for both and could also appeal to those who were fans of whatever the decanter depicted, such as the military or sports. I felt the need to ask for a second opinion.

I called my buddy Bill Thomas, owner of the famous Jack Rose Dining Saloon in Washington, DC, a spectacle of rare whiskey from all over the world. Bill has bought just about every bottle you can.

"What do you think about the Jim Beam decanters?" I asked Bill.

"I never touch them. You can't trust them," he said.

"Why?"

"If I can't see the whiskey, I don't like taking a chance on it, with the exception of your favorite—the Chessmen. Plus, there's concerns of lead, and I just don't need that hanging over our head at Jack Rose," Bill said.

At the time of this conversation, in 2018, I had heard whispers of possible lead contamination in decanters, but I always thought that only applied to the really old ones from the 1930s and 1940s. I had never considered the Jim Beam and Old Crow decanters in the lead conversation. Or perhaps I didn't really want to know.

What's the saying? Ignorance is bliss.

If I looked too far into the use of lead, a low melting-point metal, in the use of ceramic manufacturing, I might have to eliminate one of my greatest joys in life—the Old Crow Chess Piece—because I knew if I confirmed there's lead in there, I wouldn't drink it. Could you really get lead poisoning from it, though?

"You'd likely have to drink the whole decanter to get lead poisoning if there is contamination, and at that point, you'd die from alcohol poisoning instead," my doctor said.

Still, with Oscar running around the house like a wild man and Jaclyn's belly growing, I couldn't in good conscious drink Old Crow without knowing if there was lead in there.

I ordered a lead test kit. And when it arrived, I looked at it as if it were a pregnancy test: The answer would directly impact my life. Well, not really. It was just whiskey, and I frankly took it far too seriously. This was more akin to a grown man crying over a comic book or baseball card.

The swabs looked like Q-tips and turned different colors if lead was detected. I swabbed the inside of the decanter, the whiskey itself, and the inner portion of the cork topper.

Even though the packaging said the test would read instantly, I immediately placed the swabs under a piece of paper. I didn't want to see them until I was ready. I took a deep breath and reached down for the paper when Jaclyn walked into the room.

"Fred, are you okay? What are you doing?"

"Oh, yeah, just testing for lead in whiskey," I said.

"Sounds good," she replied, as if this were a perfectly reasonable statement.

Jaclyn walked out of the kitchen, and I lifted the paper. All three swabs were negative.

Such relief.

I tested my other Crow decanters. All negative. Now, this wasn't done in a scientific lab or down to parts per million, but I felt confident enough in the whiskey that I could go on sipping it. But if my hair started falling out, I most certainly would have stopped...maybe.

It was around this time I also realized how little I enjoyed the vintage spirits game. I loved history and the whiskey itself. But I absolutely loathed negotiating with people trying to sell bottles. After I completed the collection for the Bardstown Bourbon Company, acquiring hundreds of bottles for less than $100,000 total, I didn't take on any more clients and put my focus back where it belonged—on whiskey and the secrets it held. That led me right back to where I had started: the question of what happened to Old Crow.

Sure, I had determined Crow was never a doctor, even if he did make an impact on the whiskey world. But his namesake lived on in Old Crow, which was arguably the greatest bourbon made over a one-hundred-year span. I badly needed to know what happened next. Why did Old Crow taste so bad today compared to the vintage years?

I had to find the answers. But that was the least of my worries.

The vintage bottle hunting and other business ventures also had kept me so busy that I had neglected my duties as a husband, and I didn't realize it until it was almost too late.

As I traveled with sacks of cash, cashier's checks, and boxes full of booze, I had a four-year-old running around with a soccer ball and digging for worms in the backyard, and a pregnant wife home alone. I called and video conferenced when I was away, but when I was home, I was constantly on my phone or computer.

Jaclyn was sad. The man she had fallen in love with was never home. And when he was, he wasn't present as a father or husband.

I told myself I was doing it all for my family, that I needed to earn more money, to build my media business to the point where it could be sold or my name would mean something. But the truth is, that was vanity talking. I wanted to build something so badly that I had lost sight of why I was even working so hard.

It was near my fortieth birthday in 2018 that I realized what I had done, how I had wasted so much time.

Oscar, who stood hip high to me, was carrying his fishing pole at our favorite spot and tripped. The pole bent and the reel released the line, tangling on the pole and on sticks. Never one to ask for help even then, Oscar tried to take care of it himself. But when he couldn't untangle the line, his baby blues leaked tears the size of Texas. I put my hand on his shoulder and said, "Son, it's okay. First rule of fishing is to have fun. Let's not let this tangled line get in the way of that."

He shook his head in agreement, trying to fight away the tears. I managed to untangle the line, straighten the pole, and get it all squared away. After handing it to him, I asked, "Now are you ready to have some fun?"

"Yeah, Dad, I am with you."

The words cut through me, and soon my own tears formed. How many fishing trips had I missed because I had to meet a stranger in a Kroger parking lot? And when I was home, did I really take the time to be in the moment?

We caught a couple of decent fish, but the lesson of my life was served up to me on a fishing line by my four-year-old. I do not know if it was his tone of voice or the words he used. But that conversation changed me forever, and I later told Jaclyn how sorry I was for being so absent and that I was going to focus more on her, Oscar, and our new little wiggle worm due in two months.

I created a forty-day plan for prepping the house and taking care of Oscar while also caring for Jaclyn, who opted for a planned C-section this time around. We joked about going for the all-natural way again, and I ended up cussing out Ricki Lake by the end of it, still angry over how I had been brainwashed by a documentary.

I read Oscar books about being a big brother and cooked just about every night. I even folded laundry. The forty-day plan was going swell when on day twenty Jaclyn felt nauseous.

She rushed to the bathroom and began screaming. "I'm having contractions," she yelled, "and I'm puking." *This could not be happening this early*, I thought. The baby wasn't due for another month. I was only on day twenty of my "making things right" plan. I had beef Bolognese, corn fritters, and butter chicken to make, and I wanted to wax the floor so shiny you could see your reflection. And I had yet to read Oscar another book about becoming a big brother, and childproof the stairs.

"Fred, call Angela..." Jaclyn cried, before puking some more. I thought to myself about the nurse who said people don't puke during labor. "Oh yeah, well, my wife puked twice, lady," I said out loud.

"What?" Jaclyn said.

"Oh, nothing," I said, realizing I should focus on getting Oscar to his grandparents' house and calling our saving grace, the doula, who comforted Jaclyn and reminded me to not drive 100 miles per hour on the way to the hospital. This time, there would be no toughing out the pain and trying to give birth like we lived in a hut. When we arrived, Jaclyn dry heaved, with Angela informing the nurse, "Yeah, she's nauseous."

"Oh, I don't get many of those," the nurse replied.

Unlike with Oscar's birth, Jaclyn didn't seem to be in pain, likely thanks to the drugs the nurses gave her. And the doctor was incredibly thorough in explaining it all, even if I cannot remember a single word other than the question, "What music do you want to listen to for the birth?"

She chose Frank Sinatra and was wheeled off in a green gown, and I joined shortly thereafter. Unlike Oscar's birth, where everybody was intense and moving quickly, the medical team smiled, talked, and moved with ease. I guess that's the difference between an emergency and a planned, albeit early, C-section. I was holding Jaclyn's hand, looking into her glowing brown eyes, when the next thing I know the nurse said, "Look." The baby faced me, being pulled from the womb. His face was smashed, neck and limbs swirling.

They cut the cord and handed him to me. Our little guy was beautiful.

But he wasn't breathing.

He wasn't breathing.

I panicked inside. Before I could scream, two nurses grabbed him from my arms, wiped his face, and put a pump device over his mouth. Voilà, he started to cry.

When we reunited with Jaclyn, we had yet to confirm the little guy's name.

"Let's wait for Oscar and name him together," Jaclyn said.

Until then, our new little son lay in her arms and Jaclyn smiled from ear to ear. "Oh, did you bring bourbon this time?" she asked.

Bourbon runs so deep in our family veins that when we named our second son Julian, most people thought it was after Julian Van Winkle of Pappy Van Winkle. But we didn't. As Oscar said, terrifying me as he cradled the newborn, "He really looks like a Julian." Oscar didn't drop him, to my surprise, and whispered in his ear, "I am going to be the best big brother." Of course, like all siblings, it wouldn't take long for the rivalry to begin. The cradle would turn into the site of wrestling matches, and there remains an ongoing household investigation of when six-year-old Oscar pushed two-year-old Julian down the stairs. In truth, Julian likely whaled a baseball bat toward his brother's head at the time; the two are always fighting.

But as a parent, I will always cherish the moment when the two met for the first time. With Julian swaddled tightly in a hospital blanket, Oscar curled his arms underneath his brother, supported his back, and arched his feet to tilt his knees toward Julian for a firmer grip. Oscar whispered in his ear; Julian just stared at him. When I close my eyes for the final time, I hope I see this image of my family together.

They are my everything.

And I would soon face a moment that reminded me how precious life is.

CHAPTER 8

LIFE AND DEATH

A FEW MONTHS before Julian was born, a longtime distiller friend called me and asked for a favor.

"I'm launching a new brand with a celebrity group, but I can't really talk about it yet," said Dave Pickerell.

"Oh, that sounds exciting, Dave. Tell me more."

He said one simple word, a word that's so powerful to my ears that I'll stop whatever I am doing at any moment to listen to more.

"Metallica."

Since "Enter Sandman" invaded my life as a teenager, Metallica has been a part of my life, every song digging deep into my metal soul. And seeing them at Wimmer's festival in Ohio somehow made me an even bigger fan. There's nothing like your favorite band living up to your expectations!

Metallica was starting a whiskey brand? And Dave Pickerell was backing it? For me, this was two worlds becoming one.

My heart raced and I found myself short of breath. Nervous,

even. Why? What if Dave needed me to taste the whiskey to see if it was any good? What if he wanted me to help? My mind raced.

"Fred? You there?"

"Um, yeah, wow, Dave, that's amazing. I love Metallica."

"I know," he replied. I imagined Dave smiling.

I also found this partnership fascinating because Metallica's alcohol problems were once so bad that they earned the nickname "Alcoholica." The band had since stopped drinking, and I don't think there's ever been a whiskey brand started by sober celebrities. Still, that didn't matter. I loved Metallica and Pickerell. I was in.

"Well, how can I help?"

"I'd like to get you the exclusive on the band, because of your music ties, but you have some competition. So you'll need to convince their managers," he said.

The timing couldn't have been better. I wasn't actively writing or promoting a whiskey book, and I had paused my Old Crow research to focus on my burgeoning media and events business. I had just launched *Bourbon+* magazine and was in the throes of the Bourbon & Beyond event as well as an independently produced TV series on Amazon Prime called *Bourbon Up with Fred Minnick* I was also a Forbes.com senior contributor and still figuring out the world of podcasting with *Bourbon Pursuit*. The vintage spirits side hustle kept me busy, too, but nothing could stop me from landing this interview.

I wrote to Metallica's management team, Q Prime, saying I would introduce the band to the whiskey world, but that my story wouldn't really be about them as much as it would be about Dave, the whiskey icon who helped build WhistlePig, Hillrock, and now

Blackened, the name of the Metallica whiskey. I later learned that the other more mainstream media wanted to focus solely on the band and that I ultimately landed the exclusive because of my ties to Dave and my passion for whiskey.

Still, as I sat across from their famous music publicist, Steve Martin, who also repped Paul McCartney, Foo Fighters, and David Bowie, I felt a little out of my league, like I didn't belong at the table, that a music reporter from *Rolling Stone* or the *NYT* culture beat writer should cover this. I tugged at my ascot and fidgeted with the menu at a café with a view of Lake Mendota in Madison, Wisconsin, where Metallica opened their 2018 tour. Perhaps Martin noticed my nerves, because he immediately tried to put me at ease.

"You're really tackling all the angles in whiskey," he said.

"I'm trying. I think it's really cool that you all are working with Dave Pickerell," I responded.

"He seems like a great guy," he said.

"Dave is an industry icon, and I cannot think of a project better suited for him than the Metallica whiskey!"

We met up with Dave at the Madison arena. Dave wore black pants, a black shirt, and his patented black panama hat. Although Dave's belly was so round that it made it difficult for him to fit through a narrow Kentucky bourbon barrel rickhouse, he wanted to take the stairs in the backstage area. We were both winded when we hit the top.

"Damn," I said out loud, "I gotta get in shape."

Dave nodded in agreement. Truth is, the whiskey business is tough on one's health. While some elder industry leaders, such as

Elmer T. Lee and Jimmy Russell, live well into their eighties and nineties, many industry veterans have died in their forties.

I was trying to catch my breath when I saw the band for the first time, hanging out with their crew. The lead singer, James Hetfield, held a white paper cup in his hand, and I just stood there watching him, thinking, *That's the greatest thrash metal singer of all time. And I am in the same room as him*. Steve Martin must have seen my jaw drop a little. He tapped me on the shoulder and asked, "Wanna meet the band?"

As he spoke, I noticed everyone was wearing black, a tradition in music so the audience can't see people walking on stage when it's dark. In a greenish turquoise blazer and white pants, I stuck out like a sore thumb. But I needed to focus on the job, not my wardrobe. I was here to interview the greatest metal band of all time. There was just one problem: I was far too nervous.

"Yeah, but give me a minute. I need to get my notebook ready," I told Steve.

In this man's illustrious career, having been on the sets of *Saturday Night Live* and *60 Minutes*, I doubt Steve Martin ever heard a reporter say, "I need to get my notebook ready." Well, it was clear that I needed to process my nerves or there was a fifty-fifty chance this fanboy would lose his lunch. I reached into my pocket and touched the only thing I had in there—a quarter. Just like during the early mindfulness days of protecting my brain from trauma relapses, I closed my eyes and felt George Washington's head and the coin's side ridges, and focused on how warm the metal felt to my touch. This grounding technique had saved me from many bad moments, and now it helped me shake James Hetfield's hand.

James stood a couple inches taller than me, but his stature was entirely dominated by massive medieval leather bracelets that looked like they were borrowed from Conan the Barbarian. Eyeballing James, I realized in this moment why Steve and the Metallica management likely chose me over other reporters. Hetfield was sober, and there's not a *NYT* reporter alive who would not have asked James about being sober and starting a whiskey brand. While I was curious about that, I wasn't a real reporter; I was a whiskey writer. Nobody from the band ever pressured me to not ask James about what it's like to be affiliated with a whiskey while sober, but I didn't bring it up with him and planned to talk about it with the non-sober members. James jumped into it anyway.

"I hear the whiskey's good; I wouldn't know, I don't drink. Can't do that," he said, laughing.

I chuckled, too, feeling like James could also sense my nerves.

"What's it like working with Dave?" I asked.

"Dave is the Metallica of whiskey," James told me.

I talked to James for several minutes and then the rest of the band. First, the guitarist, Kirk Hammett, introduced himself to me. Slightly shorter and with seemingly glowing olive skin—seriously, he must use some serious face moisturizer—he initiated the conversation.

"Nice ascot," he said.

"Thank you. I wear them all the time. Do you wear them?" I asked, knowing he fit the bill for an ascot type. Eccentric and creative!

"Yeah, I used to wear them all the time, but they got tangled up in my guitar," he said.

I couldn't believe I had just bonded with Metallica's guitarist over ascots. What was happening?

Steve then walked me into a backstage office space, where I met with bassist Robert Trujillo, who joined the band in 2003. The management team billed Robert as the main whiskey drinker of the band. I asked him what he sipped on early in his career, as Dave sat nearby and listened.

"It was Crown and ginger and that was it," he said. "The theory with Crown and ginger—and I don't believe it anymore—was that ginger ale had less sugar than [regular soda pop]. But it had that ginger root and would have that much less chance of having a hangover. Maybe there's some truth to it, but it all revolved around the ginger root at the time, and we rolled with it."

I remember looking dumbfounded at Dave. Not because of the hangover theory, but I didn't know how to respond. Should my follow-up question be about Crown Royal? Music? I felt the nerves crawling up my leg to my stomach and into my hands. I had no time to practice mindfulness, and if I asked to take a bathroom break, the interview would be over and Steve would probably ask me to leave for a lack of professionalism.

Dave could see my hesitation. He rubbed his chin and interjected. "So we've got Crown Royal in our history. When I was at West Point, they gave me this lockbox for valuables. I grew up in the slums and didn't have money, jewels, or any of those things. I asked the [commanding officer]: 'Isn't this West Point? Don't you get in trouble if you steal?' And they go, 'Look it's not inspected. You can put whatever you want in there.' I got the largest volume Crown Royal bottle, because it's a little squatter, and put in my box. For four years, I had a Crown Royal bottle in my lockbox."

I never asked Dave if that story was true. But he somehow

knew I was struggling and saved me with the lockbox story. I asked Robert a few more questions, shook his hand, and said, "Be sure to try Blackened now with ginger ale." He laughed, and I later welcomed Lars Ulrich, who looked me directly in the eyes for every question.

Later that night, I watched Kirk, Robert, Lars, and James rock out to a sold-out arena.

I wrote my *Bourbon+* cover story on the new whiskey, Blackened, and planned to profile Metallica's relationship with Dave for Forbes. And two weeks after Julian's birth, Dave and I cut it up on camera backstage at Bourbon & Beyond. When the camera was off, I asked how he was doing.

"This Metallica whiskey is amazing," he said, which was similar to what he said when cameras rolled. But this time he paused and looked at the ground, scooting his butt up to the edge of the chair, and took a deep breath. His large belly expressed air in and out, as he gathered himself. I thought maybe he had drunk too much.

"Are you okay?" I asked.

"Yes. I just have some hypertension, but I'm on some medication."

He staggered to his feet, and I helped him out of the trailer studio.

That was the last time I saw Dave Pickerell. He passed away six weeks after the interview; I was bottle-feeding Julian when I learned he died of a heart attack in his San Francisco hotel room.

Tears coming down my face, I looked down at Julian, rubbed his chubby cheek, and just told him everything I knew about Dave: that he was a West Point graduate and likely the smartest distiller

I ever met. I shared stories about the people he didn't like and what he thought about a couple distillers he called "frauds." The man co-founded WhistlePig, Hillrock, and Blackened, and helped anybody who ever needed it. His imprint can be found at Rock Town in Arkansas, Woodinville in Washington, and Nelson's Green Brier in Nashville, among others.

"He was the James Crow of the modern distillers because of all the things he did for the industry," I said, hardly believing I was saying this out loud to my infant son. "But he was so much more than a distillery builder; I won't ever forget him, as a person. Oh, Mr. Dave was a character, Julian. He had a big round belly but still appeared athletic and had a handshake that could crack your knuckles. He also had a knack for stirring the pot. One time when he was starting a moonshine called Popcorn Sutton, named after a famous moonshiner, he told me they had no marketing budget..."

I stopped; Julian gazed at me with his reflective hazel eyes, seeming to enjoy the conversation. So I continued.

"Dave had this idea of copying the Jack Daniel's label. Not a little bit, like the whole thing. The font, size of the label, color, and bottle size. Everything. He completely ripped off Jack Daniel's, which, as you know, Julian, is the largest whiskey brand in the world. You can't go far without seeing Jack somewhere. Well, he did it. The Jack Daniel's lawyers wrote to him to cut it out. Dave didn't stop, and Jack Daniel's straight up sued Dave and his partners of Popcorn Sutton. The lawsuit made all the newspapers. And Dave said, 'That's how we launched the brand. Their lawsuit was our marketing. We pulled the bottle, which we always intended to do once they sued us, but you can't buy that kind of publicity.' So the moral of the story here, Julian, never bet against Dave... Damn, I am going to miss him."

When I looked down, Julian was asleep, and my eyes were sore. But I found myself wanting to tell Julian more. Not just about Dave, but about the other great distillers who meant so much to me. Jimmy Russell, Edwin Foote, Fred Noe, Chris Morris, Jim Rutledge, and so many others who helped me become who I am. "And there was one distiller, who I was with as he struggled through ALS. People may remember Parker Beam for his incredible golden palate and ability to make whiskey, or how he led Heaven Hill after the horrendous fire in 1996. Or maybe they'll think of the brand with his namesake—Parker's Heritage. But I'll remember the man as he fought to live, battling ALS. The courage it took for him wake up every day, to ride his bike for as long as he could and remain active. Some may think that was not how he'd want me to remember him, but I'd argue I saw his strength when others saw a man on his deathbed. He never gave up and lived with ALS for six years."

One after another, I shared the stories of people who've influenced me, outlining all the quirks of these folks, including Julian's godmother, the first female master taster, Peggy Noe Stevens. "She's the reason I have a beard, you know," I said, noticing his eyes opened when he heard her name. Then I started telling him about the early distillers.

"In the late 1800s, one master distiller named Cyrus Noble made whiskey so good that a gold miner traded his mine for the whiskey. But the story of Cyrus is one of caution, too, buddy, because he liked whiskey so much that he got drunk and fell into the mash tun. Another iconic fella, E. H. Taylor, was super important for passing the Bottled in Bond Act, and you can still find his name on bourbon bottles today with his picture. My favorite distiller of all time, Julian, is a guy named James C. Crow. You know, he's the guy I said Mr. Dave was like. And Daddy's got a file so thick on this fella I could fill your crib with papers. But I feel like I don't know nearly enough about him or if I ever will."

Julian's attention was entirely on me. At two months old, he had never seemed so focused. He squeezed my finger and cooed. "Do you want more bourbon stories?" He kicked, which was my answer for yes.

"You see, son, the industry has a long history of making stuff up. And the greatest distiller of all time was said to be a doctor. But neither I nor past researchers could find evidence that Crow was actually a doctor. The best theory is he learned some chemistry techniques here and there and put them to use when he moved to America. We do know for certain that his whiskey took off like wildfire and that Old Crow was the greatest brand of the 1800s and arguably the best quality of the 1900s. Then Jim Beam bought it in 1987 and turned it to poo poo," I said, still trying to refrain from cussing around my kids, no matter the age, which, by the way, lasted for as long as Julian was in diapers. Once a soldier, always a soldier's mouth.

I looked at Julian, his eyes closed now, and let him rest on my left pec. As I rocked, I thought about Dave, how whiskey events would never be the same without seeing him, his huge smile, and the legions of fans that came to learn from his massive distilling brain. I kissed Julian on the forehead and slowly laid him in the crib. The line between life and death is ever moving, so small. One minute we are here; the next we are gone. The loss of Dave. The love of my life, the birth of my boys, my passion for bourbon. They're all chained together in moments, bringing me to tears, laughter, and deep thought. I was putting my boy to bed, and a simple text about Dave's passing changed everything.

As I left Julian's room, walking down the stairs, I thought about how distillers live on in the brands they create, and I smiled knowing that Dave Pickerell would never be forgotten and that Parker Beam's legacy is sipped every day. It's like music: I never saw Jimi Hendrix in person, but his guitar is felt in my inner being. Distillers' recipes are their legacies. But this sentiment mattered little at the moment.

Dave's loss was also a reflection of us all in the whiskey business. He did not live a healthy life, by any means, and I was walking the same path.

I needed to lose weight, to exercise, to live to see my boys have their own kids, and to grow old with Jaclyn.

I didn't sleep at all that night.

And as I often did, I coped with anxiety by thinking about history, distillers' past. My mind went to Old Crow. It always went back to Old Crow.

What happened to this brand?

THE SCANDAL

CHAPTER 9
THE BRAND

IN MY SMALL office, several boxes of my research collected dust. From 2008 to 2016, I photocopied or printed just about every piece of information I came across about James Crow and his namesake brand Old Crow.

When I took a break from my obsession, I put the papers in boxes and just left them on my office's kitchen cabinet.

At the start of 2019, I was ready to crack open the boxes and begin the quest to find the truth, to fully understand what happened to Old Crow. But I could not fully dive into research like I had in the past. From co-owning the *Bourbon Pursuit* podcast to participating in Bourbon & Beyond planning, I was busy, juggling a calendar laden with meetings and *Bourbon+* editor deadlines.

I had to hire an assistant, Jessica, to keep my life straight. But she was far more than a scheduler and helped grow my brand within the whiskey community while simultaneously building hers.

So when I had taken my four boxes down from kitchen cabinet and spread the papers all over the floor, she was not happy.

"What are you doing?" barked Jessica, a slender young woman with brown hair and a piss-and-vinegar spirit. Truthfully, when I hired her, Jessica sort of became my de facto boss, always telling me where to be and when. She challenged me in ways I had never imagined possible.

"Um, I am looking through my old research," I said.

"Well, you're making a mess," she replied.

Yeah, before Jessica came around and whipped things into shape, my office was basically hundreds of bottles on the floor, with stacks of papers in the corner. I like clutter; what can I say?

"Maybe you should take a long lunch, because I'm in book mode and it's gonna get really dirty here," I said, chuckling.

"Ugh," she replied. "I'll clean up after you. I'm gonna get ready for tonight's tasting."

As Jessica organized the bottles for the blind tasting I was hosting that evening, I looked at every paper on the floor, separating the stories of James Crow, the human, from Old Crow, the brand. Truth is, I had moved on from James Crow himself, almost irritated with the fact I had studied a man who lived a lie. But did he really? I certainly didn't have a time machine that could take me back to the moment when Crow introduced himself as a doctor.

The whiskey industry had clearly turned Crow into a cartoon character, pulling his name through the marketing bullshit that spins this industry round and round. Would he have approved of that?

It's hard to say. In closing the chapter of Crow the person, lying on the ground and my hands folded under my chin, I looked at the only alleged photo of him, where he's with his fellow distillery workers. I said out loud: "I guess we'll never know who you truly are."

Jessica overhead my mumbling and said, "Excuse me?"

She walked out of the tasting room and saw me surrounded by papers, sighed, and said, "I see you're in your little hole." I laughed and she went back to the tasting studio.

In that moment, surrounded by my notes and papers, my entire focus went into figuring out what happened to Old Crow, the brand, and I had to begin with the greatest piece of evidence I had from the 1800s—the trademark dispute that started after the Civil War.

When James Crow died in 1856, the United States of America was in the middle of the country's greatest debate—slavery.

The 1856 presidential election pitted pro-slavery Democrat James Buchanan against Republican John C. Frémont and American Party (Know-Nothing) nominee Millard Fillmore. Buchanan supported the Kansas-Nebraska Act of 1854, which repealed laws that prohibited slavery in the territories, and the debate became one of morality and states' rights. According to the White House Historical Association, Buchanan defended slavery as a constitutional right, and he "seemed aware and comfortable with the idea of Black people working for him in ways that White people would not."[1]

The Republicans' first anti-slavery presidential candidate, Frémont, lost decisively to Buchanan, while Fillmore was a distant third. As Buchanan's agenda unfolded, especially his push for

Kansas to become a slave state, it became clear that slavery would continue to become the country's most divisive issue. And when South Carolina seceded from the Union shortly after anti-slavery Republican Abraham Lincoln won the office of president in November 1860, the writing was on the wall—a civil war would ensue.

Kentucky never officially sided with the North or South, but its young men fought for both sides. Throughout my years of researching James Crow, I've always wondered what side he would have fallen on. I like to think he would have sided with the North, pursuing freedom for the men who worked by his side, to help the man only known as Albert pursue a life of freedom. And since James Crow was not the owner of the distillery—he only worked there—I have to believe he had no financial interest in maintaining ownership of people to do his toil. And there are no records indicating he owned slaves or championed the rights to own men, while his distillery ownership—the Peppers—owned dozens of people.

Of course, it's dangerous to use a modern morality lens to judge the past, even if I know what I would have fought for. Still, when I look at that smirking James Crow in the only known photo of him, he's standing comfortably next to enslaved people, and there's testimony that he taught a Black man, presumably a slave, all of his distilling techniques. Why would he teach a slave his craft if he didn't believe in them as people? I have to believe—no, I need to believe—that James Crow sided with the North to free people from their shackles.

Alas, I'll truly never know.

But his namesake whiskey would become federally taxed

through Lincoln's whiskey tax and help pay for the Union army, while the Confederates imposed a prohibition and used much of the equipment, such as stills, to make materials for the war. The Confederates, no doubt, damaged themselves by not having access to whiskey tax revenue. In most acts of prohibition, the governments pass the laws for morality purposes. But William Robinson Jr. wrote in "Prohibition in the Confederacy," in *The American Historical Review*, that was not the case in this instance.

"Prohibition in the Confederacy was the enforced product of war conservation. It was never a high moral issue; although, indeed, we do find that the Confederate Congress twice passed acts to discourage drunkenness in the army—with no reason at all for implying abstinence in the navy and the Marine Corps. Prohibition arose from the twofold necessity of conserving grain supplies in order to feed the armed forces and of conserving the inbound tonnage of the blockade-runners in order to increase the importation of war supplies," Robinson published in 1931.

Meanwhile, the Union earned 25¢ per proof gallon of whiskey at the beginning of the Civil War and 70¢ per proof gallon toward the end. And the Confederacy faced high inflation with minimal revenue streams. It doesn't take a financial guru to theorize that if the Confederates had imposed a whiskey tax like the Union did, they would not have had to as aggressively seek outside financing to fund their army.

Of course, whiskey played only a small role in the Civil War finances, but its most heralded brand, Old Crow, did serve as General Grant's dram of choice, and remnants of Crow's barrels were found at Civil War battle sites a century later. I've jokingly said at whiskey tastings that Old Crow was like Gatorade for Union Soldiers. That tongue-and-cheek joke always felt a little classless as it left my lips, but a cheap joke can help move along an evening. The sad truth is that the original Old Crow died with its creator, and nobody's laughing at that.

Both Crow's wife and daughter died before the war's end. Thus, at the end of the Civil War, with no remaining heirs, Crow's name was up for grabs. And whiskey dealers feasted upon his name like actual crows on a roadside ham sandwich.

From the West to East and North to South, wholesalers and taverns advertised "Old Crow" whiskey for sale by the barrel. They frequently billed their whiskey as the genuine article made in Woodford County, Kentucky. Most sold through their existing barrels and then went about their business selling other whiskey, but some actually laid claim to the name Old Crow.

At the time, trademark law lacked the precedent and federal regulations to restrict multiple people from using the name *Old Crow*. Sure, some states had common law and statutes for intellectual property, but there was no federal law that could give one entity the use of a name over the other. Even when the 1870 trademark act was passed, the Supreme Court deemed it unconstitutional nearly a decade after its initial passing. Revisions would be made nearly every decade thereafter, and there were duct tape measures to allow for intellectual property law, but trademark law didn't become more narrowly tailored until the early 1900s—much too late to protect the Old Crow name.

While more than eighteen hundred individual legal letters would be sent to people accused of trademark infringement, from the end of the Civil War to 1949, there were really three major claims to the Old Crow throne, and each one was convincing in different ways. The one that emerged victorious would become a beacon for future corporate America endeavors.

The legal fight for Old Crow showcases three prominent companies: W. A. Gaines & Co. in Frankfort, Kentucky; Hellman Distilling Co. (not the mayonnaise company) in St. Louis, Missouri; and Rock Springs Distillery in Owensboro, Kentucky.

W. A. Gaines—originally Gaines, Berry & Co.—had the rights to the whiskey Crow made, acquiring the distillery along Glenn's Creek in 1867. Gaines claimed that it distilled the "James Crow" way, and that others using the words *Old Crow* did not follow the same distillation techniques used by Crow. In fact, Gaines outright called Hellman fraudsters for using imitation whiskey. I couldn't help but get a few goosebumps when I read Gaines's lawyer's oration:[2] "by reason of the inferior quality of the said liquor, the reputation of your [Gaines's Old Crow] whiskey has been greatly damaged."

I remember reading this for the first and screaming: "Yeah! Get 'em, lawyer man!" I loathed the rectifiers, people who ruined whiskey with additives, often deadly ones, and I harshly judged them with the full weight of my bourbon geek heritage. Anytime I came across a deadly historic recipe, like those that included sulfuric acid, I asked myself how my distilling heroes would react. What would Dave Pickerell say? How would Parker Beam react to this?

But in Hellman's defense, it did nothing wrong for the time. It was simply the business of whiskey back then to add impurities or acids. That's what people drank, and Gaines was trying to protect its pure, straight whiskey that would eventually dominate the marketplace. That said, Hellman was a company to be reckoned with, selling the whiskey in beautiful bottles, with vertical grooves and stamped text protruding from the glass. It also sold Crow in many varieties: Crow, Old Crow, Celebrated Old Crow, and J. W. Crow's Bourbon.

The Hellman camp was in business prior to Gaines, giving it a leg up on its Kentucky opponents, and were actively selling Crow-related whiskey during that time, laying a major blow to Gaines's argument that it only sold the genuine article. Even if Hellman sold something we would consider copycat and disgusting, it did sell it prior to 1867, the year Gaines claimed ownership of the brand. And Hellman claimed Gaines knew about its products and even that the so-called original formula of Crow was inferior, delivering more fusel oils (volatile liquids from fermentation) in the final product than its version did.

Nonetheless, the first court sided with Gaines, citing the fact that it was producing the original formula. But the appeals court seemed to care little about the actual whiskey and was more interested in who had used the name *Old Crow* first.

The judges wrote: "The evidence, without contradiction, establishes the following facts: that as early as 1862, the firm of I. and L. M. Hellman, composed of Isaac Hellman and Louis M. Hellman, were engaged in the wholesale liquor business on Pine Street in the City of St. Louis, Missouri; that as early as 1862 or 1863, on the whiskey barrels employed in their trade, they had a bird with wings spread, in imitation of a crow burned into the head of the barrel and the word "Crow," or the words "Old Crow" were burned beneath this figure."

The Court of Appeals ruled in favor of Hellman in 1908, saying Gaines didn't have exclusive rights to the name *Old Crow* and that other distillers were actually using the so-called Crow techniques, also known as sour mashing. Truthfully, when I read this ruling, I felt incredibly disappointed and my stomach twisted into a knot. How could these judges rule against the house that wanted to make great bourbon?

I think I was so angry at the Hellmans of the world because I believed their pursuit of selling imitation whiskey as Old Crow opened the door for other grifters just like them, including brands like Duffy's Pure Malt Whiskey, which made false medicinal claims. In a 1900 newspaper advertisement, Duffy's wrote: "Duffy's Pure Malt Whiskey has cured over 4 million souls in the past half of the century."[3] Among the ailments Duffy's claimed to cure: cancer, diarrhea, consumption, malaria, and "weak women." Duffy's purchased full-page advertisements in medical journals and quoted testimonies from alleged 160-year-olds.

That kind of false advertising attracted the ire of the federal government, leading to the Pure Food and Drug Act, which was the precursor to the Food and Drug Administration (FDA), to ban false medicinal claims. Duffy's Pure Malt also gave the Prohibitionists' marketing material to use in their efforts to ban alcohol. One of the leading faces of Prohibition, Carry Nation, who literally wielded axes inside bars, wrote in her autobiography: "Oh! The drunkards the doctors are making! No physician, who is worthy of the name will prescribe it as a medicine, for there is not one medical quality in alcohol. It kills the living and preserves the dead. Never preserves anything but death. It is made by a rotting process and it rots the brain, body and soul; it paralyzes the vascular circulation and increases the action of the heart."[4]

See, my belief is that if Duffy's Pure Malt Whiskey didn't exist and Hellman hadn't attempted to grow the imitation whiskey market and steal the Old Crow name, Nation and her Women's Christian Temperance Union cohorts wouldn't have had as big of a whiskey target to convince the public of an eventual Prohibition. In the grand scheme of the world, it matters little, but it's essentially "give them an inch, and they'll take a mile" when dealing with an adversary. The whiskey industry players couldn't exactly thwart the rise of Prohibition while they were also fighting among themselves.

But the law is the law. Until legal precedent was set or an Act of Congress was passed, Duffy's Pure Malt Whiskey and Hellman could thrive.

Therein is why Gaines's legal challenges were so incredibly important to modern whiskey definitions.

Neither the Pure Food and Drug Act of 1906 nor the Taft Decision of 1909 were law at the time of the first lawsuit. And while this was technically a trademark case, much of the argument centered on who—Hellman or Gaines—made Old Crow bourbon the correct way. Hellman rectified the whiskey through blends with neutral spirits and additives; Gaines bottled straight bourbon whiskey but added water to proof it down from around 107 proof to 100 proof. This case would be one of the most important legal moments for answering the question: What is whiskey?

After the United States added whiskey definitions, rectifiers challenged the laws in court, according to the brilliant book by Brian Haara, *Bourbon Justice*. "This made the lawsuits between

Hellman and Gaines a true heavyweight battle, involving back-and-forth victories, numerous appeals, reversals, and efforts by Gaines to game the legal system," Haara wrote.[5]

Gaines surely knew this when it sued for the final time in 1918, now going after Rock Springs Distillery in Western Kentucky federal courts. This time Gaines had reregistered the name *Old Crow*, and the Supreme Court decided it owned the name in 1918 and should be its exclusive dealer. The court ruled that Rock Springs and Hellman were guilty "in fraud of the Gaines Company rights and in infringement of its trademark."[6]

Sadly, once this was decided, Prohibition was on its way, and Old Crow was a juicy target for those who sought to end drinking in the United States. Carry Nation wrote that the name itself was "slandering the crow, for there is not a crow or vulture that will use a drop of this slop."[7]

The rush to ban alcohol caught fire, aligning with other political initiatives such as women's suffrage, and the United States passed Prohibition in 1919, one year after Gaines won the landmark trademark lawsuit. Perhaps Gaines spent too much on arguing its case before the Supreme Court or didn't have the energy to continue fighting to sell whiskey; in any case, W. A. Gaines closed for business upon the passing of Prohibition. And Old Crow's trademark, which Gaines had fought so hard to obtain, went up for grabs and was acquired by National Distillers.

But why would anybody want to obtain rights to sell an alcohol brand when it was illegal to sell booze?

I spent a great deal of time researching and writing about how whiskey distillers stayed viable during Prohibition. Some, like George

Remus, carved out illegal bootlegging syndicates. Others, like Gaines, went out of business. But most of them diversified their businesses and lobbied for small pockets of revenue opportunities. With the Spanish flu killing millions of people around the world in 1918 and 1919, doctors and druggists campaigned for Congress to allow for medicinal whiskey. Even during Prohibition, doctors could prescribe whiskey in most states, although so-called bone-dry states like Indiana and West Virginia remained completely without drink. Thus, whiskey had a small pocket of revenue coming in from the medical community. And believe me, people were sick back then. A lot. In fact, patients could receive a prescription once every ten days for their sickness. And much like the early days of medicinal marijuana in the contemporary world, people abused the system, obtaining prescriptions to treat maladies such as stubbed toes and headaches.

Thus, Old Crow, now under the ownership of National Distillers, had life, and it became a preferred brand for doctors to prescribe simply because people were familiar with the whiskey and it had a good reputation. Although whiskey distillation was not completely banned during Prohibition—the feds allowed for the occasional distilling to replenish medicinal stocks—the new owners of Old Crow began to produce it in Canada in the 1920s. Their advertising would leave many modern whiskey geeks dumbfounded, because today's bourbon cannot be made anywhere but the United States, according to a 1964 U.S. congressional declaration. "The old aristocracy, the great plantations and Old Crow have disappeared from the Old Dominion State. But Old Crow lives again in the Dominion of Canada—mellowed and ripened by the years—the same gladsome, fragrant bourbon that fostered friendships and kinships years ago in Richmond… Old Crow American Bourbon Whiskey, distilled in Canada of American Grain, by American distillers," the new Old Crow advertised in 1929 in the Montreal newspaper *The Gazette*.[8]

All that said, Old Crow survived Prohibition because of the brand recognition of its creator and all those who sold it. And it was perhaps the most successful brand in all of bourbon in 1933, the final year of Prohibition.

Ironically, as I was beginning to turn my research attention toward post-Prohibition Old Crow, in early 2020, the news started covering a story about a couple of cruise ships not allowed into port due to some sort of virus on board. Little did I or the rest of the world know at the time that we were about to rehash the same arguments from one hundred years ago.

Jaclyn was in the kitchen making cookies, and I was preparing for a nightly tasting on my shiny new YouTube channel, where I blind tasted flights of bourbon and ranked them. This was outside of my comfort zone. But my assistant, Jessica, really encouraged me to start a YouTube channel, because that's "where all the people get their information now." I balked, because I never wanted to become an "influencer," a word I didn't associate with my work as an author. But when my friend Clay Busch, an entertainment manager, said that YouTube was the future, I reluctantly joined and started live streams.

I stood at the foot of my bed, tying my ascot, when a news report came on the TV screen. The news ticker scrolled something like: Breaking News: Contagious Virus on Cruise Ships.

"Hey, baby, you hear about this?" I asked.

"What?"

"This virus thing. They are quarantining cruise ships," I said.

"Yeah, those things are petri dishes for disease," she said.

Within a matter of a week, the virus had been confirmed in the United States, and I attended an event where somebody had tested positive for the so-called coronavirus. The organization sent an email to notify all attendees, and we were all nervously watching the news, listening to doctors, and wondering what the hell was going on.

Soon, people around the world started dying, and the government shut down schools, businesses, and churches across the country. Nobody knew what would happen next. My friends in New York said they saw health officials dragging bodies out of apartments and lining them up in the streets. In the Kentucky countryside, sheriffs were arresting citizens for not following mandates such as closing businesses or not wearing a mask in public.

And while it seemed trivial in comparison, my livelihood was in jeopardy. Before I knew it, I had been furloughed from the majority of my revenue-making ventures. Bourbon & Beyond was gone. *Bourbon+* magazine revenue vanished from my bank account, and my events dried up.

I lost 95 percent of my income within a couple of days, and Jaclyn, now a department head at the hospital, essentially became our sole income. All my research, writing, and everything in between was on pause.

I was in survival mode, in constant fear that if something happened to Jaclyn I could not provide for our family. After all, she worked at a hospital every day, where they were enduring the first major pandemic of our lifetime.

So I did what any respectful husband and father of two young boys would do—I picked up a camera and became an influencer. For years, I hung true with pride that I was an author, an actual Smithsonian speaker, and taster. Instagram, TikTok, and YouTube were for the kids looking to become famous. I was studious, in my forties, and far too curmudgeonly to try new things. Except for the occasional YouTube tasting, of course.

Then, my livelihood withered. Bars closed. Liquor stores were open, but mostly because everybody needed a drink to cope with the world, and highly dependent alcoholics can go into seizures if they do not have alcohol in their system. I didn't realize that this "withdrawal" symptom was so prevalent that liquor stores were considered an "essential" business during the pandemic.[9] I asked Jaclyn about it.

"Are there really that many people who will actually die if they don't have a drink?"

"Yup, people get dependent on alcohol," she said. "It's really bad."

I paused, thinking about what I might be doing to contribute to this issue. Did people read my work and then chug booze? I recalled a gentleman I talked to while on a book tour. He said he drank a liter of Maker's Mark or Evan Williams a day. I laughed, thinking it was a joke, but he said, "No, it's true. My old man and I drink a bottle a day." He bought a book and a few bottles at the liquor store I was at.

"Am I helping create people with dependency?" I asked Jaclyn.

"What do you mean?"

"Like, are people becoming alcoholics because I am out there promoting it in a positive light?" I replied.

"No, you talk about the history and the positives of bourbon. People drink for reasons you can never know. You talk about tasting and being responsible. Not how to become a drunk," she said.

I nodded my head. But I felt a little shame in that moment, knowing that somebody might take my positive tasting notes as a freedom to drink as much as they want. And while I genuinely did not want people to become alcoholics from consuming my content, the only way I could earn a living during the pandemic was through virtual tastings, videos, and podcasts.

YouTube and podcasting had become my only sources of income after my events were canceled. Between my podcasts *The Fred Minnick Show* and *Bourbon Pursuit*, I was interviewing somebody every other day. But it was my YouTube live streams that became my pandemic identity, and I truly had no idea what the hell I was doing.

I bought a Sony Handycam and YouTube-connected software, and I pressed the "live" button with any bottle of bourbon in front of me, a glass, and no idea what I would say or if anybody would watch as I did a live tasting online. Then, the chat started trickling in. Hundreds, eventually thousands, of people tuned in to watch me drink. It was the darndest and most rewarding tasting I had ever experienced. All these people were home with nothing to do, and we interacted while we all drank.

At first, I hit "live" on my software and started talking. Then, as I got more comfortable with the format, I added music and started dancing as I popped bottles to sip. This was all happening in the middle of the day, and the chat feature would light up. And soon my YouTube community started drinking games.

"You have to drink every time you see an ascot," wrote Clinton Kincaide in the chat.[10]

I answered all sorts of questions in the chat, ranging from what I thought about Evan Williams 1783 (which I like) to whether whiskey is good for COVID (I'm not a doctor, but yes).

I took my share of heat, too, especially when I picked an unpopular bourbon over what the general bourbon community called a "Tater bottle." See, somebody with far too much time on their hands started calling bourbon lovers who spent too much money on bourbon "Taters." My friend Wade Woodard created a list of criteria for the derogatory term, and it included spending over suggested retail prices and listening to people like me.[11] I thought the whole thing was funny and even had Jaclyn dress as a potato for a few videos to steal bottles behind me while I was recording. Anyway, often the so-called Tater bottles, such as the ever-popular Blanton's, would lose in a live stream blind tasting and a few would sling insults at me for picking what they considered inferior bottles over those that tended to draw the hype.

But even those who disagreed with my tastings hung around for the whole stream. We were all there just sipping bourbon and trying to get through this pandemic. And for the first time in my career, I drank way too much and could feel my waistline expanding every week. The thing is, and 95 percent of the people on this planet would not believe this was true, I could only make money during the pandemic if I was sipping bourbon.

In addition to YouTube live streams, event planners booked

me for virtual tastings and would send their corporate clients tasting kits. We hopped on Zoom, and I said hi to Google one day, Amazon the next, Home Depot the next week, and so on and so on. I also sent rare whiskey to celebrities and got the opportunity to interview them, since they were also stuck at home with nothing to do. There was no way I could have booked celebs like Ludacris and Mick Fleetwood for my then-startup podcast if they hadn't been forced to sit around at home.

I spent the day tasting with my incredible YouTube community, corporate buyers, or celebrities. And at night, Jacklyn, the kids, and I took family walks around the neighborhood, which, looking back, were kind of funny.

We cooked dinner just about every night and genuinely bonded as a family. Once, Oscar and I were playing catch on the front sidewalk, and Julian, now a butterball of a two-year-old, rolled down the steps with a piece of focaccia bread in one hand, an apple fruit pack in the other, beef jerky in his mouth, and another stick of jerky sticking out of his diaper.

"Julian," Oscar laughed, "are you putting food in your diaper?"

Julian ignored him and walked straight to his bigger brother, attempting to knock the football out of his hands, and simply said, "ball," before walking back up the stairs.

"Your brother is something else, isn't he?" I said to Oscar.

"Yeah, all he wants to do is take my stuff," he said.

Well, that was true. Within in a couple days of learning to walk, Julian stole the TV remote and replaced it with something similar—a toy remote. He trotted away laughing. Day after day, the younger one found ways to annoy the elder brother.

And when the two went at it, they got under the skin of their grandpa, Charles, who started to become ill in the beginning of 2021 with various ailments. He was sensitive to their high-pitched fighting. During one family dinner, I asked to chat with Charles alone, thinking it would be a good respite from the kids. I often went to Charles with business ideas to get his thoughts.

I lit up a cigar and he smoked a pipe on the front porch.

"How's business?" he asked.

"Well, Charles, I'm not really writing much these days. I think I've become an influencer," I jokingly replied.

"Hmmm," he said, taking a huff from the pipe, likely thinking I had become a booty-shaking TikToker. Or did he not know what an influencer was? I couldn't tell by his lack of a reaction if he was judging me, annoyed, or clueless. I decided to change the subject.

"So I have this podcast now where I am interviewing celebrities."

"Oh, yeah. Any big names?"

"I just booked Terry Bradshaw and Peyton Manning," I said.

"Wow, what are they like?" he said.

"Well, Terry is hilarious. This guy has stories coming out of his ears and is not shy to tell you what he thinks about Aaron Rodgers, the Green Bay quarterback that he doesn't like!"

Charles, a casual sports fan, laughed.

"And Peyton is exactly like you'd think: super polished. His brother..."

"Oh, Eli? Anne loves him. He's a giant."

"Actually, their older brother, Cooper. He was one of those I could never tell if he was joking or telling the truth."

Charles shook his head in disapproval. He was not a fan of jokesters.

We talked about the stock market, birds, and the state of cigars. And when I saw the opportunity to bring up what I really wanted his advice on, I delved into a risky business move I was considering—the Super Bowl.

"My events business has really grown, and my team wants me to throw a Super Bowl party," I said.

"Like at the actual Super Bowl?"

"Yes, every year there's a whole slew of parties and celebrities come from all over to attend, sort of like they do here at the Kentucky Derby. Some awesome opportunities have opened up for me because of all the celebrity contact I've been having, and this is one of them."

"Sounds like a lot of work. Who's paying for it?"

"Well, that would be whoever my partner is..."

"Do you trust them? Do you have to put money in?"

"Yes, I definitely trust them. I will have some costs, but I have a guarantee I will get paid."

"Well, then, this sounds promising, but you still need to do a Column A for pros and a Column B for cons. If the pros outweigh the cons, do it. If they're even, side with how much money you'll earn."

By the time I could have a follow-up conversation about the event that would become Big Game Bourbon ventures, Charles's condition grew worse and he was hospitalized in May 2022.

When I saw him in his hospital bed for the first time, he was just skin and bone. Tubes ran from his arm, there were wires taped to his chest, and his breathing was erratic.

"Hey, Fred," he said, looking confused. He closed his eyes.

Jaclyn grabbed her dad's hand, tears dripping down her face. Charles awoke disoriented, as if he had no recollection of us walking into the room.

"Hi, Jackie," he said to his daughter. He looked at his wife of nearly fifty years, Anne.

"Do you remember the sea turtles?"

"Yes," Anne said.

"They walked on the beach under the moonlight," he said and then fell asleep again.

The family took turns being with him every hour of every day as his organs shut down. At seventy-four, he had lived longer than any other man in his family, and he fought every single day just to see his wife one more time to tell her about the sea turtles crawling on Myrtle Beach.

I was there on June 1, 2022, holding Anne's hand as she said, "It's okay, Charles. You can go now. We've had a beautiful life together." Charles's breaths became deeper, slower. At that moment, we were interrupted by the hospital chaplain, a tall, pudgy, and smooth-skinned fella with glasses and blondish-brown hair.

"Hi, would you like me to pray with you over your loved one?"

Anne and I both agreed. We bowed our heads and proceeded to await the young minister.

"Dear heavenly father, please be with..." the minister stopped and looked at Anne.

"I'm sorry, what's his name?" he asked.

How could he come into the room and not know Charles's name? I wanted to laugh, because I knew such a snafu would earn the minister a special nickname from Charles. "His name is Charles Engelsher," she said.

When the minister left, Anne and I both started laughing and joked about the possible nicknames Charles might have come up with for the clueless chaplain. We settled on "Dough Pants," giving us a lovely smile to hold during a conversation about Charles's life.

"He is such a fascinating man," she said. "He wrote books and saved so many lives as a radiologist. Whatever he wanted to do, he did."

As Anne talked, I saw Charles's chest rising and falling. Anne looked at me as Charles took his last breath. She didn't know it, but Charles was likely still there in that moment, with his spiritual hand on her shoulder as she told me about the love of her life.

Maybe she saw me looking at Charles or could feel his presence disappear, but she turned toward the bed and looked at her husband for the first time all over again.

"Oh, Charles," she said, bursting into tears, holding his hand. I placed my hand on her shoulders as the nurses came in.

Charles was gone.

Death is scary.

It comes for us all. But having seen people take their last breaths in war and then seeing how Charles passed, I would much prefer to be surrounded by loved ones, like he was. Charles was an amazing man, and his *New York Times* obituary reflected what he had done for hospitals in New York and Kentucky.

Death redirects the living.

Whenever somebody important to me died, I noticed how deeply I felt for the person I had lost and the relationship we had. David Mitts, a soldier I knew in Iraq. Dave Pickerell. Parker Beam. My father-in-law. I think of them often. And immediately after their passing, I took the tidbits they gave me from their lives and added them to my own.

Death gives us a reason to live. In nearly all stories of people on their deathbeds, those dying say they wish they spent more time with their loved ones. After I prioritized work over my family time when Jaclyn was pregnant with Julian, I vowed to never put myself in that situation again.

The pandemic helped me bond more deeply with my family. When I boarded an airplane, I closed my eyes and asked myself: *If this plane crashed, would my kids know I spent every quality minute with them that I could? Would Jaclyn know that my last breath would be thinking of her?* The minute I answered no, I started to cancel trips.

Death makes us search for our own legacy. How are we remembered when we die? Will anybody care months, or years, after? Charles's legacy was his family, but as I learned from writing his obituary, there was also another layer to his life. Charles was a man of principle who fought medical administrators to ensure proper patient care in poor areas of New York. His legacy would unknowingly live on in the people he helped.

The final breaths of our loved ones eventually make us think of our own.

As a kid, I fantasized about how I would die, imagining I would jump on a grenade to save a platoon or wrestle a bear to save a random hiker. In all scenarios, I died violently, a hero, and that death would be my legacy. As I grew older, especially in my postwar life, I lost the desire for a wild animal's claws ripping out my jugular and hoped for a peaceful passing. My wife and children are my reason for living, and I want to be on this earth for as long as I can to be with them. They make me want to be better, to build something bigger than me to perhaps pass down to them. I didn't quite know what to call this desire until I was having drinks with, of all people, the famous musician Pitbull. "Building generational wealth to pass down, my man, that's what it's about," he said, slapping me on the back and passing me the cheese tray.

Did I want to pass on money? Or did I want to pass on knowledge?

At this point in my early forties, what I could give the world was tied to alcohol, which the World Health Organization increasingly recommends we abstain from. Every other day there's a new study saying how booze kills you if you look at it sideways on skates. I am being facetious, of course, but health advocates are the new temperance advocates, and the younger generation has taken heed.

Three decades from now, I do not know if my profession will even exist.

As I was trying to determine my professional legacy and what I could leave my kids if I passed, I oddly came back to James Crow. It seemed that at every low point of my post-Iraq life, I found Crow to be a grounding influence, something I could focus my mind on when nothing else seemed to help me settle. But every time I dug into his life and the brand that was his legacy, I got pulled away to focus on new endeavors.

When I entered the Kentucky Historical Society again, I hoped this time would be different, that I would find something I missed and could complete this research without interruption.

For no other reason, I needed Crow. This research became my mindfulness practice, my method of coping with the loss of my wife's father, and it gave me a calmness to help my children through the first loss of their young lives.

So what would be my legacy?

Would I finally solve the question of what happened to Old Crow?

CHAPTER 10

ALL THINGS NATIONAL

FROM 1920 TO 1933, the United States banned alcohol's manufacture, sale, and transportation. Aside from a few exceptions, such as medicinal whiskey sales, all booze efforts in these thirteen dry years were illegal. But here's the thing: people didn't stop drinking.

Illegal drinking establishments popped up all over the country. As soon as one got busted, another one opened, all supplied by bootleggers, who sold real and fake alcohol. And when the cops arrested one bootlegger, four more popped up in their place.

Prohibition opened the door for normal everyday Americans to break the law just because they wanted a drink and helped build a network of organized crime. At the beginning of Prohibition, temperance was considered a morality issue. Toward the end, the public opinion shifted and people believed that the unlawfulness it fostered taught children not to respect the Constitution. In addition, the lack of alcohol taxes definitely contributed to the Great Depression in 1929.[1]

Just as politicians used the ban of drinking as a political plank in 1919, Franklin D. Roosevelt caught the wave of people wanting to repeal Prohibition in his 1932 presidential election. He campaigned on repeal and kept his promise. On December 5, 1933, Utah became the thirty-sixth state to ratify the Twenty-First Amendment, which repealed the Eighteenth Amendment and gave the federal government the required three-fourths majority to actually repeal Prohibition.

For Kentucky, this meant jobs and farmers supplying bourbon distillers again.

With weather-hardened faces and calloused hands, the 1930s Kentucky corn farmers plowed their fields with the help of mules, hand shucked every ear, and hauled their corn for pennies on the dollar in comparison to their grain's worth a decade earlier. Although Prohibition had ended and distilleries were up and running again in 1934, the Great Depression still had its meaty hooks in American farms, with corn going for as low as 8¢ per bushel.

Settled along Glenn's Creek in Woodford County, where James Crow would have been making whiskey in the 1800s, the Old Crow Distillery no doubt gave local farmers hope. Old Crow bought wagon after wagon, truckloads, and train cars galore of Kentucky corn, rye, and barley. The distillery's workers ground the grains with a hammer mill to make a coarse flour and filled a large mash tun with clean spring water. They cooked the grains, converting the starches into sugar. Then, they added yeast.

I imagine that as the distillers across Kentucky fired up for the first time legally in 1934, residents may have stepped out of their homes and caught the scent of corn and rye fermenting, which smells like a bread bakery crossed with a tavern. That had to be glorious!

And when they distilled the fermented mash and poured the distillate into the oak barrels, rolling them into the stone warehouses to age for several years, Kentucky had to feel whole again. While bourbon certainly couldn't save all of Kentucky corn, the stills' constant need for good ole-fashioned yellow dent corn offered consistent revenue, so much so that many of the farms that provided corn to distillers in the 1930s still do so today.

For nearly two decades, with the exception of the occasional medicinal distillation license, bourbon had been gone. And now, it roared again.

The only problem was that it would take some time for the consumers outside of Kentucky to realize the fruits of the post-Prohibition labor.

By the time Prohibition ended on December 5, 1933, most whiskey stocks had been consumed for medicinal reasons, stolen by bootlegging syndicates, or destroyed by Prohibition agents.

For the post-Prohibition market, this meant little aged whiskey was available to be bottled. As a result, distillers created a plethora of blends that could contain grain neutral spirit: essentially grain vodka, and whiskey. Blends were cheaper than straight whiskey, too, creating a diluted category that targeted consumers who didn't care about quality. Prominent brands like Four Roses, which had once only bottled straight bourbon, were forced to sell their brands as blended whiskey. And while they attempted to keep the whiskey as good as possible, they simply did not have the ability to release well-aged bourbon.

Back then, a four-year-old bourbon would have been considered top shelf.

Thus, when Old Crow advertised its four-year-old bourbon line in 1934, its parent company, National Distillers, struck a chord with the consumers of the day—Old Crow equaled quality. In addition, National Distillers pursued two prominent marketing angles for Old Crow that would seal its legacy forever. On one side, it promoted the heritage of Old Crow, really namedropping the 1800s-era celebrities, like statesman Henry Clay, and famous writers, like Hemingway, who sipped on the good stuff.

National Distillers also experimented with a new style of marketing for the time—cartoon characters. With people adopting the "living room lifestyle," centered around large radios and magazines portraying cartoons for quick laughs, the whiskey market was perfectly positioned to fall in love with a cartoon crow dressed in a tuxedo. In a 1936 internal memo, National Distillers noted: "Once this figure is created, and popularized with the public and the trade, it provides an especially effective possibility in point-of-sale advertising. Miniature 'Old Crow' models should be made—sufficiently decorative in design so that retail stores would want them in their windows and bartenders keep them on the backbar. Statuettes of this type are always sought after, and receive display far beyond that given to more conventional ideas."[2]

In 1936, National Distillers spent $122,267.50 advertising both the cute crow figure and the legacy of Crow, the man, building a double-entendre marketing style that had never before been done in whiskey.

One 1937 advertisement read: "Its superb quality has made it America's preferred bourbon."[3]

National Distillers shared Dr. James C. Crow's legacy with the lovable bird.

In one magazine advertisement, the adorable black tux–wearing Crow held a craps stick and informed readers that Old Crow "traveled in the best of company." In another ad from 1939, the regal crow, in his natural state, simply looked down, his beak pointing toward "Bottled in Bond" and his shimmering black eye staring right at whoever looked at the page. This particular advertisement promoted the "art of fine whiskey-making," and mentioned James Crow in small print.

When I saw this ad, I wondered if there had been heated internal discussions about the decision to move away from James Crow as the lead in much of the marketing and focus on the bird. Considering it did not really make much of a splash about the one-hundred-year anniversary in 1935, I presumed National Distillers wanted to get away from good ole Dr. Crow. And in fact, the small print in most of the ads did not refer to him as a doctor. Were the early managers of the brand trying to slowly soften James Crow's connection to Old Crow?

But then World War II kicked every plan in the world to the curb until the Nazis were gone.

In October 1942, the federal government ordered the Kentucky distilleries to stop making whiskey and offered them an option to make industrial alcohol for the war effort. Most of them, including Old Crow, fitted their distilleries to make what was essentially ethanol. Bourbon distillation can only go up to 160 degrees proof, while the likes of industrial alcohol and vodka must be distilled to 190.

Even though distillers wanted to win the war, some could not afford the still refit cost of about $12,000, which would be around $250,000 today, to create industrial alcohol. Those companies that could afford it pursued the path of industrial alcohol distillation, as they really had no other choice.

On the modern Kentucky Bourbon Trail, tour guides often brag about how distillers volunteered to make industrial alcohol for the war effort. But the truth is, it was another de facto Prohibition, and I doubt the industry leaders were very happy about losing production time. While they could sell the good stuff, they didn't have much choice on the production. That is, except for the big distillers like National Distillers, the parent company of Old Crow.

National Distillers owned a 35 percent stake in Standard Alcohol Inc., which had an industrial alcohol and oil arm that helped shaped the laws. And at the top of the pyramid was National Distillers' Seton Porter, who appeared on the cover of *TIME* magazine on December 4, 1933, the day before Prohibition was repealed. Porter owned more than half of all whiskey stocks nationwide at the end of Prohibition.

Porter, whom the Associated Press dubbed the "Whiskey King" in 1934, had managed railroad, oil, and food companies before he entered the whiskey business—he had no previous experience in spirits at all. In 1913, as distillers knew Prohibition loomed, the Distilling Corporation of America, often referred to as the "Whiskey Trust," was sold to the US Industrial Alcohol Co., which became the US Food Products Corporation after World

War I. When Prohibition hit, the bankers hired an engineering firm, Sanderson and Porter, to assess whether they should keep the distilleries or sell off the stocks and scraps. They kept them and appointed the younger brother of the firm's partner to lead the distilleries during Prohibition. That was Seton Porter, who didn't know the whiskey business but suddenly found himself in charge of seven distilleries, fifty-two warehouses, and 1.4 million gallons of whiskey in 1921. Porter eventually renamed the company National Distillers and somehow grew the parent company into a behemoth at a time when it was illegal to operate, for the most part.

How?

I remember discovering Seton Porter and writing on my notepad: "Who was this guy? How is he not the most famous whiskey person from this time? And what did he do that made National Distillers so prominent? Who did he know?" I had been covering whiskey history for well over a decade and can honestly say that other than a short passage here and there, I knew nothing about this guy. Whiskey history celebrates people from Porter's time period such as Pappy Van Winkle, Lewis Rosenstiel, Sam Bronfman, and the Browns. But Porter?

Like I often did with my historical discoveries, I wanted to talk to Jaclyn about this.

"So I made a huge discovery today," I told her.

"Let me guess, you found a new reason to hate vodka," she said, which was a solid guess. I mean, can there ever be enough reasons to hate vodka, bourbon's heated rival since 1958?

"No, I found this big-time whiskey exec. I didn't really know was that important when digging up material on Old Crow's parent company of the time, National Distillers," I said. Now, to my wife's credit, she really tried to remain engaged, but I could see it in her face, "Oh, boy, another dead guy history project." I had to quickly let her know that I wasn't about to jump into a new research rabbit hole.

"This is more about Old Crow, but I think he's a major reason why this brand became so famous," I said.

My working theory was that Porter foresaw trends both as an industry leader and as the president of National Distillers. What impressed me more than anything was his seemingly strategic communication tactics with two primary audiences to keep happy—shareholders and customers.

In 1932, as National Distiller shareholders became antsy about the end of Prohibition, Porter received approval from the feds to offer up a dividend of actual whiskey to shareholders, or they could keep their preferred shares and receive an extra 50¢ per share on December 1, 1934. "Due to the long period during which prohibition has been in effect, there seems to be a popular misconception regarding what constitutes good whiskey," Porter said in a statement to shareholders at the time.[4] "The raw spirits which are initially manufactured assuming the use of the best materials and methods of distillations are gradually transformed into whiskey solely by aging under proper conditions and is generally recognized steadily to improve with age. All of the company's large inventory of whiskey manufactured prior to prohibition and not already bottled has, therefore, been aged in wood for fifteen years or more. This irreplaceable inventory as now has been reduced to about 700,000 cases."

I read this statement out loud and blurted, "Absolutely genius." Granted, my dog, Remo, was the only one to hear it, but I had just found the pen of a whiskey business savant, one who not only kept shareholders happy but also let the world know how much whiskey they had and which brands would be ready to drink after Prohibition. Most whiskey people were silent at this time, likely fearing the retribution of another Carry Nation or government agents. Not Porter.

But it was Porter's post-Prohibition prowess that, I believe, shaped the whiskey landscape for the next decade. In 1934, when the public feared distillers raising prices, Porter told reporters: "Competition is going to cut prices all along the line—and almost regardless of profits."[5]

Porter was a major player behind the blends that flooded the market to keep prices down. In addition, he had all the good whiskey stocks four years and older and released them under his flagship brands Old Crow and Old Grand-Dad. You'd have thought that World War II halted Porter's cunning business plays, but I think it actually emboldened him.

With a firm seat at the government's table, he could steer the rules, regulations, and penalties of 1940s industrial alcohol. Porter had already managed an industrial alcohol company and would have known how to help his colleagues in this crisis. Even if several bourbon history books, including my own, didn't fully acknowledge Porter's role during World War II, he would have most certainly been a prominent leader for the distillers regarding industrial alcohol. But what was good for National Distillers and the larger companies was awful for the smaller distillers.

Meanwhile, the cost of fitting the stills to meet industrial alcohol specs was analogous to buying a standard four-cylinder gas vehicle off the lot and then the government mandating eight-cylinder engines. A car owner could pay for the change, but it wouldn't make sense for everyone to do so. While around 60 percent of the whiskey distillers acquiesced and made industrial alcohol, many smaller distillers did not. They sold out or shut down. But that wasn't the only problem facing small companies.

The larger companies squeezed them out of the liquor stores, too, lowering their whiskey prices and blocking them from vital distributor partnerships and prominent store placement. Eventually, the federal government sued National Distillers for violating ceiling price laws from World War II mandates. National Distillers would also be called into the Senate to testify about the price-fixing accusations. The government tried to help the smaller distillers. But by the time it noticed the likes of National Distillers circling the small companies, it was too late.

By the end of World War II, National Distillers had acquired several brands and smaller distillers, and so had Schenley, Brown-Forman, Seagram, and Hiram Walker—the other growing spirits conglomerates.

Today's liquor industry operates with the big distiller's foot upon the throat of the craft brands, which often sell a bottle for 50 percent more than the likes of Jim Beam, because their cost of goods sold is so much higher than the bigger brands' and they have more marketing dollars to spend. So not much has changed.

When I analyze the current American whiskey scene, I think it was greatly influenced by National Distillers' Porter, who championed low pricing on one hand and quality on the other, while he influenced the industrial alcohol decisions that would drive smaller brands out of business, only for his company to feast upon their carcasses.

An argument could made that he also saved bourbon.

See, in 1949, the U.S. Treasury pursued a regulation change to allow the use of secondhand or used barrels for aging bourbon. Porter not only led the fight to prevent this change, but National Distillers embarked on a social campaign promoting its conservation use of American white oak.

The distillery created a 130-acre white oak tract in the Ozarks of Missouri called "National Distillers' Cooperage Reserve" in the Seton Porter Forest in 1953, the year Porter died. From its advertisement: "White oak barrels carefully charred to an exact depth are essential to the proper aging of the many fine whiskeys sponsored by National Distillers. Slowly, gently throughout the aging process, the crisp brown layer of wood beneath the just-right char produces rich golden color, distinctive aroma and smooth mellow flavor typical of National's celebrated whiskeys. Meanwhile, Seton Porter Forest is conserved through selective cutting and replanting and its resources and natural beauty preserved for posterity. Thus, National Distillers integrates a continuing source of this raw material with the manufacturing part of its business enterprise."[6]

And once again, when I discovered this new-to-me piece of whiskey history, I was dumbfounded.

I ignorantly thought the 1930s and '40s were eras of garbage-laden lakes, smog-growing cities, and dudes in tight white T-shirts smoking two packs a day. Okay, I am exaggerating—a little. But I didn't think companies were this environmentally and socially conscious back then, and certainly not a bourbon company!

When Porter died, the executive whiskey torch was being passed to Rosenstiel, Brown, and Van Winkle, all of whom had different beliefs and ideals about where the whiskey industry was heading. I don't know if it was one of them, or a member of another prominent family or company, but somebody had the bright idea of using bourbon's folklore as its history base. Porter struck me as more of a straight shooter, talking about and preserving the elements of whiskey instead of glorifying tall tales.

Peddling false stories as truth became the norm in the bourbon world in the 1950s and '60s, such as the well-worn tale of a Baptist minister inventing bourbon and the myth of James C. Crow being a doctor. An exhaustive search shows that under Porter's reign, there were few mentions of Crow's medical prowess. But most ads after Porter's death touted the "doctor."

He may have been bad for the smaller distillers, but Porter genuinely knew how to navigate the storms thrown his way, bringing his shareholders year-after-year record profits. And boy, did National Distillers know how to make great whiskey.

Of course, it was following the path James C. Crow had laid out.

Doctor or not.

CHAPTER 11

NEW AGE

WHEN JULIAN WAS just getting out of diapers, we packed up the car and headed to the Smoky Mountains to Gatlinburg, the redneck Disney World, to visit my aunt Shannon, whom the boys had never met and I had not seen in almost ten years. She lived on a beautiful Southern homestead with an acre-sized garden of peas, tomatoes, okra, potatoes, and a few other tasty vegetables that could keep your cholesterol down.

In the back of her property stood thick brush and tall pine and oak trees as far as the eye could see. And in the front, tall weeds, tiny trees, and a man-made trench from the 1940s that had turned into a creek.

I love creeks.

When I was a kid, I played in a creek, gathering crawdads and pretending to be a soldier hiding from the enemy. When it rained, the creek flooded up to our property's lone peach tree. Other than that, it remained a steady three-foot-wide creek, although it would eventually dry up as invasive plants sucked out all the water.

So I saw this as an opportunity to take the kids up there and play. While Jaclyn and Aunt Shannon visited, the boys and I trekked the wide and muddy terrain. Oscar, now seven, jumped into the mud and fell into the little stream. Covered in yuck up to his neck and elbows, he popped up and stared at me, bursting into laughter.

"Dad, this is awesome, jump in," he belted.

Julian, a three-year-old meatball who was the size of most six-year-olds, pushed me and I slipped down the ledge. That small level of cardio caused me to breathe deeply. *My goodness, I am out of shape*, I thought. Julian, the beast, jumped square off the bank and into the softest mud spot there was.

Oscar laughed.

Julian did, too, covered up to his ankles in the pit.

But he kept sinking.

"Dad," Oscar screamed. "Julian is sinking. This is quicksand mud. We have to get him out."

I wanted to laugh, because I knew if this had happened to me as a kid, my brother or friends would start throwing rocks at me or something menacing that would require a bloody retribution, which would then lead to them retaliating by somehow tricking me into touching the neighbor's electric fence. I was actually day-dreaming of these fun childhood rivalries when Julian grunted. "Dad, I can't get out," he said, staying calm.

I walked toward him and felt the mud crawling up to my ankles, then my shins. Holy crawdads, this was deep mud. I finally got to Julian. The mud was up to his knees. I placed my hands under his chubby arms and hoisted. He barely budged. I pulled again, and I may have gotten him above the kneecap.

Oscar was more concerned than Julian.

"Dad, I'm calling the fire department," he said.

"No, son, we're fine. I almost have him."

And with one more pull, Julian was free. He went back to the house, as calm as could be, and said, "Yeah, Mom, I almost died back there. Daddy saved me in the creek."

I laughed, which I know I shouldn't have, but it reminded me of how much I loved creeks and rivers. All the memories I have of chasing my friends, throwing rocks, and actually getting stuck in the mud... I hoped this little creek incident was just the beginning of my sons' memories on or near water.

The moment reminded me, too, of how different Kentucky water was than where I grew up in Oklahoma.

Not far from where I lived was the Canadian River, a muddy catfish haven that flows into the Arkansas River. But it wasn't very wide. A tall felled oak could touch both banks in most spots of the Canadian.

So when I moved to Kentucky, my eyes could not believe the size of the Ohio River, which serves as the border between Louisville and Indiana, or Glenn's Creek, the Kentucky River tributary that James Crow settled on and that later became a hotbed for Kentucky distilleries such as Jim Beam. Glenn's Creek was the size of the Canadian River. I guess what I considered a creek growing up would have been a Kentucky puddle.

The mighty Glenn's Creek was not only a river by my childhood standards, it also served as a major marketing angle for National

Distillers in the 1950s. "The original springhouse still in use at the Old Crow Distillery," a 1953 newspaper ad touted. "Free-flowing limestone water of a certain select type, James Crow early realized, is the secret of Kentucky whiskey. For ten years he examined the streams and springs of Kentucky's famous bourbon country—and in 1835 found the crystal-clear water he had been looking for, some miles below the headwaters of Glenn's Creek. Here Crow built his first stone spring house, and here Old Crow is still made today!"[1]

These marketing campaigns painted a picture of the distillery and all the celebrities who had ever been seen sipping Old Crow. National Distillers also did something that would have likely been controversial for the time: they released an 86-proof Old Crow in 1952.

Eighty-six proof was the standard alcohol strength of the lesser brands and blends that sold on the bottom shelf. Not Old Crow, a standard 100-proof offering. If that happened today, the bourbon geeks would have been calling for Porter's head for making the decision. In fact, they did just that when Maker's Mark lowered its proof in 2013 from 90 to 84.

The difference between the contemporary and 1950s decision to lower the proof, besides the lack of internet then, was that Old Crow didn't rid its portfolio of the 100-proof. Instead, it simply created a new product that was lighter, milder, and cheaper. In addition, National Distillers released Old Grand-Dad and Old Taylor at 86 proofs, creating a house style that, in my opinion, would never be duplicated. No brand before or since has had such a cadre of flavors in such low-proof bourbons.

The 86-proof National Distillers bottles are what us dusty

hunters often chased, because the soft mouthfeel was like butter and the flavors popped with hints of Cracker Jack, caramel chew, and fig. Almost every bottle of 86-proof National Distillers I've had was like this, making it perhaps the most consistent vintage bourbon. There was also a lot of it out there, giving collectors like me an opportunity to taste the various iterations of the company.

The 1950s and 1960s were also a time of the younger generation moving away from brown spirits, such as bourbon, toward the likes of vodka and tequila. While I have much respect for tequila and the toil it takes to create, vodka's another story. I championed and later trademarked the phrase "vodka sucks," because of how badly the spirit hammered bourbon in the 1960s. And it's been well documented in my past books, videos, and public speaking events that I'd rather clip the toenails of an alligator in a sauna than drink vodka. Wait, do alligators have toenails? Anyway, the bourbon industry's attempt to appeal to vodka fans was to bottle at lighter proofs, which National Distillers did ten years before it was common to do so, and I really think that helped the company dial in its marketing angles.

One of its primary competitors, Ancient Age, produced an ill-fated campaign of drinking its 86-proof bourbon with orange juice, which is the perfect mixer for vodka but creates an acid bomb that explodes in the middle of your chest with bourbon. Old Crow, on the other hand, played up its 86-proof milder bourbon as the perfect cocktail mixer and even published a cocktail book in 1963 to tap into the cocktail culture of the time.

During this time frame, bourbon was also campaigning to become a unique product of the United States, and the industry was using the Elijah Craig folklore to help sell its cause to Congress. It's also at this time that National Distillers dug its heels in deep with nostalgic stories.

"Though James Crow's distillery produced but 2½ gallons a day in 1835, its quality made all Kentucky whiskey famous. Prior to this date distilling was a crude and haphazard process. Col. Crow revolutionized the process by introducing scientific methods, and produced a bourbon of unsurpassed smoothness and rich flavor. The favorite of Daniel Webster—lauded by Mark Twain, Henry Clay and other noted men—Old Crow's renown spread rapidly, until, following the turn of the century, it became America's best-selling bonded whiskey," the 1960s Old Crow cocktail booklet proclaimed, using the first known reference of Crow as a colonel. Perhaps the underpaid copywriter confused Crow for Col. E. H. Taylor's, another National Distillers brand?

Old Crow also maintained the socially conscious mission that Porter had started with the maintaining of the oak trees. In 1966, it embarked on one of the most unique campaigns in whiskey history—it sought to save the American crow.

Look, I love crows. In fact, I read somewhere that crows remember the face of every human who has ever wronged them and will hold grudges for up to fifteen years. They even tell their friends, so there's no crow who can be harmed by said human. That's why I've always said hi to crows and tried to feed them; I'd like to think they'd remember my goodwill and may help me if I am in a jam or maybe lost my car keys over the ridge.

Well, that's a bit off topic, but my point is I've always liked crows and found it peculiar that in the 1960s, when bourbon was about to peak, the Old Crow execs spent time and money on a campaign to save a bird that probably didn't need saving. Or did it?

—ɷ—

This line was printed in newspapers across the country through a wire service in 1966: "America's rarest bird—rarer even than the whooping crane—is a black crow."[2]

The World Wildlife Federation had determined that the crow was depleting in numbers and, like the jet-black Hawaiian crow, was down to twenty-five in Texas in the early 1960s. The federation blamed housing and apartment developments cutting into the crow's habitats, while the winter of 1964 killed so many that the wildlife organization reported the American crow was on the verge of extinction.

Granted, I learned about this 1960s crow situation through a whiskey promotion. But I couldn't help but think this was a Mandela effect, the social phenomenon that people misremember an event. So I asked a few people if they knew that the crow was endangered.

"Hey, babe, did you know the crow was on the verge of extinction in the 1960s?" I asked Jaclyn.

"You mean the bird?" she replied.

"Yes."

"Well, kind of. Seems like something I knew," she said.

"What do you mean?"

"I guess I knew there were fewer of them when I was little."

But Jaclyn and I did not grow up in the 1960s. My mom did, and she confirmed that there were indeed fewer crows back then, per her recollection, but my mother-in-law, Anne, said there were many crows in upstate New York. "But there were way more birds back then than there are today. There are fewer finches and blue jays now!"

In the age of conspiracy theories, I found myself diving deeper down the rabbit hole, digging into crow populations and what happened to them. Eventually, I had to stop, reminding myself that crow populations were not actually the subject of my research!

As for the whiskey brand, Old Crow executives paid for a national campaign seeking original bottles of Old Crow, which had been sold between 1843 and 1890. The label featured a drawing of a barrel with two crows on both sides and the bottler's name, P. Welty Co. According to the advertisement, the label embodied the Society for Preservation of the Crow's motto: "Two Crows You See. Good Luck to Thee."

National Distillers instructed readers to look for this exact bottle and mail it to the Preservation of the Crow. And the first to send the bottle in perfect condition would receive a $5,000 prize.

This ad campaign felt very much like the scene from *A Christmas Story* where Ralphie wins a decoder pin only to decode the message to drink more Ovaltine. Was the Preservation of the Crow just a marketing ploy for Old Crow?

Preservation of the Crow used the same address—25 East 73rd Street, New York, New York—as an art company, a TV production studio, and a publisher in the 1960s and 1970s, making me even more suspicious about the legitimacy of the organization.

While National Distillers certainly received a fine share of publicity for helping out the crow, I do not know how this campaign sold whiskey. This kind of oblique marketing is strategy that would play out time and again in the bourbon industry.

Meanwhile, National Distillers expanded the Old Crow Distillery, adding cookers, mash tuns, and more capacity for making whiskey. But the timing could not have been worse. Whiskey sales were finally on the verge of collapsing. In the 1960s, year after year, vodka took up more space on the bar shelf, and younger drinkers preferred to move away from what their parents drank—bourbon—while the National Distillers execs seemingly did everything but focus on the existing bourbon consumers.

When the larger companies started to push into the market, the likes of Crow Light didn't even make a dent into vodka sales. National Distillers spent millions buying ads in *Playboy*, *LIFE*, *TIME*, and other periodicals to promote Crow Light and then pulled the plug on it in 1976. This was not unique to Crow. Brown-Forman, Glenmore, and others discontinued their light whiskey brands around the same time. Light whiskey was a total abject failure, a business decision that marked the sign of the times.

About the only promising whiskey brands of the late 1960s were Wild Turkey, Jim Beam, and Maker's Mark. Unlike Old Crow, these companies did not create light whiskeys with their namesake or build up a weird sweepstakes to draw interest. Rather, they just directed their messaging directly to bourbon lovers.

Even Old Crow's greatest accomplishment of the 1960s—the chess pieces—were not intended for whiskey drinkers. They were meant to connect with the growing chess clubs. That's why four decades after their creation, I could still find full bottles at garage sales, and to this day there's enough inventory for everybody to get a taste.

After my very public love affair with Old Crow Chessmen, others tasted and discovered this deeply dark bourbon that was only 86 proof and ten years old. Its color is the most consistently discussed aspect of the Chessmen. Why was it so dark?

In truth, I didn't know. Sure, I had my suspicions. Perhaps the barrel entry proof was super low, like around 100, allowing a more soluble spirit to extract more wood sugars from the barrel. I also considered that the whiskey might actually contain stocks older than ten years old, even if it was not advertised as such. Did they add fifteen- to twenty-year-old barrels in with the ten-year-old barrels for some reason?

To find out, I went to the only person who might know.

A decade after I first tasted Old Crow Chessmen, I recorded a video complaining about the state of modern Old Crow, titled "This Bourbon Makes Me Sad." In the thumbnail, my beautiful long-flowing COVID hair touches my shoulders and my hands are tucked under my frowned face. In the comments, David Meier wrote: "The Chessmen were not actually distilled at the Old Crow Distillery."

Now, my YouTube channel gets its fair share of wacky comments and a ton of spam, like any popular channel, so I take most of these comments with a grain of salt. But this wasn't just any commenter. David bought the Old Crow Distillery in 2014 and started doing business as the Glenns Creek Distillery.

I won't lie—when I read his comment, I had a hard time coming to terms with it. The whiskey used in the chess pieces was not even from the Old Crow Distillery? The whiskey that pulled me into the fray of this ten-year research voyage, the whiskey that flipped my palate from a casual taster to an out-of-body experience and carried the Old Crow name…was not even made by Old Crow?

I felt embarrassed, as if 1960s marketers got one over on me. But I had to swallow my pride and admit I had been duped.

Still, I needed to understand what this whiskey actually was.

I met with Meier at Glenn's Creek, where the same brick of Old Crow's heyday still stood. "In 1964, they did a renovation here, and during that process, they added some more fermenters, somebody miscalculated and they got the amount of setback wrong and that threw off the recipe," Meier told me. "Employees could tell, and they told corporate, and National said to use the whiskey anyway. If you look at the Old Crow Chessman, it says 'bottled by Old Crow' not 'distilled and bottled by.'"

I held the chess piece in my hand. The ceramic was cool and the ridges felt sharper than I had recalled. I looked right at the black sticker that reads "bottled by Old Crow." In the distilling business, this is code for "you didn't make the whiskey."

Meier also introduced me to Bob Johnson, the superintendent in charge of the Old Crow Distillery when the chess pieces were manufactured. Now with his likeness on a Glenn's Creek label and in his early eighties, Johnson worked at the distillery from 1966 to 2005, although he admitted his memory isn't what it used to be. Johnson had had twelve surgeries in the past decade. "And every time they put me under, I lose a little bit of my memory," he told me. But when it came to the operations of Old Taylor and Old Crow in the 1960s, he recalled specifically that National Distillers transferred whiskey from Old Taylor to Old Crow to be bottled. The Old Taylor facilities, now named Castle & Key, were just down the road from Old Crow. "The barrels were transferred to the warehouses. When they come to the cistern room (where barrels are dumped to be bottled), they noted it was transferred [from Old Taylor to Old Crow]," Johnson said.

However, Johnson never saw the decanters being bottled, because that simply wasn't his job. "I never knew what was being bottled. My job was the warehouses and making sure 500 barrels were ready to get processed at a time," he told me.

With Meier's and Johnson's critical information, I walked away from the former Old Crow Distillery convinced that the whiskey I fell in love with was actually Old Taylor. How could I have not seen this?

After all, I not only knew about this "bottled by" trick to deceive consumers about where something was distilled, but I also covered the massive class action lawsuits in the early 2010s that went after whiskey brands for taking off the state of distillation that's required on all bourbon and straight whiskeys. The brands used clever language like "produced and bottled by" but did not disclose in what state it was distilled. And since covering this practice, I always scanned labels for the state of distillation. Yet, somehow the vintage Old Crow got the better of me, probably because it does notate "Kentucky Straight Bourbon," which is clearly establishing the state at which it was distilled. But I failed to see there was no "distilled" next to the "bottled by," which should have been a huge red flag.

I had fallen into the trap of trusting a whiskey brand. Because it was vintage, because I figured that if the old-timers said they made the whiskey, it had to be true. Was it possible that I did notice the label on the bottle, but the whiskey inside lit up my soul so much that I was willing to ignore it?

I didn't know.

Since Old Crow's whiskey was becoming known to be lower quality in the 1960s, the execs simply made the call to fill the chess pieces with Old Taylor. And since nobody really cared about authenticity or transparency back then, they got away with it.

This revelation took an emotional toll on me. I had built so much around my whiskey life, thinking Old Crow was the greatest whiskey I had ever tasted—and in the end, it wasn't even Old Crow. I felt like a fraud.

So I did what I always do when I screw up: I talked to Jaclyn.

"I messed up," I said, coming into the kitchen the day I found out about the Chessmen.

"What?" she said, sounding concerned. Jaclyn sat down at the table. I sat too. She grabbed my hand.

I took a deep breath. "You know how I love Old Crow," I said.

"Yes..." she said slowly.

"Well, the whiskey I fell in love with is not even Old Crow," I said.

"Are you serious?" she said.

"Yes. It's awful, right?"

"For God's sake," she said, letting go of my hand and standing up. "You had me seriously worried that something was wrong."

"Well, this is wrong. I've built up this obsession with Old Crow, but the whiskey I was drinking was actually Old Taylor. You know, the brand that's named after Col. E. H. Taylor, who was also a cattle rancher. He was a big part of the Bottled in Bond Act of 1897."

"I know who he is, Fred. You're just making this out like it's a problem. You're likely the only person on earth who cares. Was it true that the whiskey in the Chessman was the greatest whiskey you've ever tasted?"

She was right. From my experience, people only care if something tastes good. For most casual drinkers, the history of whiskey was a nice addition to the story, but the main squeeze was how good was the juice.

"Yes, that's true," I said. "It remains the greatest bourbon I have ever tasted."

"Then what's the big deal?"

"I was wrong. Should I make a public apology?"

"For Pete's sake. This is ridiculous."

"What? I messed up."

"You didn't have key information about the whiskey in question when you said it was the best whiskey ever. Now you have that information. You don't need to apologize for this. Just be honest if it ever comes up again."

"So this isn't a problem?"

"No. But I love you. Now give me a kiss."

Jaclyn always knows how to make me feel better. But I reflected a lot on Old Crow after that. And not from a research perspective—but just how much I built up this vision of what the brand was and what it stood for. I built this story in my head that it was one of the bestselling, best-tasting bourbons ever, culminating with the iconic chess piece. But I was wrong on so many levels. Dr. James C. Crow wasn't a doctor, and the chess piece didn't even contain Old Crow whiskey.

And the truth is, the bourbon industry has always been perfectly comfortable telling tall tales to sell whiskey or to spin a story in favor of the industry. Whether it was selling a folk legend, like Crow being a doctor, or falsely claiming an original formula, whiskey's DNA is lying about its DNA. That was until the likes of Cowdery and other writers started coming out of the woodwork and uncovering the true histories through lawsuits, congressional testimony, and interviews with old-timers who didn't care about exposing the truth.

Even with people chronicling every detail in American whiskey today, new companies still find ways to make up backstories and lie about their whiskey origins. It's one of the most absolutely frustrating things in covering this incredible business.

But no story ever hit me harder than discovering that the Chessmen did not actually contain Old Crow.

As I ruminated on it, I did have one glowing new revelation. The production error occurred in the 1960s, as did the crow conservation movement and the chess pieces.

What else might have happened to the brand over the past several decades?

In my career, I've tracked whiskey history through wars. The Revolutionary, Civil, World War I, and World War II all are well-represented in my books. But I had never really looked into Vietnam. Perhaps that's because it's never come up in my interviews, and the Vietnam War isn't exactly a fun topic for a distillery tour.

So the "Old Crow" I loved turning out not to be Old Crow at all just may have been the greatest thing to happen to my research. Because it opened a door I didn't see coming—Vietnam.

CHAPTER 12

VIETNAM

WHEN I WAS a kid, I remember watching Vietnam War movies and pretending to be like the soldiers in my backyard. I hid behind bushes, jumped into the shallow creek, and crawled through pockets of mud with my BB gun slung over my shoulder. And when I was hanging with my fellow BB gun warriors, I cut the sleeves off my T-shirt so my meaty arms could be seen from far away in the event the enemy was near. *That'll intimidate them, for sure*, I thought, *just like the cool soldiers in the movie* Platoon*!*

I'd flip open the top of my Shasta, the generic soda pop of the Minnick household, and slam it just like the soldiers—or really, actors—did in the base scenes. Some movies showed all sorts of parties in Vietnam, from drugs to booze and brothels to love affairs. That portrayal turned out to be a disappointment once I joined the military as an adult. We didn't have any of that crap in Iraq! Hell, we had to bootleg our alcohol into the country with the fear of being court-martialed under the General Orders. I remember sitting in my bunk and wishing we could party like they did in Vietnam.

And boy, not only did they not have to illegally transport their alcohol in country, but the government also made sure they had access to the good stuff—Old Crow, which employed a team to solely work with the government to make sure their whiskey was available to soldiers.

I mean, can you imagine that?

Vietnam veteran Tom Equels, a Cobra helicopter pilot, told me that he received a monthly ration card that allowed him to buy a pint of whiskey at the Post Exchange (PX). There was also a beachside Quonset hut outfitted as a bar. "We would fly three or four combat missions a day. As a gunship pilot, I was exchanging fire with enemy combat and that's stressful, which is why pilots accounted for a little more partying than you may see than with other people," says Equels, who used whiskey as a literary device in his novel *The Horseman's Tale*, about a Vietnam veteran recovering from the war.

The ration card looked like a lacquered sheet my grandma might have gotten at church bingo, a four-sided, folded bluish-gray card that sported a shield with a sword and opened to a "US Military Assistance Command, Vietnam" offering beer, liquor, wine, tobacco, and a slew of bigger items, such as a TV and typewriter.

"Whiskey was like a $1.15 a pint. Cigarettes were the big one," Equels recalled. In fact, one full side of the ration card was dedicated to smokes.

The whiskey industry coveted these nineteen- to

twenty-five-year-old soldiers fighting in Vietnam, one of the bourbon industry's last growth demographics. In fact, while bourbon sales were down 30 percent in some markets in the late 1960s, soldiers bought more than three million bottles from 1966 to 1969 in Vietnam with their rations. Jim Beam was the category leader with 1.5 million sold, and National Distillers' brands Old Grand-Dad and Old Crow finished in the top four.[1] Every distillery knew creating fans in the military was the strongest growth potential for their product, and many hoped to capture the loyalty of drafted soldiers looking for a relief from the stresses of war.

But there were no normal importers bringing in bourbon and other spirits. Doing business in Vietnam required working with shady third parties who knew how to maneuver several governments at one time to get a case of bourbon in front of a soldier who didn't know if he'd live another day.

Jim Beam worked through a former CIA operative with a checkered past named William J. Crum, whom *TIME* magazine dubbed the "Money King of Vietnam."

Born in China to American parents, Crum started his empire working in Korea as a liquor distributor, selling bourbon to Post Exchanges (military commissaries) during the lead-up to and throughout the Korean War. Crum expanded into all exported goods, but not through normal channels. He allegedly built a smuggling business that sold everything from headphones to whiskey to the U.S. military retailers. And although he was investigated for kickbacks and smuggling, the charges were dropped and Crum, according to *TIME*, said: "Everyone has a price...whether he be a private or a four-star general."[2]

National Distillers worked with a company called Envoy-International Asia, managed by Glenn Faulks, a former army officer, who knew how to navigate the military through proper channels. But he noted in a 1970 memorandum that the liquor business was "corrupt and fickle" in Southeast Asia.[3] I am not sure if Faulks incriminated himself, but he definitely had knowledge of the illegal system that put whiskey in the Vietnam market.

Crum controlled the market and developed a system of kick-backs, where noncommissioned officers managing the bars in Vietnam received $1 per case of whiskey purchased by the U.S. military. Generals, sergeant majors, and lower-ranking soldiers all were caught up in a scheme to defraud the government and accept bribes from the likes of Crum and Faulks.

The key difference between the two, however, was that Faulks cooperated with the federal investigation, while Crum evaded sub-poenas and became the U.S. government's central focus in building a case against the corrupt system selling goods to American sol-diers. Faulks would certainly face scrutiny, fines, and embarrass-ment for his role, and Crum's name would be dragged through the mud in the media, but the feds ultimately placed their focus on the clients—Jim Beam and National Distillers—which were providing bribes at a much higher level.

Jim Beam awarded college scholarships to the children of gov-ernment procurement officers in Vietnam, although supposedly there was no conflict or "no strings attached whatsoever,"[4] testified Mel Peterson, who also said Jim Beam executives were not aware of the Crum profits they raked in from Vietnam.

In addition to other gifts linked to Beam, National Distillers' presents to government buyer families included a $1,400 vacation, pool chemicals, an Abercrombie & Fitch Town and Country rotisserie for cooking chickens, and a slew of other items that would make home life more comfortable.

Throughout the hearings and investigation, one bribe after another was revealed, and Crum quickly became the scapegoat for the whole scandal. And at the center of it all was Jim Beam, whom Crum told would make the No. 1-selling bourbon in Vietnam. Beam paid for PX personnel's official trips and put them up in villas throughout Southeast Asia. The letter that seemed to have proved Crum's guilt to Beam came in 1965, when Crum wrote Peterson about courting Air Force buyers.

"I showed them the brand-new house I am decorating for them, and they are absolutely delighted," Crum wrote. "We are getting along like peas in a pod and they are real sharp operators so I feel we are going to get a lot more action than we did in the past. Believe me, I am practically moving right in with these boys without jeopardizing our reputation. Got them a delightful four-bedroom house, which I am doing the living room in natural rush rattan, installing wall-to-wall rush carpet and bamboo bar.

"Also, I include in the rent the cook and two maids, utilities and other local expenses so they pay me in dollars twice a month at quite a saving. The cook is a real pro and their cuisine will be only second to none in Southeast Asia."[5]

Crum, who earned a 10 percent commission on $2.3 million sold of Jim Beam, later hid from officials on his yacht and would die in a mysterious house fire six years after a three-hundred-page 1971 Senate investigation report placed blame on him and the U.S.

military for creating a system that allowed for such "corruption, criminality and moral compromise."[6]

While National Distillers faced ridicule for the scandal, most of the blame directed at National was actually deserved by Faulks's firm. In fact, the National Distillers' representative, more so than any other civilian, seemingly outlined how the scheme worked and told investigators what rocks to look under for information on people taking kickbacks. And when the dust settled and the media set their attention on Jim Beam, not Old Crow, perhaps it was because of the utter arrogance the Beam executive offered in testimony.

Peterson never denied the bribes and made it out like it was all part of the job, which for some in the liquor business, it is. "We hoped our products would be purchased because of this," Peterson testified in regard to building villas for military buyers. "I have to get my whiskey in the marketplace to create a demand for it."[7]

Peterson's in-country agent, Crum, would appear on Mike Wallace's *60 Minutes* segment to proclaim his innocence, but this only upset the Senate committee more and placed a bigger bullseye on Beam.

According to the Committee on Government Operations's report conclusions, Peterson had acted improperly when he encouraged Crum to obtain favored treatment for Jim Beam products from PX personnel living in the villa.

"Peterson and the James Beam Co. itself unhesitatingly accepted the profits from the Vietnam sales promoted by William Crum. By the same token, they should be made to bear certain of the responsibility for actions Crum implemented for the sake of their products," the report said.

The committee further chastised Beam and its executive, Peterson, for encouraging Lou Bernard, the civilian buyer for the Far East Locker Fund in Tokyo, to stockpile three thousand cases of Jim Beam, free of storage charges, in expectation of a shortage in Vietnam. In return, Peterson arranged for Bernard's son to receive a college scholarship financed by the Blum-Kovler Foundation that was headed by the president of Jim Beam and the former chairman of the board of the company. "The impropriety of this kind of indirect gift is plain. Such practices should be subject to the same prohibitions and the same penalties as the giving of gifts and gratuities directly, as set forth in military regulations," the committee wrote.

While Jim Beam felt the committee's fury for nearly two full pages of the ten-page conclusion, National Distillers' scathing was only one sentence long, and that fell under the purview of its agent paying bribes to warehouse workers. Thus, Jim Beam took the brunt of the criticism.

And while this whole Vietnam black market ordeal would lead to significant government purchasing overhauls, the committee clearly would not have taken such a strong stance if Crum had testified and if Peterson had not been so brazen about the effort to bribe officials. They wanted a military head to put on a platter. And on more than one occasion, the general of the army's chief of staff was discussed in testimony. Did Crum, a former CIA operative, have special deals lined up with higher-ups? Is that why he evaded interrogation?

His "house fire" death only deepens my suspicions. If social media existed then, all the conspiracy theorists would have sounded off on how a former CIA asset died in a house fire. I've studied this PX saga and have come to my own conclusions as it relates to the whiskey market. Jim Beam was on the rise at the time, while National Distillers was on the verge of moving on. In 1972, they would close several bourbon-related operations, including Old Taylor—which, it turns out, made the greatest whiskey I have ever tasted—and would begin to diversify their portfolio and marketing spends. Beam was all in on bourbon; National Distillers was on the way out. I don't agree with their methods, but the investment Jim Beam made in Vietnam paid off, because those veterans would drink Jim Beam for years to come.

I have also wondered why it was Beam that took the brunt of the heat. Sure, Peterson was a little cocky and National Distillers seemingly cooperated with federal officials more than Beam did, especially with Crum dodging the interview requests, but many people who either received bribes from or worked for National Distillers agents pled the Fifth Amendment to avoid incriminating themselves. If this happened in today's media landscape, the *Saturday Night Live* cast would have a five-minute bit about National Distillers buying a government buyer's wife a rotisserie and pool cleaning supplies. How did they prevent the same ridicule?

Faulks openly shared that the liquor system in Southeast Asia was corrupt, and his team members shared with investigators exactly how much in kickbacks it took to sell a case of whiskey to the PX exchange in the 1960s. It is definitely possible that National Distillers' agent fed information on Crum to keep the attention on Jim Beam and off them.

It certainly would explain why the Beam and National Distillers rivalry went deeper than traditional sales rivalries. And it wouldn't have been the first time distillers ratted on one another for their own benefit. Pappy Van Winkle, after all, went scorched earth on his competitors in the price-fixing hearings of the 1940s.

But my greatest takeaway from the Vietnam era is how badly Jim Beam wanted to fight for every case sale of whiskey while National Distillers was promoting to new markets via chess pieces, crow conservation, and light whiskey. Sure, the Vietnam deal was a black eye for Jim Beam, but it was one of many promotional efforts to capture military-aged men with bourbon, while National Distillers withdrew from that market and put its focus on other categories.

It reminded me of the old adage: "Don't forget who brought you to the dance." Jim Beam cared deeply about the bourbon drinker. National Distillers was moving on.

I was deeply disappointed that National Distillers would have thrown in the towel. Surely, the workers at Old Crow had a little more fight in them. I knew the market was changing, moving away from bourbon in the 1970s, but Old Crow couldn't just give up.

Then, on a random drive home one day with the kids in the back seat, Julian swung a miniature baseball bat and thumped Oscar in the arm. Julian was four and Oscar was eight, but only five pounds separated the two. Oscar instantly retaliated, punching Julian on the thigh.

"Stop it," Jaclyn ordered.

They ignored her, and Julian poured a full can of soda water on his older brother and then threw the can.

"You little piece of..." Oscar said as he head-butted his brother and proceeded to take off both their seat belts for a full-tilt driving wrestling match.

"Enough," I barked, pulling the car into a Walgreens parking lot. "Boys, what are you doing?"

"Julian started it, Dad," Oscar said.

"No, I didn't."

"Yes, you did."

They pushed each other.

I wanted to laugh. I think Jaclyn wanted to laugh, too, but she's far more mature than I am and knows we cannot show the boys any wiggle room in these delicate moments.

"Boys, how long can you fight? Seriously, you can't do this forever."

"Yeah, we can, Dad. We're brothers," Oscar said.

That's when it hit me. Oscar and Julian will never. Ever. Stop. Fighting. They don't hate each other, and hopefully they never do, but the long-standing sibling rivalry will carry on when they're in their twenties, thirties, forties, and beyond. People are just wired that way. We want to prove to our parents that we're better than our sibling, and business rivals spar until the bitter end.

Even though National Distillers closed several Kentucky facilities after the Vietnam ordeal, I suspected Old Crow had to put up a bit more of a fight, just so National Distillers could stick it to Jim Beam one more time.

There was something about my own personal evolution, too, with this Old Crow research. It started early in my career and had been an up-and-down ride that led to disappointment, intrigue, and several shocking finds. I had now entered the 1980s, the decade Old Crow would soon fall to the bottom shelf, while its fierce rival, Jim Beam, blossomed with the likes of Hank Williams Jr. parading Beam on stage to drink with his "rowdy friends."

By now, I knew the Old Crow whiskey quality had declined, the marketing tactics had failed, and National Distillers was checking out of the Old Crow business. Its facilities were built prior to the 1972 update to the Clean Water Act, which restricted where it could dump coal ash and wastewater, and all its warehouses were in the floodplain. In 1978, a flood filled a warehouse three ricks high, about twelve feet, and barrels of whiskey were floating out of the warehouse, Bob Johnson told me.

That means National Distillers was struggling to market Old Crow and its dated facilities made it a prime target for acquisition. Little did I know, though, the company that would buy it, its bitter rival Jim Beam, was the more desperate of the two.

CHAPTER 13

OH, CANADA!

AT THE DAWN of the 1980s, the alcohol industry faced significant scrutiny, and the Reagan administration actually tried to deregulate the whiskey business. Since Prohibition, the government had kept excise agents on distillery sites at all times. These excise agents, also known as gaugers, kept track of all the proofs and made sure there were no illegal activities happening at the distillery. This was the federal government's way of keeping track of weights, barrel inventory, and authenticity of whiskey to ensure the product being advertised on the label matched what was actually in the bottle. At every distillery in the country, the agent on-site had a set of keys to the stillhouse, warehouses, and cistern room, where the whiskey is dumped from the barrel.

The Bureau of Alcohol, Tobacco, and Firearms also made sure that every booze label contained accurate claims and there were no illegal additives included in the product. This regulation process cost taxpayers money, and Reagan saw no need to keep these agents on payroll and wanted to send the responsibility of alcohol administration to the states.

When the Senate held hearings on abolishing the Bureau of Alcohol, Tobacco, and Firearms, which oversaw the liquor industry, state administrators and distillers pushed back, essentially proving to the public that elected officials have no idea how the alcohol industry works.

"The product integrity that BATF provides by on-site inspections, laboratory testing, record audits, and regulatory guidance has assured the American public that both imported and domestic alcoholic beverages they purchase contain what the label claims," testified Ed Soderman, a state official for the Department of Liquor, Licenses and Control for Arizona. "This assurance is assumed without question by the public that the products they purchase are not contaminated by foreign or harmful substances and are similar to other products so labeled. The majority of alcoholic beverages sold in any state are not produced within its borders. Again, it would be next to impossible for a state to attempt to ensure the products manufactured in another state are in compliance with the laws and regulations. States have no authority to make out-of-state on-site inspections and would have to accept a producer's representations and establish a consistent and questionably efficient duplication of testing procedures."[1]

The truth is, those federal employees befriended the distillery workers and often helped prevent mistakes, such as accidentally mixing a rye and a bourbon in a holding tank. Distillery execs and lobbyists testified that they wanted to keep the federal government in their existing role, because they were essentially de facto consultants. Norman Hayden, the president of the Old Fitzgerald Distillery, testified that keeping things the same or replacing the ATF with a similar government body was the best means to protect the public. "The need to protect this source of a great amount of government revenue and to protect the public is best served by one cohesive unit having ready expertise in all aspects of the alcohol beverage industry laws and regulations," Hayden declared.[2]

The government ended up listening to the likes of Hayden and maintained an agent presence at distilleries, but it slashed budgets to the point it eventually eliminated agents on-site and tax stamp requirements. So it was a deregulation by defunding, of sorts. In an interview with me, Hayden blamed that moment for the "shit show that is whiskey today."

Hayden, who passed away in 2022, believed that the modern whiskey business got away with more false claims, such as claiming a product was the first distillery in a state when it was not true, than it had back in his day, because there was no longer sufficient oversight. Indeed, a brand could claim in advertisements it was the most award-winning whiskey in the country and nobody, outside of a few bloggers, would fact-check it.

However, that deregulation moment came on the heels of bourbon's decline, and many believe it's the reason why distillers started experimenting with barrel finishing, where the whiskey is taken from the original barrel and placed in a used one. While this process certainly adds new flavors from the secondary barrels, such as former port and cognac casks, I do not think the federal agents would have allowed such experimenting if they were still on the premises in the modern age of bourbon. In addition, in the early

1980s, distillers became more creative in their marketing, creating specialized products, such as single-barrel and small-batch offerings, which may have never been allowed if the Reagan administration hadn't pursued deregulation.

Age International created the concept of "single barrel" (when the product only contains one barrel) in 1984 with Blanton's, a new brand named after the former George T. Stagg CEO Albert Blanton. And in 1987, Jim Beam marketed the term *small batch*.

The only problem was Canada.

In the 1980s, as the U.S. government withdrew regulations over the spirits industry, Canada increased its regulations and began regularly testing products for ethyl carbamate, a compound that can occur in fermented beverages under certain conditions, such as significant contact with copper during production. The Canadian government said ethyl carbamate caused cancer. Now, I vaguely knew about ethyl carbamate being a carcinogen because of this nifty quote from Matt Strickland, distiller of Iron City in Pennsylvania: "The cancer risks of EC have been assessed over the years on mice, but no studies have been done on humans. Currently, EC is listed as a Group 2A carcinogen, meaning it's 'probably carcinogenic to humans.' This is just below the Group 1A rating of 'fully carcinogenic to humans.' 'Probably carcinogenic' is enough for me to say that I don't want it in my drink."[3]

The FDA studied what causes ethyl carbamate for nearly thirty years and concluded that when it comes to whiskey, wrong barley types and copper in the still cause the carcinogen to form.

Canada began testing for the compound in 1979 and established a regulation in 1985 that distilled spirits could contain no more than 150 parts per billion of ethyl carbamate.

From here, the Canadian government began testing every wine, beer, and spirit sold in the country. If a brand popped too high in its sample testing, the government ordered the bottles off the shelf. Dozens of wines, sherries, and brandies were hit, but only three bourbons.

Jim Beam contained nearly double the country's legal limit of ethyl carbamate; Ezra Brooks barely hit 175 parts per billion; and a tiny brand called Lionstone with only 200 bottles in Canada was over the limit, but its amount was not reported.

Prior to my research, I had no idea about an entire country ordering Jim Beam off its shelves in the 1980s. This Canadian ban could have been potentially as cataclysmic for Jim Beam as World War II distilling mandates, especially if other countries followed suit.

South Korea, a prominent bourbon market, added similar regulations a few years after Canada did, and the U.S. FDA assembled a committee to reduce ethyl carbamate in distilled spirits that saw nearly 400 parts per million of the compounds in domestic whiskey samples in 1988. While this clearly was an industry-wide problem, Jim Beam was the face of ethyl carbamate overages in Canada.

Every 1980s Jim Beam executive had to be concerned that other countries would adopt Canada's mandate. If they did, it would all but shut Jim Beam down.

One company happened to own many whiskey brands that tested comfortably under the 150 parts per million requirements—National Distillers. Johnson said Old Crow's ethyl carbamate levels were 45 parts per million, which were six times less than Jim Beam's. "We don't have no copper," Johnson told me. "That's one of the things that always shocked the hell out of people when I tell them National did not use copper in their stills." Not only was copper used in distillation equipment, but it's also one of the hallmark marketing pieces to American whiskey history. In the 1800s, distillers marketed their whiskey as "copper distilled," and consumers believed that the copper helped make the whiskey smooth. To this day, the copper still is celebrated in American whiskey, with dozens of brands placing copper in its name. It's the base metal inside most prominent stills!

But apparently, too much copper in making whiskey leads to a carcinogen that stopped Beam from selling in Canada in the 1980s. And I couldn't help but wonder: *Was this why Beam really bought National Distillers' bourbon portfolio?*

Surrounded by police officers, John Candy's character Burton Mercer ordered an "orange whip" in the 1980 film *The Blues Brothers*. The vodka, rum, and triple sec cocktail, a dump truck of a drink, was a sign of the times: People liked sweet drinks. Even the manliest of manly dudes like the Blues Brothers were sipping that sweet concoction.

And at nearly every bar in the country, some sort of liqueur was drawing center shelf attention. In the early 1980s, cordials and liqueurs were the fastest growing categories in spirits and had even passed bourbon in total case sales.

In 1984, a company the bourbon fans will know all too well—Sazerac—introduced three new lines of liqueurs: Vieux Carre, a coffee and chicory liqueur; Capistrano, a hazelnut cordial; and Aspen Glacial, a blue-colored peppermint sweet drink. The company president at the time, Peter Bordeaux, told media that the oversupply of neutral spirits helped spark the cordial movement after World War II with brands creating new liqueur types and flavors. "That boom is obviously continuing," he said in 1984. "Liqueurs are being served over ice cream, in coffee and with other drinks to make exotic flavored beverages which are enjoyed any time of the day. The only limit to the use of liqueurs is one's own imagination."[4]

Most spirits companies were rushing to start a liqueur brand because the sales were explosive and the product was so inexpensive to make. All you needed was to start with a grain neutral spirit, add something sweet, and voilà, you have something you can bottle with a few preservatives. The category was an absolute quick cash cow, as proven by Bailey's, which grew from forty thousand cases sold in 1979 to one million in 1983.[5]

Spirits executives no doubt looked at the rise of liqueurs similar to that of vodka. It just sort of came out of nowhere and was propelled by the younger generation, who loved sweet soft drinks. Jim Beam executives must have known that if they didn't start a significant liqueur portfolio they would be left in the dust.

And sitting with the most lucrative portfolio in all of spirits was National Distillers, holding the DeKuyper line of liqueurs, which covered every sweet category. National also had interests in chemicals and energy, having diversified its portfolio significantly. In fact, when analysts discussed its earnings potential with potential stock market players, they rarely even led with their spirits division.

In reality, National Distillers was no longer a bourbon company at its core. By the early 1980s, it was checking out from the spirits game altogether. And it held onto one of the most coveted liqueur lines in all of spirits—DeKuyper.

Even though the twenty-one to twenty-five-year-olds loved them because sweet drinks reminded their palates of the sodas of their youth, and National had the multimillion case sales of DeKuyper, the distillery saw an opportunity to completely divest from spirits and focus on its energy efforts.

Enter the golden child of bourbon in the 1980s: Jim Beam, whose executives feared its bourbon sales were about to collapse and rushed to diversify its offerings.

After a failed attempt to buy Southern Comfort from Brown-Forman, Jim Beam pursued National Distillers' cordials.

"DeKuyper was so hot," Mike Donohoe, the national sales director for Jim Beam at the time, told me in a phone interview.

Donohoe, a former professional football player for the Green Bay Packers, recalls walking into a conference room with his fellow Jim Beam execs. Jim Beam was part of the American Brands, a cigarette company, and its meeting rooms were filled with ex-athletes who now worked liquor.

In fact, Jim Beam historian Jim Kokoris says the sales team then loaded up on athletes, in part, because they could keep up with the iconic master distiller Booker Noe, who was known to stay out late and have a good time. "All the younger sales guys were college athletes. I used to hang out with these guys on the road, and those nights were pretty wild. Their whole goal was to try to drink as much as Booker," Kokoris recalled.

I can easily imagine a smoke-filled meeting room packed with ex-jocks reliving their glory days with a bottle of bourbon on the table and all sorts of inappropriate jokes being shared.

At any rate, in 1985, Jim Beam executive vice president Rich Reese, a former Major League Baseball player, Donohoe, and then-CEO Barry Berrish, among others, began investigating what it would take to buy the DeKuyper line from National Distillers. They quietly talked to their distribution partners and came away thinking the liqueur trend would last another decade, at least, and that the DeKuyper sales would diversify their portfolio to the point that Beam could weather the drop in bourbon sales they were anticipating. They were ready to make an offer for DeKuyper line.

Meanwhile, Jim Beam would soon be alerted to the ethyl carbamate issues in Canada that could decimate the brand if other countries adopted similar policies. When it made its initial offer to National Distillers for DeKuyper, Beam had no interest in Old Crow.

But to its surprise, National wanted to sell everything.

National desired to offload its dated facilities and sagging bourbon brands and focus on its chemical and propane companies. If Beam would bite, it had the opportunity to rid its entire drinks portfolio in one fell swoop.

Then, as Beam was considering the counteroffer, it was hit with the ethyl carbamate news. The timing was perfect for both sides. As Donohoe told me, "the whole [ethyl carbamate] thing was resolved with very little business lost."

But when Beam purchased National for $545 million in April 1987, the carcinogen was not mentioned in the press release or the follow-up stories. The headlines focused on the fact that National Distillers, a company built by a man who had once been featured on a *TIME* magazine cover, was leaving the spirits industry entirely.

"We've sold our birthright," company spokesperson Richard Tilghman said. "We're a very different company now."[6] National was now a company focusing on polyethylene resins, while Jim Beam genuinely cared about the spirits business and knew how to grow its portfolio. This acquisition was the end of one era and the beginning of another.

And if this sale had never happened, I do not think the bourbon boom would have ever taken off, for a few reasons.

Jim Beam was arguably the most important parent company of the twentieth century, with its "small batch" portfolio creating an entirely new category for bourbon. And at the time of Beam's launch of Booker's in 1987, its warehouses were filled with bourbon that would soon be illegal in Canada and South Korea, and would eventually fall under major U.S. scrutiny. There's no way the small batch portfolio could have launched if it didn't figure out its EC levels, and I don't think Jim Beam even would have survived the fallout if it couldn't fix the problem quickly. That would mean Buffalo Trace Antique Collection, Parker's Heritage, Four Roses Limited Edition Small Batch, and any number of other limited edition small batch releases never would have existed.

If Beam didn't get over this hurdle in 1987, the largest brand in bourbon would have been taken off the board, and the industry would have remained a bottom dweller in the spirits space.

Instead, Beam immediately put the National Distillers whiskey into its own product lines, solved its Canada issue, and launched the Small Batch Collection whiskey program in 1992, forever redefining how whiskey was marketed.

The National Distillers whiskey saved Jim Beam, whose parent company, which was then Fortune Brands, purchased Maker's Mark in 2005. Both Beam and Maker's Mark, I believe, spearheaded the 2000s bourbon boom through their marketing of affordable bourbons, such as Booker's, Knob Creek, Maker's 46, and many others, while other distilleries mostly received attention for their hard-to-obtain and rather expensive products, which grew the market with the upper middle class. But Beam never moved away from keeping bourbon affordable and in the hands of the working class, bourbon's crown jewel of the consumer.

If Beam didn't acquire National Distillers, who knows what would have happened to Old Crow's whiskey stocks or Jim Beam's fate with its ethyl carbamate issues. Thus, Jim Beam's 1987 acquisition was the most important business move of the past one hundred years in American whiskey. It saved two companies. But neither Beam nor National got credit for this bold move.

Instead, we historians negatively painted Jim Beam's legacy for dismantling Crow.

After all, Jim Beam followed a rigid plan for each National Distillers' brand to complement its sales of Jim Beam. Old Grand-Dad and Old Taylor were meant to box out Jack Daniel's, and to take attention away from Old Forester. As for Old Crow, it was relegated to the bottom shelf to compete with Ten High and Walker's Deluxe, two rotgut blended whiskeys that couldn't hold the original Old Crow's label dust. This was something all of us Old Crow fans always knew, but to read it in an internal memo and hear people talk about it, that hurt on another level.

"Jim Beam had competed so hard with Old Crow for so long that when they got their hands on it they wanted to kill it, but they couldn't because it still had fairly decent sales," said bourbon historian Chuck Cowdery, who actually worked with Jim Beam after the acquisition to write sales guides on the brands. "But Beam did not put one penny behind Old Crow. They put their lowest quality whiskey that was barely legal under the label."

Almost overnight, the Old Crow brand transformed from composite four- to eight-year-old bourbon to three-year-old barely drinkable whiskey.

When I first started my Old Crow research, another prominent historian, Mike Veach, told me Jim Beam's handling of Crow was "criminal." That always stuck with me. Veach, like Cowdery, was a mentor to me, and I carried that "criminal" mantra throughout my every archive visit, interview, and newspaper search, always believing in the back of my mind that Jim Beam had gutted and destroyed Old Crow. In a sense, it did.

And I and others hated Beam for it. We had all fallen in love with pre-Beam Old Crow whiskey. It just hit us differently than anything else.

But the more I learned, the more I realized Beam had done nothing wrong. It put Old Crow out of its misery.

National Distillers didn't care about the bourbon category anymore, let alone the Old Crow brand, and pissed away all that great whiskey with poorly managed marketing campaigns.

Maybe Beam did hold a grudge from the Vietnam era. Maybe

it needed the whiskey to bolster its exports. Or perhaps it planned to use National Distillers' whiskey to jump-start Knob Creek, the flagship of the Small Batch Collection.

The more I learned, the less I found myself hating Jim Beam for killing what I considered to be the greatest bourbon I had ever tasted. Hell, the Old Crow I fell in love with wasn't really Old Crow at all.

I spent nearly two decades of off-and-on research to prove that Jim Beam had intentionally gutted my favorite brand. While that is partly true, my final take is that if Beam hadn't bought National Distillers, the bourbon industry would not have made its comeback in the 1990s and early 2000s.

In the early 1990s, Jim Beam's small batch portfolio started the wave of new products that would garner fans across the globe. And if it hadn't had National Distillers' whiskey to play with, who knows if this category ever would have taken off?

We certainly know National would not have done a thing with that beautiful bourbon. It was checked out of the spirits category entirely.

I know how to admit when I am wrong. While I would like to see Jim Beam bring back Old Crow with the same grandiosity it has Old Grand-Dad and Old Overholt in recent years, its executives should not be persecuted for mishandling a brand that meant so much to me. But also, what does that say about me?

I had this Old Crow research compulsion for so long. I told myself that this history needed to be written, and it helped me focus on something other than my own problems. But truthfully, I did not know why I was so obsessed. And now that it was over, what was I going to do?

I grabbed an Old Crow Chessman, jumped in my Ford Escape, and drove to the Versailles, Kentucky, cemetery.

CHAPTER 14

SAYING GOODBYE

JAMES C. CROW died on the Johnson farm distillery along Glenn's Creek, close to where Glenns Creek Distillery is located today. The details of his burial site are not clear, but there is a small cemetery near the Castle & Key Distillery, which was once Old Taylor. The only known details about Crow's original burial site was that it was along Glenn's Creek, and that grave site is a stone's throw away from the creek. Is this cemetery where Crow was originally buried?

It's plausible.

Nonetheless, Crow's wife later moved his remains to the Versailles Cemetery, which is cut between the two main roads of the small, yet wealthy, town near Lexington.

Crow is buried in section B2, where a towering oak fell on a couple of headstones in 2023. One monument was broken in half and several smaller ones were bent, cracked, or completely knocked over.

Crow's headstone, perfectly erect, looks as though it has been out to sea, discolored by splotches of white and green lichen.

The inscription says: "James C. Crow. Died April 28, 1856. Loved life."

It was cold, almost freezing, the day I visited. As I poured a couple ounces of whiskey onto the soft mushy ground, which was strange considering how cold it was, I wondered if even a little drop would make it down to his casket. "Cheers, my friend," I said, raising my metal cup to the gravestone and then to my lips. The quick splash against my gums fell underneath my tongue, caressed my cheeks. Soon, the sensation covered my whole palate and the flavors just erupted with the greatest bourbon I had ever tasted. One more time.

I touched the gravestone. Its edge was rough and sharp. I wanted to drag my finger across it but feared I'd cut myself and likely get some sort of weird disease only transmissible at graveyards. Is that a thing?

And then, I just started talking.

"Hey, James C. Crow. Wanted to thank you for what you did for bourbon. I mean, we know you're not a doctor. Did you tell people you were a doctor?

"Whatever you were, there is no doubt you knew how to make whiskey and that you changed how whiskey was made. That sour mash technique is now used by just about every American distiller.

"And boy, did people love Old Crow. There was this one fella trying to bribe his constituents with shots of Old Crow just to vote for him. Yeah, that's illegal now."

I took another swig of whiskey. It hit the back of my throat, nearly missing my tongue. When it's cold, I kick it back a little quicker so I can get my hands back in my pockets.

"In fact, people loved Old Crow so much that all sorts of people laid claim to the name. People who worked with you testified about how you made whiskey. I wondered, too, is there any more information on Albert, the black man you taught how to distill?"

What am I doing? I am asking a grave question. Well, why not? I've gone this far. I'm literally standing at this dude's grave after spending two decades studying him and the brand named after him. Besides, there's nobody here to see how silly this looks.

"I tried, but I couldn't find much on Albert. Learned about him through one of the lawsuits I was telling you about. The last one went all the way to the Supreme Court. While you have your name all over a bourbon brand, you are also forever tied into U.S. trademark law. I bet that's what you really wanted for your life."

I laughed, again fully knowing how weird this would appear to anybody within earshot. And then I went on telling Crow, or his tombstone, about my research and all the wild turns it took over a decade.

I looked down at my cup.

"Oh, it's empty. Give me a second, James. Can I call you James?"

I went back to my car and grabbed another pull for my graveside chat. Took a swig and kept catching up with my friend. And I just kept chatting about his life and how his name became the most important brand in bourbon history.

"I wonder how you would feel about getting marketed the way you did. I mean, I hope you were cool with crows, the bird, because they practically had you two intertwined at one point."

I squatted and pressed my hands in the grass. I took another swig.

"James, I don't go to cemeteries often, and they always creep me out. So maybe that's all that's going on here. Damn, it's cold!"

I started to wonder, *if I had known the whiskey in the Old Crow Chess Piece was not really from the Old Crow Distillery, would I have been as obsessed with James C. Crow?*

"Probably not," I said, looking at the grave. "But I am glad I was."

The tears welled up. There was no stopping them.

"Tracing your life and brand gave me purpose when I didn't feel like I had any. I left much of my life in war. I'll never be that person again. And I was so angry that I nearly killed myself. Finding you gave me something to hunt for for nearly twenty years."

I looked at his grave one more time and then tilted my head toward his wife, Catherine, and daughter, Elizabeth. They were buried next to him within ten years of his death. In one recounting of James C. Crow's life, a friend of his said he died penniless.[1] But I think he died rich, with the love of his life in his heart and a daughter he likely rocked on his knee and read poetry to. Did he want to live to see her grow old? Of course. But don't tell me a person with a family died "penniless." They had purpose, a reason to live far greater than money.

I realized that all this time my quest to know more about James C. Crow was nothing more than me searching for myself. I guess some people climb a mountain, run a marathon, or backpack through Europe. I followed a man to his grave and connected to his family and the whiskey he made, because that's what I care about.

One of these days, like my buddy James, my bones will rest

underground, with only a stone marking my spot in sea of graves. I hope that the love of my life, Jaclyn, is buried next to me long after I pass and that my boys have kids of their own and find somebody who loves them as much as Jaclyn and I love each other.

I touched Crow's grave one more time and said, "Thank you for everything. Thank you for helping me find myself."

Tears streaming down my face, I called Jaclyn.

"Hey, babes," she answered.

I sniffled.

"Are you okay?" she asked.

"Just really love you, baby."

"Awe, I love you too."

Nearly twenty years ago, I almost took my life to hide from the pain I was facing. And now, here I was at a graveyard, finally fully understanding the journey I had taken. I know why God spared my life. And my purpose was never to be a bourbon writer and discover some plot against a forgotten brand. It was to be with my two boys, day after day, reading to them, playing catch with them, teaching them to ride a bike, helping them learn a single leg for their first wrestling tournament, and showing them how to become good and respectable men. It's to softly scratch Jaclyn's back during a boring movie and wait an hour in the Target pickup line because she needs me to.

"Hey, would you like to go to Chip and Cheese for dinner?" I asked Jaclyn after a brief moment of silence.

"Oh, good idea," she replied.

At our favorite Mexican restaurant Limon Y Sol, which we nicknamed "Chip and Cheese" because Julian guzzled the cheese sauce and smashed the chips as a toddler, the Minnick boys kicked one another underneath the table, Oscar flicked a spit wad at his brother, and Jaclyn looked at me with her big brown eyes while sipping a tequila drink. We let the boys do their thing and just looked at one another. I could feel my heart racing faster.

She reached across the table, touching the top of my hand.

"I love you, Beans."

EPILOGUE

NOT LONG AFTER my suicide attempt, we sold the downtown condo where I nearly ended my life. Before we moved out, I stood in the bathroom and looked at the shower. I ran my fingers along the rigid doorway, and I sat on the edge of the tub. I nearly took my last breath here. Now, I caressed the smooth porcelain and vowed "never again."

I would never have predicted my journey, but I found peace in a therapy chair, happiness in a barbecue potato chip, and an unknown tasting talent that has helped me bring joy to others around the world. Sometimes when I am on stage explaining taste mindfulness to a crowd, I pause, look at my hands and think *Look at how far we've come.*

But I could not have made it without Jaclyn. Not only did she save my life, but she also inspired and pushed me in the direction I am today. When our family takes long car trips, with Julian and Oscar wailing on one another, I catch Jaclyn's brown eyes and we when our eyes lock.

Of course, the journey is ongoing, and I can't stop working to become a better person.

While my taste mindfulness journey and family life were at all-time high points, I was obese.

In 2022, while waiting for a plane, I felt my tight shirt untuck from behind and a cool breeze find my posterior. My pants were tight. My shirt barely fit, and I couldn't button my blazer without the risk of a popped button whacking some stranger's head.

I weighed 255 pounds, the heaviest I had ever been, and my belly protruded like it was another person eager to eat a whole cake. I blamed the pandemic, with live stream tastings every day. All those bourbon calories went straight to my hips. But the truth is, after my military career ended, I had let myself go, never finding a healthy hobby that could keep the weight off.

So there I was waiting in line to board and wondering, *How can I get in shape?*

A few days before, I had a bourbon dinner at Watch Hill Proper, an epic American whiskey bar, and I noticed one of the attendees had cauliflower ears. I had wrestled until my freshman year of high school and always love to chat it up with fellow wrestlers.

"Did you wrestle?" I asked.

"No," he said. "Jiujitsu."

Ah, yes, wrestling's more deadly distant cousin. Arm bars, chokes, ankle locks, and throws. Wrestling, an Olympic sport, is all about takedown and pin; Brazilian jiujitsu, a martial art, is self-defense from every position and became famous when Royce Gracie went through the UFC like a hot knife in butter in the 1990s and early 2000s.

"I've thought about doing something like that," I said. "I used to wrestle."

"You should give it a shot. I'm one of the black belts at MADE," said Andy Waner, a bourbon fan who would plant the seed for the next obsession of my life.

As we started boarding, I thought about that conversation and my physical self and the state of who I was. And this person, well, I felt like a pudgy pillow of what I used to be.

I made a quick phone call.

"Hey, I am interested in jiujitsu," I said when the person at MADE answered.

"Great. Let's get you started," said Garrett Watson, whom I would come to know as the enthusiastic owner.

"But I'm in horrible shape. Should I get in shape first?" I said, knowing full well that if I hung up the phone without an appointment I probably wouldn't call back. Was I trying to already get out of it?

"Nah, you should do it. You can only really get in shape for jiujitsu by doing jiujitsu," he said.

I committed, scheduled a private session, and showed up a few days later with no understanding of this art of strangulation.

I eventually moved from private lessons to a class, where I completely dedicated myself to the martial art. I've lost more than forty pounds since I started my Brazilian jiujitsu journey and am now a blue belt, and it was the last piece of the puzzle to finding the real me.

I do believe that correcting my physical woes not only helped my body, it also improved my mind, to the point I had the courage to write this book.

I found jiujitsu late in life, but it's important to me that my boys see Jaclyn and I focus on our physical health. We go to the gym regularly as a family, and both boys wrestle.

As for Old Crow, well, Jim Beam still keeps it on the bottom shelf with no public mention of ever doing anything with it. By now, all the old-school fans are mostly gone, and the new Old Crow has built a loyal following of people wanting three-year-old Kentucky bourbon for $12.

They did hold a press event in New York a while back to celebrate the affordability of Old Crow, and my buddy Aaron Goldfarb was covering it for VinePair. He asked the Jim Beam representative if they planned to bring back the Chessman series, and the rep had never even heard about the iconic line. I laughed when I read Aaron's closing of his story: "Indeed, at a recent press event, a Jim Beam executive grilled me on ideas for selling more White Label, seemingly having no interest in my thoughts on how to sell other brands in its portfolio, but especially Old Crow, which I continued to bring up."

"Have you considered just releasing an all-new Chessmen series?" I finally asked her.

She didn't know what I was talking about.[1]

I am no longer mad at Beam, after all, for how Old Crow fell to the wayside. Like I discovered writing this book, it was never about the bourbon. It was about me.

Speaking of the bourbon world, though, when this journey began, America's spirit was on the rise and I was there when it supplanted vodka as the top-selling category in some parts of the world. Oh, it was glorious, and it's been a true honor bringing insightful information, history, and clever tasting notes to enthusiasts. But now, bourbon is again beginning to show signs of collapse. A 2025 *Wall Street Journal* article cited the following reasons for the boom's bust: "The growing popularity of anti-obesity drugs, cannabis and low- and no-alcohol drinks is increasingly hurting sales too. The U.S. Surgeon General recently said alcohol should carry cancer warning labels, a recommendation that if enacted could hurt sales for an industry already contending with a pullback in drinking by younger people."[2]

After this article was published, Brown-Forman, owner of Jack Daniel's and Woodford Reserve, announced layoffs of 12 percent of the global workforce and the closure of its main cooperage facility. Truth is, I don't know where bourbon's heading.

In addition, throughout 2025, bourbon sales tanked in Canada after several Canadian provinces issued a ban on the sale of American spirits in retaliation to the 25 percent tariff on Canadian goods. From late February to late August, Ontario, Quebec, Manitoba, Nova Scotia, Newfoundland and Labrador, Prince Edward Island, and British Columbia ordered government-run liquor stores to remove U.S.-made alcohol, which resulted in a 66 percent dip in all American spirit sales in the United States' northern neighbor. While I took no satisfaction in this, the more recent Canadian sales offered credence to what could have happened to distillers in the 1980s with the Ethyl Carbamate situation.

So, what's bourbon's future? My dear friend, the late bourbon promoter Dave Sweet said that bourbon's collapse began when they stopped focusing on their customers who helped build the industry. Before his passing in early 2025, Dave told me that the bourbon industry's woes were directly linked to executives forcing cases sales of products consumers wanted and that they overvalued chain stores instead of working with mom-and-pop operations. Couple Pepper Dave's theory with health concerns, tariffs, and the younger generation not drinking as much, and I suppose that's a recipe for a bourbon bubble busting.

I just know I love what I do. And one day, I'll see ole James Crow up near the pearly gates and I plan to ask him: "So were you a doctor?"

Recipes

In the early 1960s, National Distillers executed a national cocktail campaign to promote Old Crow. The small booklet, "The Best Bourbon Drinks Are Made With Old Crow," was distributed to liquor stores around the United States and promoted the "Great American Bird Toast:"

May you always have an eagle in your pocket…
A turkey on your table…
And Old Crow in your glass.

No doubt, this little toast was shared with Old Crow fans back in the day. These are some of my favorite cocktails from that little book. And my personal favorite: The Brown Derby, which was not included in the Old Crow book.

High Ball

1. Fill glass with cubed ice.
2. Add in 1.5 ounces of bourbon.
3. Slowly pour ginger ale or club soda over ice.
4. Stir slowly.

Manhattan

1. 1 ounce of sweet vermouth
2. 2 ounces of bourbon
3. A dash of bitters
4. Stir in ice and strain in a chilled glass.

Whiskey Collins

1. Juice of 1 lemon
2. 2 teaspoonfuls of sugar
3. 1.5 ounces of bourbon
4. Shake with cracked ice. Strain into glass with ice. Then pour soda water over ice.

Bourbon on the Rocks

1. Fill old-fashioned glass with ice cubes.
2. Pour 2 ounces of bourbon over ice.
3. Add a twist of lemon peel.

Whiskey Punch

Servings: 12

1. Fill punch bowl with ice.
2. 6 juiced lemons
3. 8 juiced oranges
4. 2 tablespoons of sugar
5. 3 ounces of curaçao
6. 1.5 bottles of bourbon
7. Add fruit.
8. 2 quarters of club soda
9. Stir.

Ward 8

1. 1 juiced lemon
2. ½ juiced orange
3. 0.5 ounces of Grenadine
4. 1 ounce of bourbon
5. Shake with ice and strain into glass with ice, fruit, and club soda.

The Brown Derby

Note: This is my favorite bourbon cocktail.

1. 2 ounces of bourbon
2. 1 ounce of fresh squeezed grapefruit juice
3. 0.5 ounces of honey syrup
4. Aggressively shake and strain in a coup glass. Garnish with a grapefruit twist or honey stick.

Reading Group Guide

1. What about returning from war makes it so difficult for veterans to reacclimate to "normal" life? Are there ways society could make it easier on veterans?

2. Have you ever tried online dating? What have your experiences been like?

3. How do you like to enjoy food? Are you able to pick out every distinct flavor? What about with alcoholic beverages, such as wine or bourbon? Are you able to discern the "fruity" or "chocolate" notes the bottle specifies?

4. What flavors or dishes remind you of other times in your life—your childhood, previous vacations, school, etc.?

5. People would buy the Old Crow Chessmen sets for the decanters rather than for the liquor itself. Is there something you like to collect for aesthetic purposes as opposed to what it was originally created for (such as trading cards, coins, or shoes)?

6. How much did you know about the history of any kind of alcoholic beverage before reading this book? Do you think schools in the United States purposefully avoid the subject in classrooms? Should this kind of history be taught more often?

7. Fred and Jaclyn had very specific plans for how they wanted the birth of their child to go, but in the end, they had to throw those out and go with the flow. Is there a time in your life when you had planned something down to the last detail, only to have to adjust when the time came?

8. In becoming more of a prominent figure, Fred faced many unfair critiques and eventually decided to use those critiques to motivate himself to be better. How well do you take criticism? When is criticism helpful, and when is it simply cruel or unproductive?

9. Have you ever bought something online that, when it arrived, wasn't as you expected or hoped? How did you deal with that situation? Are there ways to ensure what you're buying online is exactly what you want?

10. Confrontations with failing health forced Fred to really think about how he was living and what he would leave behind. Do you think about your own legacy? Is there something you would like to be remembered for?

11. How important is your physical health to your mental health? Do you find that when you feel more comfortable in your body that you also feel better about yourself in general?

A Conversation with the Author

What was the writing process like for this book?

This is my ninth book. I can honestly say this was the most difficult and rewarding book I've done. I shared very personal stories that only my wife, therapists, and I knew. Opening up about my early postwar life made me vulnerable to those moments. But I have worked so hard to move on from these instances that neither the reaction to the war nor the war itself can control me.

The truth is, I was afraid to tell this story because some things are just too personal to share. Now that it's out there, my kids will one day know about it. But I was determined to explain what had happened to me, how I felt, and my suicide attempt because I just felt like my story could help somebody else. As I noted in my acknowledgments, this empowering feeling came from beginning to share my taste mindfulness story on the *Today* show. I received so many messages from therapists and people suffering from PTSD that my story had helped them.

And while I had written about my PTSD struggles before, I always kept the suicide attempt away from the public in fear of judgment. Those people telling me how I helped them with my taste mindfulness story: They gave me the power to show this side.

Of course, the book is just not about the personal struggle. That part of my life was only the beginning of the story. I thoroughly enjoyed telling the story of how I got into bourbon, especially Jaclyn's influence on me and the discovery of Old Crow. I loved the research for this book and how it linked all my past works and personal life together. As a matter a fact, this book allowed me to actually research Old Crow. I had spent so much time sidebarring other books' research. To have dedicated time on this book was awesome.

And at every turn, I found something new. I do hope that another researcher can one day build on what I found. If somebody can find out what James Crow was up to in New York and Pennsylvania in the early 1800s, they will tie up the only loose end that's still eating at me.

My favorite part of the book is reliving the birth of my children and the special people who've influenced my adult life. So in a lot of ways, writing *Bottom Shelf* was like creating a time capsule of my life and an obsession that only made sense to me.

Has learning about the history of Old Crow changed how you view bourbon now?

Yes. My deep dive into James C. Crow and the twentieth-century Old Crow made me really angry at the people who made marketing decisions in the mid- to late 1950s. These are the people who really spun the Dr. Crow angle into something bigger than it was. This is the same era where people blasted the folktale of Elijah Craig inventing bourbon through an accident in 1789, which I covered in my book *Bourbon*. I once laughed at these tall tales, but research for this book introduced me to Seton Porter, who, I believe, would have created a more wine-centric marketing world for whiskey. From what I could tell, Porter wanted to discuss ingredients and how whiskey was made, and talk about the true aspects of whiskey. Not made-up stuff. Unfortunately, he died before the shenanigans became mainstream. So this book's given me a bitter taste for how bourbon was and continues to be marketed when the truth is as, or more, compelling than the folklore.

Are there any other subjects you'd like to take a deeper look at?

This is my first narrative in the bourbon space, and I'm excited to see what doors *Bottom Shelf* may open up. I really credit Wright Thompson's *New York Times* bestselling book *Pappyland*, which I edited in his manuscript phase, for opening up the public's interest in whiskey narratives. Until recently, people only wanted scholarly-like histories in bourbon. Now the fun can begin, and we can tell some stories!

Do you think you could ever find a new favorite bourbon? Or a new favorite outside of bourbon?

I don't think I will ever find a bourbon that dominated my palate and soul like Old Crow did then. But if there's something that could do it, it's a rare rum. I wrote *Rum Curious* a decade ago now, and I just absolutely love rum.

Is there a place you're hoping the alcohol industry will go in the future? Any new innovations or experiments on the horizon?

Well, the alcohol industry is trying to figure out how to thrive in a world with legal cannabis and an era of healthier lifestyles avoiding alcohol. Truth is, this industry's business model doesn't allow for flexibility and the three-tier system hurts them in times of change. When consumers can order pharmaceutical goods from India, China, Idaho, or wherever and have it delivered to their door, there's an expectation that they should be able to have alcohol shipped to them. But because of the post-Prohibition laws, every state legislates alcohol differently, and, as of this writing, the majority block shipments from retailers or distilleries in other states. Thus, the industry needs to figure out how to modernize its laws or it will fall victim to failure to change. Because, believe me, plenty of people want to sip something. They just don't necessarily want to go to a liquor store for it. So, as simple as it sounds, the industry needs to find a legal way to ship.

What would you like readers to take away from your story?

Now, that's a tough one. I am not one to say how others should perceive my work. But putting my most personal moments out there was direct result of mental-health professionals thanking me for showing my taste mindfulness story. When I think about it, every page of this book was my long road of coping with PTSD, loss, and life. I hope somebody can read my story and relate to it. We only got one shot at this thing called life. If my story ever helps somebody, that's the greatest compliment I can receive.

Notes

CHAPTER 2: TO KENTUCKY

1 In 2015, when addressing members of the media about bourbon, Senator Mitch McConnell (KY Republican) referenced this quote. He said: "The history of Bourbon whiskey and the legend of Henry Clay have long been intertwined. It is said that whenever Clay went to Washington, he carried a barrel with him, to 'lubricate the wheels of government.' Clay is also credited with writing the first historical recipe for the mint julep." However, while the senator is not the first to use this quote, nobody using it has the original source. The Henry Clay Center said it does not know where it came from. The earliest record I have found of the quote actually comes in an 1897 national ad campaign for Old Crow bourbon. Henry Clay died in 1852.

CHAPTER 3: OBSESSION

1 University of Louisville Archives, *Spirits*, April 1935, 29.

2 Alcohol and Tobacco Tax and Trade Bureau, "Federal Alcohol Administration Act of 1935," last updated May 13, 2025, https://www.ttb.gov/business-central/trade-practices/federal-alcohol-administration-act-historical-background. According to the Alcohol and Tobacco Tax and Trade Bureau: "The Twenty-first Amendment to the Constitution, repealing Prohibition, achieved ratification with unanticipated speed by December 5, 1933, catching Congress in recess. As an interim measure to manage a burgeoning legitimate alcohol industry, by executive order under the National Industrial Recovery Act, President Franklin D. Roosevelt established the Federal Alcohol Control Administration

(FACA). FACA, in cooperation with the Departments of Agriculture and Treasury, endeavored to guide wineries and distilleries under a system based on brewers' voluntary codes of fair competition. FACA was relieved of its burden and effectively vanished from history after just twenty months, when President Roosevelt signed the Federal Alcohol Administration (FAA) Act in August 1935 and Treasury once more found itself regulating the alcohol industry.

"Although Prohibition was officially over, the era's lingering effects continued to shape the federal policies for decades. On March 10, 1934, Justice's Prohibition enforcement duties folded into the infant Alcohol Tax Unit (ATU), Bureau of Internal Revenue, Department of the Treasury. At the same time, Federal Alcohol Administration (FAA), functioning independently within Treasury, was carrying forward its mandate to collect data, to establish license and permit requirements, and define the regulations that ensure an open, fair marketplace for the alcohol industry and the American consumer. In 1940, FAA as an administration merged with the ATU, but the FAA Act continues today as part of the foundation of TTB's enabling legislation."

3 From 2008 to 2013, eBay went from a thriving marketplace for bourbon sales to being caught up in a scandal where kids bought booze. Two sources that show the fall of eBay for alcohol: Susanna Kim, "Kids Can Buy Alcohol on eBay," ABC News, October 30, 2012; and Geoff Kleinman, "eBay Bans Alcohol Sales—Other Whisky Auction Alternatives," Drink Spirits, September 25, 2012.

4 The U.S. federal definition of light whiskey: "Whiskey produced in the U.S. at more than 80% alcohol by volume (160 proof) [but less than 95% alcohol by volume (190 proof)] and stored in used or uncharred new oak containers." Alcohol and Tobacco Tax and Trade Bureau, "Class and Type Designation," in *Beverage Alcohol Manual: A Practical Guide, Basic Classification and Labeling Requirements for Distilled Spirits*, chapter 4 (Washington, DC: U.S. Department of the Treasury, n.d.), https://www.ttb.gov/system/files/images/pdfs/spirits_bam/chapter4.pdf.

5 "Old Crow Has Unique Gift Idea," *The Pantagraph*, October 4, 1969, 12.

CHAPTER 4: FINDING CROW

1 *The Dominion News*, June 18, 1969, 9.

2 Woodford County Historical Society, James C. Crow burial plot.

3 "Old Jim Crow's Little Still House," *The Courier-Journal*, September 5, 1897, 23.

4 The first known recipe of sour mash used in whiskey came from Catherine Spears Carpenter Frye. Her 1818 recipe was in her family bible and noted in the author's book *Whiskey Women: The Untold Story of How Women Saved Bourbon, Scotch, and Irish Whiskey*. The original source is located at the Kentucky Historical Society under Carpenter Family Papers.

5 Testimony in *W. A. Gaines & Co. v. Kahn*, 212 U.S. 572. Max Kahn was the administrator of the Estate of Abraham M. Hellman. Thus, his name is listed in the header of court dockets, but Hellman Distilling Co. is the primary target.

6 "Bad Whiskey," *Alexandria Gazette*, July 27, 1846, 2. This article encourages the Port Tobacco, Maryland, health board to look into bad whiskey causing sickness. During this time frame, many were beginning to preach temperance for the physical ills alcohol caused.

7 In the 1906 lawsuit *W. A. Gaines & Co. v. Hellman Distilling Co.*, Richard H. Whittington, a storekeeper gauger in Frankfort, Kentucky, testified that the recipe for Old Crow in Crow's lifetime was corn and malted barley without citing exact recipes. The oldest advertisement discovered, to date, of an Old Crow in this time frame (1835–1856) was twelve years old.

8 "Crow Whisky," *The Frankfort Commonwealth*, December 2, 1851, 3.

9 "Old Crow Whiskey," *The Times-Picayune*, October 8, 1856, 3.

10 1906 lawsuit *W.A. Gaines & Co. v. Hellman Distilling Co.*

11 This anecdote also appeared in the author's book *Bourbon: The Rise, Fall, and Rebirth of an American Whiskey*.

12 Dolph Honicker, "Little 'B' Acted Big in Bygone Days," *The Tennessean*, December 8, 1963, 44.

13 Alexander K. McClure, *Abe Lincoln's Yarns and Stories* (Chicago: John C. Winston Co., 1901).

14 Jack Sullivan, *Bottles and Extras*, January–February 2007, 59–61.

15 Alcohol and Tobacco Tax and Trade Bureau, "Class and Type Designation," in *Beverage Alcohol Manual: A Practical Guide, Basic Classification and Labeling Requirements for Distilled Spirits*, chapter 4 (Washington, DC: U.S. Department of the Treasury, n.d.).

16 1906 lawsuit *W.A. Gaines & Co. v. Hellman Distilling Co.*

CHAPTER 5: WHO WAS JAMES C. CROW? THE TRUTH

1 Mrs. Jo Currie correspondence to Samuel Thomas, June 2, 1995, Samuel W. Thomas papers, Archives and Special Collections, University of Louisville, Louisville, Kentucky, Box: Bourbon businesses and families.

2 Mrs. Jo Currie correspondence to Samuel Thomas.

3 On behalf of the author, John McGee of Wheech Scottish Ancestry Services executed James C. Crow's genealogy.

4 "Account of the Parish of Dirleton," in *The Statistical Account of Scotland, 1791–1799*, ed. Sir John Sinclair, vol. 6 (Edinburgh: William Creech, 1793), 389–402, commissioned by the Ordnance Survey.

5 *Records of Sun Fire Insurance Company*. (This record is held by London Metropolitan Archives: City of London.)

6 *Records of Sun Fire Insurance Company.*

7 Post office records indicated he received mail in Versailles, Kentucky, in 1820. However, previous reports and testimony suggest he didn't move to Kentucky until 1825.

8 John Allen, "Extract from Letter," *Aurora General Advertiser*, June 26, 1812, 2.

9 *Buffalo Patriot and Commercial Advertiser*, May 28, 1816, 3.

10 "James Crow, The Renowned Distiller of Woodford County," *Woodford Sun*, September 2, 1971. This is a reprint from a letter authored by E. J. S. and published by the *Woodford Sun* on December 9, 1870.

11 *Kentucky Gazette*, August 17, 1820, 1.

12 *The Commonwealth*, December 3, 1839, 3.

13 "Number Visit Crow Grave," *Lexington Herald-Leader*, June 30, 1938, 115.

CHAPTER 6: FAME AND ILLEGAL ACTIVITY

1 ABC News, "eBay Begins Removing Alcohol Listings After '20/20' Report on Teen Buyer," ABC News, September 21, 2012, https://abcnews.go.com/Business/kids-buy-alcohol-ebay/story?id=17280467.

2 Tim Elliot, "Prospect Police Looking for Man Who Fired Shot Outside Day Care," WLKYNews.com, January 13, 2015.

CHAPTER 7: LEGIT—SORT OF

1 Fred Minnick, "Kentucky Legislature Considers Vintage Spirits Law," *Fred Minnick* (blog), February 12, 2017.

CHAPTER 9: THE BRAND

1 Daniel Leon, "The Households of James Buchanan," White House Historical Association, October 13, 2022.

2 United States Supreme Court. *Records and Briefs of the United States Supreme Court.* Vol. 241, *W. A. Gaines & Co. v. Hellman Distilling Co.*, 11. Washington, D.C.

3 *The Indianapolis News*, June 16, 1900, 18.

4 Carry Amelia Nation, *The Use and Need of the Life of Carry A. Nation* (Topeka, KS: F. M. Steves & Sons, 1909), 131.

5 Brian F. Haara, *Bourbon Justice: How Whiskey Law Shaped America* (Lincoln: Potomac Books, an imprint of the University of Nebraska Press, 2018), 49.

6 Prepared by Brian Haara, author of *Bourbon Justice*:

CASE CITATION	WINNER	QUOTES FROM OPINIONS AS CITED IN *BOURBON JUSTICE*
W. A. Gaines & Co. v. Kahn, 155 F. 639 (E.D. MO, 1907)	Gaines	"I am satisfied that this was done by them for the purpose of deceiving their customers as to the character of the whiskey offered by them. They marked the barrels "Crow," and also used a picture of the bird on some of the packages. It was an attempt to palm off on the trade an inferior whiskey, made under the name of "Crow;" they well knowing at the time the superior quality of the whiskey manufactured on Glenn's Creek, in Woodford county, KY. It was unfair competition, in that they sought to make others believe that they were selling the genuine "Old Crow" whiskey, when, in fact, they were offering an inferior production of their own"
Kahn v. W. A. Gaines & Co., 161 F. 495 (8th Cir. 1908)	Hellman	"no unprejudiced mind can read the evidence in this case without the impression that the conception of a trademark in the words 'Crow,' or 'Old Crow,' did not enter the minds of Gaines, Berry & Co. prior to 1870."
cert denied W. A. Gaines & Co. v. Kahn, 212 U.S. 572 (1908)	Hellman	NA
W. A. Gaines & Co. v. Rock Spring Distilling Co., 179 F. 544 (W.D. KY, 1910)	Gaines	Procedural victory only—kept Hellman out of the case as a party.
W. A. Gaines & Co. v. Rock Spring Distilling Co., 202 F. 989 (W.D. KY, 1913)	Hellman	Case dismissed. The court found it "altogether incorrect" for Gaines to have asserted, in its 1909 trademark application, that it had used the "Old Crow" name since 1835, because the actual year of first use was 1867. Similarly, the court ruled that it was "altogether incorrect" for Gaines to have asserted that no other similar trademark had been used by anyone else, when Gaines—at the very least because of the Missouri lawsuit—*knew* that Hellman had been using the "Crow" name since 1863.

CASE CITATION	WINNER	QUOTES FROM OPINIONS AS CITED IN *BOURBON JUSTICE*
W. A. Gaines & Co. v. Rock Spring Distilling Co., 226 F. 531 (6th Cir. 1915)	Gaines	The deception by Hellman, and the new limited use of "Old Crow" by Gaines to apply only to straight bourbon and rye whiskey, satisfied the Sixth Circuit that Rock Spring (and therefore Hellman) should be prevented from using the "Crow" name for any straight whiskies.
Rock Spring Distilling Co. v. W. A. Gaines & Co., 246 U.S. 312 (1918)	Hellman	Without much explanation, the United States Supreme Court ruled that separate trademarks for "straight" whiskey and "blended" whiskey could not be maintained and that Hellman—*not Gaines*—owned the trademark rights to the "Crow" name.

7 Carry Amelia Nation, *The Use and Need*, 187.

8 *The Gazette*, May 14, 1929, 20.

9 Max Jordan Nguemeni Tiako and Kelsey C. Priest, "Yes, Liquor Stores Are Essential Businesses," ed. Michael D. Lemonick, *Scientific American*, March 27, 2020, https://www.scientificamerican.com/article/yes-liquor-stores-are-essential-businesses/.

10 Fred Minnick, "EH Taylor Four Grain Bourbon, Four Roses Limited Edition 2014, and Russell's Reserve 10-Year-Old," YouTube, https://www.youtube.com/watch?v=0gSZZF9K1UY.

11 Wade Woodard, *Tater-Talk* (blog), December 31, 2017, https://tater-talk.com/2017/12/31/welcome-to-tater-talk/.

REASONS YOU ARE A WHISKEY TATER...

1. Buy spots in a whiskey raffle when the bottle is 20% over market
2. Pay secondary mark up price for any bottle that has just recently become scarce, ie age stated EC 12, when you passed it up on shelf less than 6 months ago
3. Instaflip bottles only to buy them back within a month
4. Own a full set of Orphan Barrels
5. Buy blended whiskeys in plastic handles while "dusty hunting"
6. Purchase a bottle of whiskey because a shelf talker mentioned it 'won' an award
7. Selling whiskey in the secondary market because your wife makes you, have bills to pay, or any reason having to do with poor money management skills

8. Put ice in a Glencairn
9. Refer to anything Van Winkle or from Stitzel-Weller as "Pappy"
10. Purchase any Pappy & Co merchandise

CHAPTER 10: ALL THINGS NATIONAL

1 Joseph Bishop-Henchman, "How Taxes Enabled Alcohol Prohibition and Also Led to Its Repeal," *Tax Foundation* (blog), October 5, 2011, https://taxfoundation.org/blog/how-taxes-enabled-alcohol-prohibition-and-also-led-its-repeal/.

2 Internal documents from National Distillers, 1936.

3 *The Escanaba Daily Press*, Advertisement: "The Preferred Bourbon of Henry Clay," September 25, 1937, 15.

4 Associated Press, *The Morning News*: "Dividend Ordered in Whiskey Stock," August 15, 1932, 7.

5 Paul Harrison, *Marshfield News-Herald*: "Better and Cheaper Liquor Is Near At Hand," February 9, 1934, 5.

6 *Fortune Magazine*, Advertisement: "90,000 Acres of Beauty…and Staves, Too," June 1943, 57.

CHAPTER 11: NEW AGE

1 *Tucson Citizen*, Advertisement: "Old Crow Makes History With A Lighter, Milder Bottling At A Lower Proof!", September 15, 1953, 3.

2 *Statesville Record and Landmark*, "Black Crow: Rarest U.S. Bird," February 5, 1966, 3.

CHAPTER 12: VIETNAM

1 United States, Congress, Senate, Committee on Government Operations, Permanent Subcommittee on Investigations, *Fraud and Corruption in Management of Military Club Systems: Illegal Currency Manipulations Affecting South Vietnam; Report* (Washington, DC: U.S. Government Printing Office, 1971), 97.

2 "The Nation: The Money King of Viet Nam," TIME, March 8, 1971, https://time.com/archive/6838604/the-nation-the-money-king-of-viet-nam/.

3 United States, Congress, Senate, Committee on Government Operations, *Fraud and Corruption*, 225.

4 United States, Congress, Senate, Committee on Government Operations, *Fraud and Corruption*, 232.

5 United States, Congress, Senate, Committee on Government Operations, *Fraud and Corruption*, 232.

6 *The Journal Times*, "The Military is To Blame," November 5, 1971, 10.

7 *The Reporter-Times*, February 19, 1971, 1.

CHAPTER 13: OH, CANADA!

1 United States, Congress, Senate, Committee on Appropriations, Subcommittee

on Treasury, Postal Service, and General Government, *Proposed Dissolution of Bureau of Alcohol, Tobacco, and Firearms: Hearings before a Subcommittee of the Committee on Appropriations, United States Senate, Ninety-seventh Congress, Second Session* (Washington, DC: U.S. Government Printing Office, 1982), 5.

2 "The Nation: The Money King of Viet Nam," *TIME*, March 8, 1971, https://time.com/archive/6838604/the-nation-the-money-king-of-viet-nam/.

3 United States, Congress, Senate, Committee on Appropriations, *Proposed Dissolution of Bureau of Alcohol*, 39.

4 Matt Strickland, "It's Time to Take Ethyl Carbamate Seriously Again," *Distiller Magazine*, October 16, 2019, https://distilling.com/distillermagazine/its-time-to-take-ethyl-carbamate-seriously-again/.

5 *The Monitor*, July 27, 1984, 17.

6 *Daily News*, October 17, 1984, 134.

7 *The York Dispatch*, April 9, 1987, 28.

CHAPTER 14: SAYING GOODBYE

1 "James Crow, The Renowned Distiller of Woodford County," *Woodford Sun*, September 2, 1971. This is a reprint from a letter authored by E. J. S. and published by the *Woodford Sun* on December 9, 1870.

EPILOGUE

1 Aaron Goldfarb, "What Ever Happened to Old Crow, Once the 'Pinnacle of American Whiskey?'" VinePair, August 7, 2024.

2 Saabira Chaudhuri, "America's Bourbon Boom Is Over. Now the Hangover Is Here," *Wall Street Journal*, January 13, 2025.

Index

C

M

Acknowledgments

This is a book I've always wanted to write. But I just didn't know how to organize it.

In 2022, book writing was far down on my list of revenue generators. I had built a prominent tasting and events business, and my content world was taking off. But in my heart, I was an author. I hadn't published a new book since 2018, and I knew I had one left in me. So I was telling my events booking agent Andrew Goodfriend this, and he said, "I got a guy." Goodfriend is an old-school entertainment agent who had represented everybody from Anthrax to Simon & Garfunkel.

He introduced me to Marc Gerald and Leah Petrakis of Europa Content. They represented books for Kevin Hart, Corey Taylor, and Jet Li, among other celebrities. We had an introductory Zoom call, where Marc said I reminded him of their client Steven Rinella, host of the Netflix Original *MeatEater* and author of several bestselling meat books. I took that as a great compliment, and they asked me to come back with several book ideas. I had five, and they were not sold on any of them. But in the buildup of one of my ideas, they heard me talk about a brand I really loved that had fallen from its once-great height. "Tell me more about Old Crow," Marc said.

So I did, and I mentioned my Old Crow taste mindfulness story.

"That's your book," Leah said.

We spent a year going back and forth on the arrangement and flow of the chapters. So when I tell you that this book would not have happened without my literary agents, I am underselling it. Marc and Leah dug this thing out of my brain, which is a level of awesome I cannot truly explain.

So thank you to Andrew for always having "a guy" in his Rolodex. And to Marc and Leah for investing so much time into this project to make it a success.

To my manager, Clay Busch, thank you for putting up with my lack of work in other areas while I wrote this. I wouldn't be here without your constant support and push to make me better.

To my ShoreFire PR team (Rebecca Shapiro, Jaclyn Childress, and Olivia Troutman), you all may not know this: You helped put this into motion by getting me to publicly talk about my PTSD and taste mindfulness. If you hadn't suggested I do the *Today* show feature in 2021, I would have never had the courage to write this book! And thank you to the *Today* show, especially Craig Melvin, for telling my story so beautifully.

Eric Carrico, buddy, cemeteries make me nervous. Thank you for helping me navigate Versailles's graveyard so I could talk to James Crow.

My good pal Brett Atlas gave me my last Old Crow Chessman. If not for sips from this last bottle, I probably could not have written this book.

Those little nips helped with the research, for sure, but I also had help with the actual research pros when I was unable to travel or find what I needed in an archive.

To John McGee, thank you for coming out of retirement to help me navigate the Scottish archives in Crow's early life. Once again, your Wheech Scottish Ancestry Services were an incredible ally for my research.

Thank you to Dr. Roseann Hogan for assisting in the research of Crow's Philadelphia and New York days.

And of course, there's the special bond between writer and editor. I am so thankful Marc and Leah introduced me to Anna Michels, editorial director for Sourcebooks. She's molded my writing and helped shape *Bottom Shelf* into a truly special, meaningful project. Without Anna, this book would probably have become an Old Crow business story, which was what other editors wanted when I shopped it under the original title, *Finding Crow*. But Anna really wanted to hear more about the journey, the self-discovery, and the true story of an alleged Dr. James C. Crow. Thank you, Anna, for believing in me and helping this dream come true.

Of course, from the start of my career to its publication, this book took twenty years to complete. And there was one person with me the whole time: the love of my life—Jaclyn.

Thank you, Manbreaker!

About the Author

Wall Street Journal bestselling author Fred Minnick discovered his bourbon passion after returning home from the Iraq War to become one of the world's leading tasters. Cofounder of the Bourbon & Beyond music festival with Danny Wimmer Presents, American Spirits Council of Tasters, and *Bourbon+* magazine, he's raised more than eleven million dollars for causes through bourbon and serves on the board of the Honorable Order of the Kentucky Colonels. His books, including *Whiskey Women* and *Bourbon*, earned international acclaim, while Fred is a cohost of the *Bourbon Pursuit*, *Pin It Forward*, and *Fourth & Neat* podcasts, as well as the host of a popular whiskey YouTube channel. Once sipping bourbon backstage with Metallica, Fred has appeared on *Top Chef*, *Pawn Stars*, and the *Today* show. He lives in Louisville, Kentucky, with his wife and two kids, practicing Brazilian jiujitsu and rocking ascots—never together.